SARAH WATERS

Contemporary Critical Perspectives

Series Editors: Jeannette Baxter, Peter Childs, Sebastian Groes and Sean Matthews

Guides in the *Contemporary Critical Perspectives* series provide companions to reading and studying major contemporary authors. They include new critical essays combining textual readings, cultural analysis and discussion of key critical and theoretical issues in a clear, accessible style. Each guide also includes a preface by a major contemporary writer, a new interview with the author, discussion of film and TV adaptation and guidance on further reading.

Titles in the series include:

J. G. Ballard edited by Jeannette Baxter
Ian McEwan edited by Sebastian Groes
Kazuo Ishiguro edited by Sean Matthews and Sebastian Groes
Julian Barnes edited by Sebastian Groes and Peter Childs
Sarah Waters, edited by Kaye Mitchell
Salman Rushdie edited by Robert Eaglestone and Martin McQuillan
Ali Smith edited by Monica Germana and Emily Horton
Andrea Levy edited by Jeannette Baxter and David James

SARAH WATERS

Contemporary Critical Perspectives

Edited by
Kaye Mitchell

B L O O M S B U R Y
NEW DELHI • LONDON • OXFORD • NEW YORK • SYDNEY

First published in India 2018
First published 2013

Bloomsbury Academic India
An imprint of Bloomsbury Publishing Plc
BLOOMSBURY, Bloomsbury Academic India and the Diana
logo are trademarks of Bloomsbury Publishing Plc

This edition published with permission from Bloomsbury Publishing Plc,
50 Bedford Square, London, WC1B3DP, UK

British Library Cataloguing-in-Publication Data
A catalogue record for this book is available from the British Library.

Library of Congress Cataloging-in-Publication Data
Sarah Waters : contemporary critical perspectives / edited by Kaye Mitchell. pages cm. – (Contemporary Critical Perspectives)
Includes bibliographical references and index.
ISBN 978-1-4411-8084-1 (hardcover) – ISBN 978-1-4411-9941-6 (pbk.) –
ISBN 978-1-4411-2021-2 (epdf) – ISBN 978-1-4411-2752-5 (epub) 1. Waters, Sarah, 1966–-Criticism and interpretation. I. Mitchell, Kaye, editor of compilation. PR6073.A828Z86 2013
823'.914–dc23
2013000254

ISBN 978 93 87863 68 2
10 9 8 7 6 5
For sale in the Indian subcontinent only

Bloomsbury Publishing India Pvt. Ltd
Second Floor, Building No. 4
DDA Complex LSC, Pocket C – 6 & 7
Vasant Kunj, New Delhi 110070
www.bloomsbury.com

Typeset by Newgen Imaging Systems Pvt Ltd, Chennai, India
Printed and bound in India by Replika Press Pvt. Ltd.

Contents

Foreword

Adapting Sarah Waters

Andrew Davies

I had never heard of Sarah Waters when Sally Head, the independent producer, sent me a copy of *Tipping the Velvet*, with a little note saying she thought it might tickle my fancy. This was in 2002 and I was on my way to the Banff Television Festival in Canada. I started reading the book while sitting outside the Banff Railway Hotel, with a view of those ridiculously spectacular snow-covered mountains right in front of me. I have to confess that I didn't raise my eyes to the mountains very often, nor did I attend many of the screenings and conference meetings. I didn't want to waste a minute away from Nan and Kitty and Florence – this was truly a new world for me, a brilliantly successful evocation of the hidden underworld of 1890s London. I could tell that Sarah was steeped not only in the classic Victorian novel, but also Victorian literary pornography. Yes, this was right up my alley all right. The moment I decided that I absolutely must dramatize this book was when I read the scene in which our heroine appears in the top half of a Guardsman's uniform, red cap and black shiny boots, and nothing else except a giant leather dildo. This, I felt, was something that needed to be seen on screens throughout the country. And so I accepted the commission and started work.

The authors I collaborate with have generally been dead for a long time, and that, on the whole, is how I prefer it. It can be a tricky situation when the screenwriter feels the need to be ruthless with a text, and some novelists quite understandably don't like their creations mucked about with. I was nervous about meeting Sarah for that reason, and also because I didn't know how she'd feel about an old white heterosexual man adapting her wonderful book. But I needn't have worried. Sarah is very clued up about film and TV and the difference between film and the novel. And she was quite happy about my adapting *Tipping the Velvet*: she had enjoyed watching some of my earlier efforts, particularly *Moll Flanders*, which, come to think of it, included a lesbian episode that Defoe had unaccountably forgotten to write himself.

At this time *Tipping the Velvet* was in the early stages of becoming a crossover hit. Sarah, she told me, had never expected her book to be displayed on any shelves except the gay and lesbian section. She had wanted simply to write the sort of book she'd enjoy reading herself – one of the best reasons for writing a book – and now it was turning out that all sorts of people were enjoying it too. Not surprisingly: although the book is wholeheartedly and intensely about women who love other women, it renders the experience of its characters so vividly and powerfully that it tells us universal truths about love, the search for identity and the sheer joy and pain of life itself.

Working on the script was a joy, and one of the least problematical adaptations I've done. That's because Sarah writes so visually, and dramatically too. I was able to take most of her dialogue straight off the page and put it in the script. It was useful, too, to be able to consult Sarah about points that puzzled me, such as 'how would a girl who loves girls bring herself to play the part of a male prostitute giving oral sex to elderly gentlemen?' Actually I can't remember what advice Sarah gave me on this point, but we must have done something right, because after the show aired I received a letter from a 100-year-old man in Halifax telling me it was his favourite bit of the whole thing.

Affinity had been published by this time, and I loved it, I think, even more than I loved *Tipping the Velvet*. Spooky and heart-rending, and wickedly subversive. I optioned it myself, and spent years trying to set it up with a film, eventually making it as an ITV film with Anna Madeley and Zoe Tapper – it received much less publicity that *Tipping the Velvet*, but I am very proud of it. Sarah herself appears briefly in it, as she does in *Tipping* – if you didn't notice before, check the DVD. In *Tipping*, she's in the theatre audience in the final scene, and in *Affinity* she passes Margaret in the street.

I've continued to enjoy and admire Sarah's novels, and a couple of years ago I had the pleasure of discussing *The Little Stranger* with her in front of an audience at Warwick Words. She was funny, and as usual very sharp and incisive, and by the end I realized that I hadn't really understood the book at all, so I sat down and read it all over again. That's one of the great things about her: like Jane Austen, she bears repeated readings, and you always get something extra each time. Really my only complaint about her is the length of time that elapses between each book.

So hurry up, Sarah. We're waiting.

Series Editors' Preface

The readership for contemporary fiction has never been greater. The explosion of reading groups and literary blogs, of university courses and school curricula, and even the apparent rude health of the literary marketplace, indicate an ever-growing appetite for new work, for writing which responds to the complex, changing and challenging times in which we live. At the same time, readers seem ever more eager to engage in conversations about their reading, to devour the review pages, to pack the sessions at literary festivals and author events. Reading is an increasingly social activity, as we seek to share and refine our experience of the book, to clarify and extend our understanding.

It is this tremendous enthusiasm for contemporary fiction to which the *Contemporary Critical Perspectives* series responds. Our ambition is to offer readers of current fiction a comprehensive critical account of each author's work, presenting original, specially commissioned analyses of all aspects of their career, from a variety of different angles and approaches, as well as directions towards further reading and research. Our brief to the contributors is to be scholarly, to draw on the latest thinking about narrative, or philosophy, or psychology, indeed whatever seemed to them most significant in drawing out the meanings and force of the texts in question, but also to focus closely on the words on the page, the stories and scenarios and forms which all of us meet first when we open a book. We insisted that these essays be accessible to that mythical beast the Common Reader, who might just as readily be spotted at the Lowdham Book Festival as in a college seminar. In this way, we hope to have presented critical assessments of our writers in such a way as to contribute something to both of those environments, and also to have done something to bring together the most important qualities of each of them.

Jeannette Baxter, Peter Childs,
Sebastian Groes and Sean Matthews

Acknowledgements

Thanks are due first and foremost to Sarah Waters herself, who was generous with her time and energy in making herself available for an extensive new interview for this volume and in responding to various little biographical and textual queries with impressive alacrity and disarming modesty. She also, most importantly of all, wrote the fabulous novels that I have rediscovered and enjoyed afresh in the editing of this collection: thanks Sarah!

Thanks to Andrew Davies for somehow finding time in his astonishingly busy schedule to write a characteristically exuberant foreword for this volume.

Thanks also to David Avital and Laura Murray at Continuum, for their patience and enthusiasm throughout the process of editing the book, and to the series editors – Jeannette Baxter, Sebastian Groes and Sean Matthews – for commissioning the volume in the first place.

I have been fortunate enough to gather an excellent array of contributors, from the United Kingdom and beyond, and would like to record my heartfelt thanks to them, too, for their promptness and equanimity (in the face of my doggedly pedantic editorial demands), and for the liveliness of their scholarship, which makes the book what it is. Any errors or omissions are, of course, my responsibility alone.

Thanks to my fantastic colleagues and students at the University of Manchester, who continue to make the daily grind more joy than travail.

Finally, enormous gratitude, big love and a sizeable slap-up dinner are due to Kate Graham who, in addition to providing unstinting emotional support and humorous distraction, did various vital research-assistant-type tasks to bring the manuscript together, including the compilation of the timeline, the hunting of elusive reviews and the transcription of the world's longest interview.

Contributors

Natasha Alden is Lecturer in Contemporary British Fiction at Aberystwyth University. Her research interests include contemporary realism, historical fiction, memory studies and queer writing. She has published on Emma Donoghue, Pat Barker and Ian McEwan, and her monograph *Reading Behind the Lines* is forthcoming from Manchester University Press in 2013.

Andrew Davies is an award-winning writer and screenwriter, whose numerous film and television credits have made him a household name in the United Kingdom. He is probably best known for his adaptations of *Pride and Prejudice* (1995), *Vanity Fair* (1998), *Tipping the Velvet* (2002) and *Bleak House* (2005) for the BBC, and *Emma* (1996) and *Affinity* (2008) for ITV. Davies also collaborated on the scripts of *Bridget Jones's Diary* (2001) and *Bridget Jones: The Edge of Reason* (2004). In his early career, he wrote children's fiction and television series, including *Conrad's War* (1978), which won the *Guardian* Children's Fiction Prize, *Marmelade Atkins* (1979 books; 1981–4 series) and *Alfonso Bonzo* (1986 book; 1990 series).

Susan Alice Fischer is Professor of English at Medgar Evers College of The City University of New York. She is Cross-Cultural Literature Coordinator and teaches British literature, contemporary London literature and literary theory. She is the Editor of the online *Literary London* journal and Co-Editor of *Changing English: Studies in Culture and Education* (Routledge), both peer-reviewed. She has written extensively about contemporary women's London narratives; she also writes about British national identity in contemporary literature and culture.

Sarah Gamble is Reader in English with Gender at Swansea University, United Kingdom, where she teaches courses in contemporary women's writing, gender theory and the gothic. Her particular research specialism is the work of Angela Carter, on whom she has published two monographs – *Angela Carter: Writing from the Front Line*, and *Angela Carter: A Literary Life*. She has also published articles on a variety of other women writers, including Sarah Waters, Pat Barker and Michele Roberts. She is currently writing a book on Angela Carter and the gothic, and conducting archival research into Carter's poetry.

Monica Germanà is a writer and Senior Lecturer in English Literature and Creative Writing at the University of Westminster. Her research interests and publications concentrate on contemporary British literature, with a specific emphasis on the Gothic and gender. Her publications include a monograph, *Scottish Women's Gothic and Fantastic Writing* (EUP, 2010) and a special issue of *Gothic Studies* on contemporary Scottish Gothic (November 2011). She is currently co-editing the Continuum New Critical Perspectives volume on Ali Smith while working on a monograph exploring the politics of body and dress provisionally titled 'Bond Girls: Body, Style, and Gender'.

Jerome de Groot teaches at the University of Manchester. He is the author of *Royalist Identities* (Palgrave, 2004), *Consuming History* (Routledge, 2008) and *The Historical Novel* (Routledge, 2009).

Kaye Mitchell is Lecturer in Contemporary Literature and convenor of the MA Contemporary Literature and Culture at the University of Manchester's Centre for New Writing. She is the author of *A. L. Kennedy: New British Fiction* (Palgrave, 2007) and *Intention and Text* (Continuum, 2008), along with numerous articles on contemporary literature, gender and sexuality and critical theory. Her current book project is an investigation of the politics and poetics of shame in literature and theory since the 1990s.

Emma Parker is a Senior Lecturer in English at the University of Leicester. She has published on Kate Atkinson, Margaret Atwood, Toni Morrison, Angela Carter, Jeanette Winterson, Michèle Roberts, Rose Tremain, Linda Grant, Valerie Mason-John, Graham Swift, Martin Amis and Will Self. She is editor of *Contemporary British Women Writers* (D. S. Brewer, 2004) and is currently co-editing, with Mary Eagleton, Volume 10 of *The Palgrave History of British Women's Writing: 1970–Present Day*. She is a founder member of the Contemporary Women's Writing Association and Co-Editor of the journal *Contemporary Women's Writing*.

Rebecca Pohl studied English and History in Potsdam, Berlin and London before taking up a teaching position at the University of Stuttgart. Currently she is working on her doctoral thesis at the University of Manchester. Her research investigates the relation between space and sexuality through the prism of the labyrinth in contemporary women's writing. Rebecca has published on Victorian visual culture and is the translator of Reiner Bucher's *Hitler's Theology* (Continuum, 2011).

Chronology of Sarah Waters' Life

1966	Sarah Waters born in Neyland, Pembrokeshire, Wales on 21 July.
1977–79	St Michael's RC Secondary School, Middlesborough, Cleveland.
1979–84	Milford Haven Grammar School, Milford Haven, Pembrokeshire, Wales.
1984–87	Studies BA (Hons) English and American Literature at the University of Kent.
1987–88	Studies at Lancaster University for an MA in Contemporary Literary Theory.
1988–89	Assistant Bookseller at the Owl Bookshop, Kentish Town, London.
1989–2000	Library Assistant for Camden Libraries, London.
1992–95	Studies for a PhD in English Literature at Queen Mary, University of London. Begins to write fiction.
1994	Publishes '"A Girton girl on a throne": Queen Christina and versions of lesbianism, 1906–1933', *Feminist Review*, 46 (1994): 41–60.
1995	Publishes '"The most famous fairy in history": Antinous and homosexual fantasy', *Journal of the History of Sexuality*, 6.2 (1995): 194–230. Awarded PhD for thesis entitled 'Wolfskins and Togas: Lesbian and Gay Historical Fictions, 1870 to the Present'.
1996	Publishes 'Wolfskins and togas: Maude Meagher's *The Green Scamander* and the lesbian historical novel', *Women: A Cultural Review*, 7.1 (1996): 176–88.
1996–99	Associate Lecturer at the Open University.
1998	*Tipping the Velvet* published by Virago.
1999	*Affinity* published by Virago. *Tipping the Velvet* wins the Betty Trask Award, the Library Journal's Best Book of the Year, the *Mail on Sunday*/John Llewellyn Rhys Prize, and is included in the *New York Times* Notable Book of the Year list.

2000 Co-authors, with Laura Doan, 'Making up lost time: contemporary lesbian writing and the invention of history' in David Alderson and Linda R. Anderson (eds), *Territories of Desire in Queer Culture: Refiguring Contemporary Boundaries*, (Manchester: Manchester University Press, 2000), pp. 12–28. *Affinity* wins the Somerset Maugham Award for Lesbian and Gay Fiction, the *Sunday Times* Young Writer of the Year and the Ferro-Grumley Award for Lesbian and Gay Fiction. It is shortlisted for the *Mail on Sunday*/John Llewellyn Rhys Prize, the Lambda Literary Award for Fiction, the Arts Council of Wales Book of the Year Award and the American Library Association GLBT Roundtable Book Award. *Tipping the Velvet* wins the Lambda Literary Award for Fiction and is shortlisted for the Ferro-Grumley Award for Lesbian and Gay Fiction.

2002 *Fingersmith* is published by Virago. Waters wins the British Book Awards Author of the Year and *Fingersmith* is awarded the Crime Writer's Association Ellis Peters Historical Dagger and is shortlisted for both the Man Booker Prize for Fiction and the Orange Prize for Fiction. *Tipping the Velvet* adapted by Sally Head Productions for the BBC into a three-part serial, first shown 9 October. Andrew Davies writes the screenplay.

2003 Named by *Granta* as one of the 20 'Best of Young British Novelists'. Voted Author of the Year by publishers and booksellers at the British Book Awards and at the BA Conference. Wins the Waterstone's Author of the Year Award. The television adaptation of *Tipping the Velvet* wins a GLIFF award (Best Feature) at the Austin Gay & Lesbian International Film Festival. Rachael Stirling (Nan) wins Best Actress Award and Geoffrey Sax wins Best Feature Award at the Dallas OUT TAKES festival and also a Eurola Award at the Hamburg Lesbian and Gay Film Festival. The adaptation wins a TRIC Award (TV Drama Programme) at the Television and Radio Industries Club Awards and is nominated for a BAFTA TV Award (Best Original Television Music) and an RTS Television Award (Visual Effect – Digital Effects) by the Royal Television Society, UK.

2004 The television adaptation of *Tipping the Velvet* is nominated for a GLAAD Media Award (Outstanding Television Movie or Mini-Series).

2005 *Fingersmith* adapted by Sally Head Productions for the BBC into a three-part serial, first shown 27 March. Elaine Cassidy (Maud) and Aisling Walsh are nominated for an IFTA Award (Best Actress in Television and Best Director – TV Drama/Drama Series, respectively) at the Irish Film and Television Awards.

2006 *The Night Watch* is published by Virago and is shortlisted for both the Man Booker Prize for Fiction and the Orange Prize for Fiction. The television adaptation of *Fingersmith* is nominated for a BAFTA (Best Drama Serial).

2007 *The Night Watch* wins a Lambda Literary Award and is shortlisted for both the British Book Awards Book of the Year and the James Tait Black Memorial Prize (for fiction).

2008 *Affinity* is adapted by Box Productions for ITV, first shown 28 December. Andrew Davies writes the screenplay. Anna Madeley (Margaret) wins a Golden Nymph Award (Television Films – Best Performance by an Actress) at the Monte-Carlo TV Festival. Zoe Tapper (Selena), Anne Reid (Mrs Brink), Anna Massey (Miss Haxby) are all nominated for Golden Nymph Awards (Television Films – Best Performance by an Actress). Vincent Leclerc (Theophilus) is nominated for Golden Nymph Award (Television Films – Best Performance by an Actor).

2009 *The Little Stranger* is published by Virago, and is shortlisted for the Man Booker Prize for Fiction and nominated for the Shirley Jackson Award. The television adaptation of *Affinity* is nominated for a GLAAD Media Award for Outstanding Television Movie and a Canadian Society of Cinematographers Award for Best Cinematography in TV Drama.

2011 *The Night Watch* is adapted by the BBC; it is first shown on 12 July.

2012 Provides the Introduction for the Virago Modern Classics new edition of Sylvia Townsend Warner's *Lolly Willowes*.

INTRODUCTION

The Popular and Critical Reception of Sarah Waters

KAYE MITCHELL

Sarah Waters is one of the most successful and best-regarded literary authors currently working in the United Kingdom, and she enjoys both huge popularity and glowing critical reviews in this country and beyond. Waters' critical success is evident in her 2003 listing in the prestigious *Granta* 'Best of Young British Novelists' issue and in her impressive haul of prizes (which includes the Betty Trask Award, the John Llewellyn Rhys Prize, the Lambda Literary Award for Fiction and the James Tait Black Memorial Prize). Three of Waters' novels – *Fingersmith* (2002), *The Night Watch* (2006) and *The Little Stranger* (2009) – have been shortlisted for the Man Booker Prize, with both *Fingersmith* and *The Night Watch* also shortlisted for the Orange Prize. Although *The Little Stranger* lost out to *Wolf Hall* in the 2009 Booker contest, in the run up to the prize it was outselling all the other longlisted titles by 50 per cent; in October 2002, *The Guardian* proclaimed *Fingersmith* 'the most popular Booker contender with the book-buying public', according to figures garnered from Waterstone's (Pauli 2002).

Popular Reception

On its publication in 1998, *Tipping the Velvet* attracted gleeful reviews describing it as 'a sexy and picaresque romp', and suggesting that it inaugurated a genre all its own: the 'bawdy lesbian picaresque novel' (Steele 1998). At the same time, *Tipping* was claimed as the continuation of a lesbian literary tradition, with Waters' work compared to that of Jeanette Winterson. As Peter Kurth at *Salon* magazine averred: 'This is the lesbian novel we've all been waiting for' (Kurth 1999). As these examples indicate, Waters was initially pigeonholed as a lesbian novelist, albeit one who might 'entice new readers' to the 'lesbian historical fiction' genre (Emma Donoghue, cover blurb). Nevertheless, as her reputation and readership have grown, Waters' major achievement – in the eyes of newspaper critics, anyway – has been to transcend whatever narrow generic boundaries and markets may have been assigned to her at the outset, and her subsequent novels have received subtler readings and near-universal acclaim. Thus, reviewers of *Affinity* praise Waters' 'consummate skill in evoking a sense of place' (Willard 2000) as well as her convincing creation of atmosphere – the *Guardian* reviewer finding it 'sexy, spooky, stylish, [. . .] a wonderful book' (Thomson 1999). Reviewing *Fingersmith,* fellow novelists Julie Myerson and Adam Mars-Jones are full of praise for Waters' plotting which is, in Mars-Jones' estimation, 'dazzlingly convoluted' (Mars-Jones 2002). Hinting at the critical shift already taking place in the assessment and categorization of Waters' work by the time of *Fingersmith*'s publication in 2002, Myerson asserts that: 'I hesitate to call it lesbian, because that seems to marginalize it far more than it deserves. Suffice to say, it is erotic and unnerving in all the right ways' (Myerson 2002), while Jane Perry observes of Fingersmith that the 'lesbo-Victorian romps' label 'doesn't remotely do justice to this dark, labyrinthine and utterly engrossing novel' (Perry 2003).

It is not exactly that such labels are unjust – in fact, Waters herself deployed them, albeit often in a tongue-in-cheek way, in the early days of her publishing career – but rather that they elide or cover over some of the nuance and skill of Waters' writing. As Jenny Turner elucidates, in the pages of the *London Review of Books*:

> 'Frissony', 'pastiche' and 'lesbo-Victorian' are all terms Waters herself has used in self-description – though generally not all of them at once – and they are both accurate enough and unfair. The [early] books are indeed pastiches: Victoriana as a queer theorist might perform it, with costumes by Judith Butler, prisons and madhouses by Foucault. They are indeed frissony, being peopled by young women just becoming aware of their sexuality, in scenarios involving much disguise and dissembling, and silky drawers with slits. But the books are less theatrical, less formulaic than the labels make them sound; Waters is not at all one of those writers setting out to profit from what Henry James called the 'fatal cheapness' of period fiction. Her work is always rich in feeling, and clever and precise. (Turner 2006)

It is this precision and cleverness which are perhaps overlooked in reviews of Waters' early novels, but which come to the fore in the popular assessment of her more recent work. Thus, by the time of the publication of *The Night Watch* in 2006, Waters had both an established popular readership and a notable critical profile – the latter now less dominated by terms such as 'romp', 'picaresque', etc., and less narrowly focused on the novel's lesbian content. Most reviewers of *The Night Watch* comment on the extent to which it is a departure for Waters: the change of historical setting, the fuller cast of characters, the more 'realist', muted style, the switch from first person to third person, the novel's 'defiantly unglamorous mood' (Tait 2006), the relative absence of shocks and reversals. In Philip Hensher's assessment, '*The Night Watch,* with its austerity-period and wartime setting, is certainly quite a risk', but a successful one nevertheless: 'Waters emerges from it as a still-more-characterful and boldly flavoured novelist', and *The Night Watch* is 'a truthful, lovely book' (Hensher 2006).

In the reviews of *The Night Watch* and *The Little Stranger* we find also a greater attention to Waters' use of period detail which, however, 'never overwhelms the simple, passionate human story' (Feay 2006). Thus, Justine Jordan comments that, 'Her ability to bring the times to life [in *The Night Watch*] is stunning, whether through smell – the "talcum powder, permanent waves, typewriter ink, cigarette smoke, BO" of the typing pool, the "unwashed feet, sour mops, bad food, bad breath" of prison – or through her minute enumerations of her characters' physical lives' (Jordan 2006). Hensher admiringly observes that, 'Waters avoids the obvious. There is no talk of "butch" and "femme" and not a lot about ration books', and speculates that, 'so convincing an illusion must be the product of a deep immersion in the period', particularly in the *literature* of the period (Hensher 2006). Indeed, numerous literary influences and comparisons abound in the reviews of Waters' writing, ranging from Victorian writers like Dickens and Wilkie Collins, to postwar novelists such as Denton Welch and Elizabeth Bowen, and contemporary authors including Angela Carter and Margaret Atwood. For Michèle Roberts, Waters is writing 'in the feminist tradition that draws on both male and female writers for inspiration' (Roberts 2006); given Waters' attention to gender (as keen a focus as sexuality in her work), it is perhaps no surprise that reviewers also invoke influences such as Charlotte Perkins Gilman and Virginia Woolf. Waters herself has commented that she writes for 'someone who is a big reader, because the books often have references, either semi-submerged or more overt, to other novels, or perhaps to other traditions of writing' (Armitt 2007: 117) and in the interview in this volume she details some of her literary tastes and influences (from Sylvia Townsend-Warner to Kazuo Ishiguro), conceding that her work is, to some extent, a kind of homage to her favourite authors.

In the reviews of *The Little Stranger*, it is Waters' keen understanding of class that draws praise from reviewers, with Hilary Mantel reading this 'masterly' novel as 'a perverse hymn to decay, to the corrosive power of class resentment as well as the damage wrought by war' (Mantel 2009), and Tracy Chevalier concluding that, 'Waters's persistent picking apart of class is fascinating, making the downfall of Hundreds and the Ayres more poignant than any ghosts ever could' (Chevalier 2009). As is clear from the critical writing on Waters that I will discuss below, class has been a central preoccupation of Waters' work from the outset and it is a mark of her talent that her novels consistently engage with this thorniest of issues while remaining utterly compelling and intricately plotted, never laboured or didactic.

Undoubtedly, the most significant factor in bringing Waters' work to a wider readership has been the adaptation of her novels for film and television. To date, four of her five novels have been adapted, with the fifth – *The Little Stranger* – currently in development as a feature film with Potboiler productions. As Ann Heilmann and Mark Llewellyn observe, the Andrew Davies adaptations of *Tipping* and *Affinity* have 'ensured that, for critics at least but also one suspects for the larger audience, Waters's work has somehow become "classicized" through the process, right down to the Hitchcockesque cameos' (Heilmann and Llewellyn 2010: 242). Davies came to the project with a track record that included such landmark literary adaptations as *Pride and Prejudice* (BBC 1995) and *Vanity Fair* (BBC 1998); his adaptation of *Tipping the Velvet*, produced by Sally Head's production company, aired on BBC Two between 9 and 23 October 2002, sparking immediate, occasionally scandalized, interest.

In interview Waters has commented that:

> Without wanting to sound cynical about it, in the best possible way I think it suited everybody's agenda: it gave Andrew the chance to do something a bit more daring than usual; it gave the BBC the chance to do a period drama, which they're terribly good at, but – just in case people are getting a bit bored with the period drama format – it gave them the chance to make it a bit saucy, to 'sex it up' a bit. (Armitt 2007: 125)

The tension between the polish of the BBC period drama and the near-unprecedented explicitness of the lesbian content has been central to the reception of the adaptation. As Heather Emmens writes, 'The BBC serialization of [*Tipping the Velvet*] in 2002 marked a milestone for the mainstream portrayal of lesbian characters', yet the adaptation tended to mould the work into more acceptable (heteronormative) forms, feminizing the character of Nancy Astley in a way that 'renders the spectacle more transparent than transgressive', and presenting sex scenes that 'evoke the pseudo-lesbian imagery of heterosexual pornography' (Emmens 2009: 134, 136, 137). As a result, the series gained a good deal more tabloid coverage than most literary adaptations, with *The Sun* newspaper running its own five part Page 3 series titled 'Victorian Secrets', which included explicit references to the adaptation of *Tipping* (Emmens 2009: 139). If such attempts to neutralize or domesticate the more radical elements of the original work – with its cross-dressing, gender play and unapologetic lesbianism – are all too predictable, they were at least not the only responses to the adaptation. Emmens discusses also the parody sketch by female comedy duo French and Saunders, 'Tippin' o' the Velveteen', featuring 'Miss Titty Saunders' and 'Miss Nancyboy French', which aired two months after *Tipping the Velvet*, as part of a Christmas special on BBC One. The parody, claims Emmens, 'ruthlessly mocks the BBC serial even as it subverts notions of male fantasy' and 'deflates the sensationalist media treatment of lesbianism' (Emmens 2009: 142). The mere existence of these further tabloid/parodic versions of *Tipping* in the public sphere goes some way to explaining the kind of popular currency that Waters' work has attained – and the role that the television adaptations have played in this. The fact that the adaptation of *Tipping* proceeded to amass a clutch of awards and nominations at lesbian and gay film festivals in addition to garnering a BAFTA nomination in the United Kingdom (for its music), suggests that the occasionally salacious content did not militate against more dissident and/or nuanced readings.

Waters herself is 'sanguine' about the processes and compromises of adaptation, asserting, in the interview for this volume, that:

> It's fascinating to see how the scriptwriter does it: what has to stay, what has to go, the compromises that get made, all the things the adaptation can bring to the novel. I think TV adaptations can sometimes tidy up messy books, so, for example, I think *Tipping the Velvet* benefited from that – I think Andrew brought something to it that made it work very well on screen and made it lots of fun. Some things do get lost on the way but that's inevitable – it's a translation.

Subsequent adaptations of *Fingersmith* (2006, Sally Head Productions for the BBC), *Affinity* (2008, again with Andrew Davies as screenwriter/adaptor, Box Productions for ITV), and *The Night Watch* (2011, BBC) have cemented Waters' public profile as a purveyor of literate, plot-driven period dramas, yet the shifts that reviewers have noted in her books (the move to a more 'austere', serious style, the more downbeat focus) have been evident also in the adaptations and the responses to them. In the same period, the presentation of lesbian relationships on prime-time television has become, if not common, then at least less likely to provoke outraged or titillated responses. Reporting from the set of the BBC adaptation of *The Night Watch* in 2011, Chloe Fox of *The Telegraph* observes that:

> Almost a decade ago, when Andrew Davies's adaptation of Waters' first novel, *Tipping the Velvet*, aired on the BBC, eyebrows were raised. When news releases told of the BBC's plans to run a drama serial that featured swearing and the use of dildos, the *Daily Mail* reported that viewers began to protest. 'Yes, it did cause a bit of splash, didn't it?' Waters says. 'But that was a long time ago and I don't think the same thing would happen now. And besides, *The Night Watch* is so much more restrained in its way.' (Fox 2011)

Critical Reception I: Historical Fiction and Neo-victorianism

Waters' novels are ripe for critical analysis because of their ambitious and insightful use of historical material and popular genres; they touch on topical themes of history, memory, trauma, sexuality, gender and class. Although accessible, these are generically and formally inventive novels – cleverly pastiching elements of sensation fiction, gothic fiction, the postwar middlebrow woman's novel and the country house novel, and employing backwards narration, complicated plotting, sly intertextual references and unreliable narrators. As Waters herself concedes: 'I've always brought to the books I've written the sorts of issues I know literary departments are interested in talking about: class and gender, sexuality, and playing around with literary tradition. The books lend themselves well to being analysed, I suppose, because I write them with my old literary critical background somewhere still in my head' (Armitt 2007: 125).

In particular, Waters' novels have been crucial in the development of historical fiction as a genre, contributing to its enormous increase in popularity in recent years – on the 2009 Booker shortlist on which *The Little Stranger* appeared, for example, every single novel could be classified as a 'historical novel'. Critical discussion about Waters' fiction has centred on what *kind* of historical novelist she is: the extent to which she is concerned with historical accuracy or authenticity, or is actively revising the histories that she relates. Arguably all historical fiction betrays a degree of self-consciousness, a degree of necessary inauthenticity. As Jerome de Groot explains:

> The historical novelist [. . .] explores the dissonance between then and now, making the past both recognisable but simultaneously unfamiliar. Historical novelists concentrate on the gaps between known factual history and that which is lived to a variety of purposes. The spaces scholars have no idea about – the gaps between verifiable fact – are the territory for the writer of fictional history. (de Groot 2008: 217)

Waters' novels are marked by such a 'dissonance', and in her case, the 'spaces scholars have no idea about' allow her to unearth hidden lesbian histories or even to insert lesbian stories into history. In the interview in this volume she asserts that the 'fragmentary nature' of lesbian history and the 'undecidability of lesbian relationships' are 'frustrating' for the historian – but 'fantastic' for the novelist. The questions that Waters and Laura Doan ask, in their co-authored chapter on lesbian historical fiction, have circulated around Waters' own creative work:

> On what terms does history appeal to the lesbian writer and how is the past negotiated in lesbian literary production? Should the popular novel be a site to recuperate the names and lives of 'suitable' or famous lesbians of the past, or is it better approached as a starting-point to invent a 'history' haunted by the present and understood to take its authority from the imperatives of contemporary lesbian identities? Should we read lesbian historical novels as 'performative' rather than 'descriptive' texts – as indices to the myths and fantasies through which lesbian culture is maintained and reproduced? (Doan and Waters 2000: 13)

Waters' fiction, I would suggest, engages in processes of both recuperation and invention; it is both 'performative' and 'descriptive'. The historical settings of all of Waters' novels pre-date the politicization of sexual identity that would emerge with gay liberation, yet her writing is notably informed by this political work, and the identities that Waters is interested in undeniably possess a political, collective function. This tension between a responsibility to the accurate representation of the past and an awareness of more recent developments in queer culture runs through Waters' work and through the critical discussion of it. So, writing on *Affinity*, Rachel Carroll asserts that:

> On the one hand, *Affinity* is a historically grounded and plausible reconstruction of marginalized women's histories: the spinster, the spirit medium, the working-class servant. On the other hand, it is characterized by a fidelity to the sensibilities of late-nineteenth-century literary conventions, specifically those of the sensation novel. The past is then experienced both through the framework of revisionary feminist historiography and through the past's own conventions of representation; the novel's attempt to reconstruct a 'lost' past is qualified by a consciousness of the ways in which the meanings of the past change with every attempt to 'return' to it. (Carroll 2006: 143)

To that tension between fidelity to the past and awareness of contemporary concerns, then, we must add a privileging of literary representation and literary conventions: Waters' knowledge of the past is largely mediated by, as well as communicated through, literary forms and genres.

Their self-consciousness about the construction of history and the 'meanings' of the past has led to Waters' early novels being characterized as 'neo-Victorian' (see, e.g. Arias 2009; Gamble 2009; Llewellyn 2009; Heilmann 2009/10; Yates 2009/10; Carroll 2010; Heilmann and Llewellyn 2010; Mitchell 2010). As Lucie Armitt and Sarah Gamble explain, 'in texts such as these, history is not just revisited but revised, and the form of the nineteenth-century novel not reproduced, but reworked' and the reworking is informed by a (contemporary) political impulse (Armitt and Gamble 2006: 141). Waters' is not the first neo-Victorian novelist, but her work has been prominent in the emergence and development of 'neo-Victorianism' as a category of fiction and as a critical category, featuring often in discussions of 'what is involved in this re-creation of history, what it means to fashion the past for consumption in the present' (Mitchell 2010: 3).

Analyses of the neo-Victorian novel have tended to take Linda Hutcheon's concept of historiographic metafiction as a starting-point (see Hutcheon 1988 and 1989), treating this sub-genre of the historical novel as necessarily critical and self-conscious. Yet neo-Victorian fiction is not isomorphic with historiographic metafiction – as Louisa Yates claims, 'the neo-Victorian paradox of authenticity versus anachronism, re-vision versus reproduction, is playful rather than radically confrontational', suggesting that *Tipping the Velvet* cannot therefore be 'straightforwardly classified as historiographic metafiction' (Yates 2009/10: 191). Rather it 'reproduces the cultural landscape [of the Victorian period] even as it re-vises the sexuality of those who inhabit it' (Yates 2009/10: 189).

Some of the discussions of the relationship between past and present in Waters' fiction have attended, in particular, to the novels' deployment of the word 'queer' (see, e.g. Carroll 2006; Jeremiah 2007; Koolen 2010; and de Groot in this volume). Mandy Koolen, in her reading of *Tipping*, not only notes how the repetition of 'queer' 'playfully reminds readers that rather than being a period piece, this novel belongs to the realm of contemporary historical fiction', but she also stresses how this term invokes both historical uses of 'queer' and present uses, setting up 'continuities and discontinuities between experiences of same-sex desire then and now' (Koolen 2010: 374). Rachel Carroll suggests, however, that the use of the term 'queer' throughout *Affinity* is absolutely 'in keeping with late-nineteenth-century usage to denote the odd, the peculiar, and the strange' (Carroll 2006: 143), and she claims that 'the modern usage of queer is not anachronistically evoked in *Affinity*', even though 'the reader cannot help but be aware of its [. . .] late-twentieth-century appropriation as affirmative and subversive' (Carroll 2006: 144).

Although Waters' more recent novels shift their focus from the nineteenth century to the postwar period, traces of the Victorian remain. Writing on *The Little Stranger*, Ann Heilmann claims that Waters 'embeds neo-Victorian Gothic within her forties context', reading the novel as '[adapting and subverting] the Victorian paradigm of the haunted house' (Heilmann 2012: 38, 41). Heilmann argues that, 'Waters's project of the nostalgic/traumatic return to the past is teased out in a multifaceted mirror game with our contemporary period's rememorizations of the dual legacies of the "golden age" of the Victorians and the "broken age" of the postwar forties' (Heilmann 2012: 41). Again, this reading implies that what we find in Waters' fiction is an enduring tension between historical and contemporary demands, that the texts not only express a desire for the past but also reflect upon the significance of that desire in the present.

Critical Reception II: Gender, Sexuality, Class

The publication of *Tipping the Velvet* coincided with the rise of queer theory within the academy and Judith Butler's notion of performativity is a crucial reference point for critical readings of Waters' early work. As Butler argues in *Gender Trouble* (1990), 'If gender is something that one becomes – but can never be – then gender ought not to be conceived as a noun or a substantial thing or a static cultural marker, but rather as an incessant and repeated action of some sort' (Butler 1999: 152). She subsequently delivers her theory of 'performativity' to account for this 'incessant and repeated action' by which gendered subjects are brought into being; furthermore, she notes how 'the notion of an original or primary gender identity is often parodied within the cultural practices of drag, cross-dressing, and the sexual stylization of butch/femme identities', presenting such 'cultural practices' as at least potentially subversive (Butler 1999: 174).

As Helen Davies notes, 'it has become a critical commonplace to note the influence of Judith Butler's theories of gender as performance on the music hall world of male impersonation as depicted in *Tipping the Velvet*' (Davies 2012: 117). Thus, Emily Jeremiah focuses on the novel's engagement with 'a performative notion of gender' – evident in Nan and Kitty's cross-dressing, and in the 'numerous references to performance and theatricality' (Jeremiah 2007: 137). Stefania Ciocia, meanwhile, comments on the oppositions within the novel 'between acting and living', the 'ongoing play between appearance and reality, deceitful surfaces and hidden depths', and discusses the importance of London as a backdrop, claiming that 'Nancy's development is closely connected to her gaining the ability to master the city *as a stage*' (Ciocia 2005). For Sarah Gamble, the centrality of drag and questions of performance to *Tipping* offers an opportunity for a consideration of the neo-Victorian novel as itself a 'performative' genre. Gamble claims that, 'novels that place the theme of gender performativity at the centre of the narrative expose the neo-Victorian project in its entirety as a form of masquerade', suggesting that it is not coincidental that 'the neo-Victorian novel has flowered alongside developments in gender theory' (Gamble 2009: 128).

The opportunities offered by performance – for the expression of deviant desires and the playing of different gender roles – are not unequivocally to be celebrated, however. Thus Koolen claims that Waters, 'provides a more ambivalent depiction' of cross-dressing in *Tipping the Velvet* than is offered by contemporary drag-king theorists' (Koolen 2010: 382), and most critics see Nan as undergoing a process of development that, finally, moves her away from the sphere/practice of performance – the possibilities of which can only be limited (see, e.g. Wilson 2006), with Davies claiming that Waters is '"talking back" to Judith Butler's work, as she indicates that the subversive intentions of queer theory do not necessarily translate into a Victorian context' (Davies 2012: 137).

If the early critical reception of Waters' work tended to align it with the queer theoretical context out of which it apparently emerges, more recent readings of her later fiction find Waters' affiliations and allegiances harder to fathom. Thus, Claire O'Callaghan avers that the pearl symbolism in Waters' fiction '[highlights] the value of queer theory in deconstructing hetero-patriarchal conceptions', but shows also how 'Waters retains an allegiance to the categories *woman* and *lesbian* that are central to lesbian-feminist politics' (O'Callaghan 2012: 34). And Paulina Palmer tends to read Waters as a 'lesbian feminist' author rather than a 'queer' one, citing an interview (Jardine 2005) in which she presents herself as consciously writing 'in relation to a lesbian canon, a lesbian tradition' and asserting that Waters, 'although aware of the provisionality of identity categories, nonetheless recognises their usefulness' (Palmer 2008: 70, 72).

The question of Waters' relationship with feminism runs through the critical reception of her work. Undeniably, each of her novels engages with issues of gender politics in some manner and each evinces a feminist interest in women's lives, bodies, histories and relationships. Yet Waters' doesn't shy away from presenting female characters who are duplicitous or untrustworthy – as Armitt and Gamble aver, although 'powerfully woman-centred in her focus, Waters nevertheless refuses to idealize her female characters who [. . .] often combine criminality and the occult' (Armitt and Gamble 2006: 141) – and there is a degree of ambiguity in her handling of crucial feminist concerns such as pornography, female agency and maternity. Reading the 'matrilineal narratives' of *Fingersmith* 'and the mother-daughter relationships they define as a comment on the (dis)continuities between feminist pasts and presents at the turn of the millennium' (Muller 2009/10: 111), Nadine Muller nevertheless concludes that:

> While utilising the familial feminist metaphor of matrilinealism, *Fingersmith* simultaneously undermines its very concept and the cross-generational continuity between feminist waves thereby implied: for the novel's daughters, any affiliation to their mothers is not biologically given, but psychologically constructed. (Muller 2009/10: 123–4)

Critical readings of *Affinity* attend, in particular, to Waters' use of Victorian spiritualism, not only as a metaphor for an invisible yet insistent queerness, but also as a vehicle for the exploration of nineteenth century femininity (see, e.g. Carroll 2006; Davies 2012). Again, though, the feminist interest in female agency does not result in a wholly celebratory portrayal of female relations in this novel, as Margaret increasingly becomes Selina's 'mouth-piece' and 'puppet', and both women, ultimately, are revealed to be more or less in the power of the manipulative servant, Ruth Vigers (Davies 2012: 132). As Carroll concludes, in a reading that anticipates the connections made between haunting and class anxieties in *The Little Stranger*, 'the domestic servant is exposed as the true ghost in the house, her class invisibility making possible the exercise of transgressive power' (Carroll 2006: 143).

This concern with class-relations is to be found in all of Waters' novels and it is an increasing focus in the critical writing on her work. Koolen ascribes the differences between lesbian communities in *Tipping* to class, while finding the novel too uncritically 'celebratory' of working-class communities (Koolen 2010: 392) – a point that could hardly be made about her subsequent novels. O'Callaghan suggests that pearl symbolism is used by Waters in the service of arguments about class, as well as in depictions of lesbianism, citing Mrs Ayres' great aunt's comment that female servants 'come to one as specks of grit' and 'ten years later they leave you as pearls' (Waters 2009: 73; O'Callaghan 2012: 26). Heilmann, like most reviewers of *The Little Stranger*, reads the novel as an exploration of class anxieties and resentment, speculating on whether Betty and Faraday together might 'constitute a composite emblem of the working class striking back' (Heilmann 2012: 49–50). As these examples suggest, the themes of gender, sexuality and class are utterly intertwined and utterly to the fore in all of Waters' fiction, but her handling of these topics is always alert to contradiction, ambiguity and irresolution.

Critical Reception III: Reading and Writing

In various interviews, including the one for this volume, Waters has acknowledged the inaugural influence of Chris Hunt's *Street Lavender* (Gay Men's Press, 1986) on the writing of *Tipping the Velvet*. Among critics, Louisa Yates offers the most detailed reading of *Tipping*'s vital intertextual relationship with *Street Lavender*, citing the emphasis on theatricality and performance in both novels and the shared interest in the burgeoning Socialist movement of the late nineteenth century; both Willie (of *Street Lavender*) and Nan are kept by wealthy lovers, both 'model Antinous for the benefit of a wider audience', and both 'have a queer sexuality reminiscent of Oscar Wilde – modern, yet subject to resolutely Victorian morals', with Nan displaying – like Willie – 'a similar lack of shame and a conspicuous absence of any self-reflexive analysis of her sexuality' (Yates 2009/10: 194). As the reviews cited earlier in this chapter demonstrate and as the critical writing on Waters confirms, literary allusions and references are interwoven through all of Waters' fiction, leading Davies to read Waters as 'ventriloquial' in a positive rather than pejorative sense, suggesting that 'ventriloquial repetition has the potential to be interpreted as a form of critique or transformation' (Davies 2012: 114). Davies proceeds to read *Tipping* and *Affinity* through intertexts such as *The Bostonians*, *Trilby*, *The Picture of Dorian Gray* and *De Profundis*; other critics have located influences and intertexts as various as Anne Brontë and George Eliot (Wilson 2006), or *Moll Flanders* (1722) (Ciocia 2005), in addition to the usual reference points such as Dickens and Wilkie Collins (Palmer 2008).

If Waters' novels engage in self-conscious dialogue with their influences and intertexts, presenting themselves as always alert to their generic inheritances, they also, frequently, take reading and writing as key themes in order to explore questions of sexuality, gender politics and power. In her first three novels, claims Palmer, 'the acts of reading and writing in which [Waters'] characters engage mirror, in metafictional fashion, the kind of activities that she herself performs in constructing the text' (Palmer 2008: 70), while Beth Palmer asserts that the 'awareness of material culture' to be found in Waters' novels is directly derived from her nineteenth-century sensational intertexts (B. Palmer 2009: 87). But if these texts-within-texts look to the past, they also have a knowing, contemporary resonance, and thus the 'diary entries and suffrage magazines pertinent to women's history (e.g. in *Affinity* and *Tipping*, respectively), along with reference to the reading and production of lesbian erotica (e.g. in *Fingersmith*), introduce topics and debates relevant to present-day lesbian culture' (Palmer 2008: 83). Again the books can be seen as mediating between past and present concerns in their construction of lesbian histories.

If literary texts and the very act of writing are, here, held up as values in themselves and sources of pleasure and enjoyment, they are not necessarily records of, or routes to, the truth. Armitt and Gamble, reading *Affinity* as 'a novel of letters', observe how Selina and Margaret's journals are not only mutually dependent but also asymmetrical – written at different points in time, with quite different motivations and different relationships to truth and trustworthiness (Armitt and Gamble 2006: 152; see also Gamble on narrative unreliability and asymmetrical doubling in *Fingersmith*, in this volume). The story emerges through the interaction of the two journals, but ultimately we must come to question the trustworthiness of each. Paradoxically – or perhaps predictably – this unreliability of the written word in Waters' fiction is due, in large part, to its connection with desire. Beth Palmer notes how, 'in *Affinity* the physical process of writing itself becomes strangely sexualized' (B. Palmer 2009: 92), but this eroticization of the written word is perhaps most marked in *Fingersmith*, a text whose engagement with discourses of pornography has made it one of Waters' more complex and challenging novels. Thus, Kathleen Miller asserts that, 'through the inversion of the gendered hierarchies involved in reading and writing, *Fingersmith* offers a corrective to the inheritance of a male-dominated pornography trade', by providing us with an ending in which Maud re-inhabits her uncle's library and becomes herself a writer of lesbian erotica (Miller 2008: npg, para 3). On Miller's reading, *Fingersmith* demonstrates that, 'female-controlled writing and reading creates an erotic literature of love, inclusion, and equality rather than female degradation' (Miller 2008: npg, para 2). However, Nadine Muller counters that 'this ending [. . .] is much less liberating if we consider the previously established links between literacy, exploitation and oppression', the fact that it is Maud's literacy, and her 'meticulous handwriting' that lead to her original confinement with her uncle at Briar (Muller 2009/10: 122). In my own discussion of this novel (see Mitchell 2013), I explore the ambivalent status of the library of pornography in *Fingersmith*, arguing that the motif of the archive or the library occupies a much more troubled and equivocal position within contemporary queer fiction than recent theories of the radical potential of queer archives might lead us to expect. What these divergent readings reinforce, however, is the richness of Sarah Waters' work and its enduring susceptibility to critical analysis. As this book goes to press, the critical excitement and outpouring of opinion about Waters' fiction, whether in the media or in the pages of academic journals, shows no sign of abating.

An Overview of the Collection

This volume of essays seeks to go beyond the parameters of the neo-Victorian as a framework for reading Waters' fiction, while still recognizing the importance of the Victorian period for Waters and the significance of her contribution to the genre of historical fiction. In the essays that follow, Jerome de Groot considers Waters' understanding of history and manipulations of genre by reading her fiction (particularly *Tipping the Velvet* and *The Night Watch*) alongside her early critical scholarship on historical fiction, considering the extent to which she practises what she preaches. In her chapter, Natasha Alden provides a historicized reading of *The Night Watch* which analyses it alongside and through vital literary intertexts of the 40s and 50s – such as Henry Green's *Caught* (1943) and Mary Renault's *The Charioteer* (1959) – as well as more recent memoirs of the period (e.g. Barbara Bell's *Just Take Your Frock Off* (1999)). Alden concludes that such texts provide a rich and complicated source material for Waters, and she seeks to unearth the 'empathic unsettlement' of Waters' own writing in *The Night Watch*. Susan Fischer, meanwhile, provides a different kind of comparative reading of Waters that is similarly alert to her influences, setting *Affinity* and Virginia Woolf's *Night and Day* side-by-side, noting their protagonists' careful negotiation of crucial London spaces – the middle-class home, the public streets – and mining Waters' novel for its feminist potential.

Matters of space and time have been crucial to the forms and themes of Waters' writing and most of the chapters here attend, in some way, to the particular locations, moments and spaces in which Waters' fiction is set: Victorian Chelsea, wartime London, the crumbling country house, the prison, the Borough, the queer subcultural spaces of the 1890s. Two chapters in particular take space and/or time as their main focus. Rebecca Pohl's discussion of *Affinity* seeks to extend the labyrinth/panopticon readings of Millbank in its development of an argument about the materialization of space and sexuality. Taking the thread as a starting point, Pohl demonstrates how desire is materialized through the repeated practice of walking and how the motion of twisting, a recurrent motif in the novel, ties together space and queer sexuality. My own chapter on *The Night Watch* examines both the treatment of time as a topic *within* the novel and the nature and effects of the backward narration *of* the novel. In this way it moves on from discussions of lesbianism's 'invisibility', by developing Annamarie Jagose's analysis of lesbianism as a 'problem' of sequence and derivation and bringing into play recent conceptions of 'queer time' in its consideration of the novel's presentation/enactment of anachrony.

As the reviews cited in this introduction indicate, the intricacies of Waters' plotting and her ingenious manipulations of the reader go some way to accounting for both her popular appeal and the susceptibility of her writing to academic analysis. In her chapter, Sarah Gamble assesses the particular, pleasurable, experience of reading and re-reading *Fingersmith,* analysing the novel's moments of 'misdirection', its asymmetrical 'doubling' and its self-conscious musings on knowledge, truth and narrative reliability. In so doing, Gamble draws out the sophisticated narrative techniques that structure Waters' oeuvre as a whole and shows that the spatial considerations that inform so much of her imagery extend also to the space of the text itself.

Understandably, much of the critical writing on Waters to date has focused on her early novels, *Tipping the Velvet* and *Affinity*. In this volume, in addition to extending this existing criticism, the contributors also offer detailed analyses of Waters' more recent fiction, particularly *The Night Watch* and *The Little Stranger.* Gender and class have, of course, been central preoccupations in Waters' writing, utterly intertwined with her interest in presenting and inventing lesbian lives and histories. In Emma Parker's chapter on *The Little Stranger,* she considers the gender and class implications of the country house novel – and Waters' own subversion of this typically heteropatriarchal and elitist genre – by reading the novel alongside intertexts such as *Brideshead Revisited* (1945) and *Rebecca* (1938) and by attending to its subtle re-figurations of relationships of class, gender and sexuality (e.g. the queer undertones of Roderick's exchanges with Faraday). Class and gender remain key aspects of Monica Germanà's reading of the same novel, but are combined there with an attention to fashion which, again, seeks to draw our attention to the specificities of the period in which *The Little Stranger* is set. Thus Germanà discusses the influence of Christian Dior, the lure of the New Look dress and the role of fashion in moulding and expressing class aspirations in this period.

These nuanced, insightful critical readings of Waters' work are bookended by a foreword and an interview. In the former, renowned writer and screenwriter Andrew Davies reminisces fondly about his experiences adapting *Tipping the Velvet* and *Affinity* for the screen and delivers his own vibrant take on the appeal and popularity of Waters' fiction. In the lengthy, engaging interview with Waters, conducted in March 2012, she discusses, among other topics: her initial attraction to the late-Victorian period; her research processes and key literary influences; her views on historical fiction; the importance of London as a setting for much of her fiction; the evolution of her writing since the late 1990s; the 'class agenda' in her novels; and the enormous changes in the literary world and publishing industry over the course of the last decade and a half. She also drops some tantalizing hints about the content of her work in progress, the as-yet-untitled and much-anticipated sixth novel. If the interview and the collection as a whole provide a detailed reflection on Sarah Waters' career to date, they also gesture forwards to her continuing and developing interests and to the critical paradigms that might both shape and be shaped by her writing in the coming decades.

CHAPTER ONE

'Taking Back the Night'? Feminism in Sarah Waters' *Affinity* and Virginia Woolf's *Night and Day*

SUSAN ALICE FISCHER

Chapter Summary: Sarah Waters' second novel, *Affinity* (1999), explores lesbian identity and the possibility of connection between women of different classes. This search for self and desire recalls not only Elizabeth Barrett Browning's narrative poem *Aurora Leigh* (1857), to which Waters' novel directly alludes, but also, as this chapter details, Virginia Woolf's *Night and Day* (1919), with which it shares thematic preoccupations developed through similar spatial and temporal configurations. In *Affinity*, as in much of Waters' work, night-time allows for covert queerness to emerge and for the lesbian protagonists to resist social norms. Similarly, in Woolf's novel, daytime marks the conventional, whereas night allows the unconscious and real self to emerge. The middle-class female protagonists of both novels move through clearly demarcated London spaces – interiors, streets and river embankment – as they locate themselves and their desires beyond the norms of social convention.

Keywords: *Affinity*, lesbianism, Virginia Woolf, London, space, class, desire.

Night-time in much of Sarah Waters' work represents a space for covert queerness and for resistance to the many ways in which society literally and figuratively imprisons her protagonists, particularly because of their gender, sexuality and class. *The Night Watch* (2006), for instance, narrates the Blitz of London in reverse chronological order and recounts the ways the characters – lesbians or other outsiders – resist their marginalization by finding spaces, often under cover of darkness, in which they can be themselves. As a wartime ambulance driver, protagonist

Kay navigates London's streets at night with a freedom she could not otherwise experience.

Similar temporal and spatial preoccupations permeate Waters' *Affinity* (1999), in which one of the main characters is 'doing time' in Millbank Penitentiary. The ways that time and space are configured here recall Virginia Woolf's *Night and Day* (1919), and parallels between the two novels are numerous. The surname of Waters' protagonist – Margaret *Prior* – suggests a harkening back to some previous model, and Waters retrospectively writes a 'prior' novel about how women – and specifically lesbians – were restricted during the Victorian era, and class divides are also central to her work (see Armitt and Gamble 2006: 156; Kohlke 2004). Woolf's earlier feminist novel resonates with Waters', and each text shows the subversive potential of night. Yet ultimately a rather different vision emerges.

Affinity is not a rewriting of *Night and Day*, and indeed, the text most obviously evoked is Elizabeth Barrett Browning's narrative poem, *Aurora Leigh* (1857). Waters directly references the text as Margaret Prior reads the poem in the novel and secretly refers to herself as Aurora. Browning's poem, like Waters' novel, concerns the unlikely alliance between an upper-middle-class woman who attempts to 'assist' her working-class 'sister' who has fallen upon hard times (see also Kohlke 2004: 165, n. 16). The upper-middle-class poet Aurora Leigh and the working-class Marian Erle travel to Italy – hence the destination and passport in the latter's name in Waters' novel – where they live together with Marian's baby who is the product of a rape, a tragedy originally set in motion through the trickery of the wicked Lady Waldemar. Browning's poem involves the protagonist Aurora finding her true love, Romney Leigh, and explores the ways that different classes are kept apart.

Julia Briggs reports that Virginia Woolf read *Aurora Leigh* in 1931. She was so interested in Browning's work that she not only proposed an essay on the poem for *The Yale Review*, but she also wrote about the poet's dog in her novel *Flush: A Biography* (1933) (Briggs 2006: 272). While this work comes well after her novel *Night and Day* (1919), Woolf's interest in the issues the poem raises is already present in her early work. Indeed, '*Aurora Leigh* is quite as preoccupied as Woolf herself was with [. . .] the role of the woman as artist, the effects of class on how women were expected to behave, and the need to speak more openly of the bodily experiences' (ibid.).

Whether Waters draws specifically upon *Night and Day* for her novel remains open to speculation. However, the ways that Woolf uses time and space in her novel, and much of her other work, reverberate in *Affinity*. As the past haunts the present in Woolf's work, many elements of Waters' novel seem visited by the ghostly spectre not only of Browning's poem, but also of Woolf's writing. Drawing upon aspects of Woolf's own life, *Night and Day* (1919) resonates in her later writings, such as *Street Haunting: A London Adventure* (1927) and *Mrs Dalloway* (1925), which focus on wandering London's streets as a process of reflection and an exploration of the inner self. Like the narrator in *Street Haunting*, the protagonist in *Night and Day* moves through London spaces – its interiors, streets and river embankment – as she attempts to locate herself and her desires. Night-time also represents the unconscious world where she can remove herself from societal restrictions.

Protagonists Margaret Prior in *Affinity* and Katharine Hilbery in *Night and Day* are both upper-middle-class women in their late twenties living in their parents' houses on Cheyne Walk, who enter alternative, and differently classed, London spaces in an effort to break free of societal norms that restrict them as women and, in Margaret's case, suffocate her as a lesbian. Less experimental than Woolf's later work, *Night and Day* is third person omniscient, while *Affinity* is narrated in two voices (and set in two different fonts). The first, predominant and seemingly more reliable voice is Margaret Prior's, while the other, Selina Dawes', is at first reading more opaque. Armitt and Gamble write that their two journals:

> . . . enjoy a privileged relationship to authority: they are self-affirming and, as such, we are at no time actively encouraged to challenge the truth-value of any of the material inscribed in them. Furthermore, their mutual dependence derives from the fact that, without its partner, each of the two narratives lacks closure, narrative 'sense' only becoming possible by reading one half through the other. (Armitt and Gamble 2006: 152)

In setting these two narratives side-by-side, and allocating more space to Margaret's upper-middle-class voice than to Selina Dawes' working-class – and more transgressively queer – narrative, Waters is perhaps luring her reader into the same sort of trap that Margaret ultimately falls for. At first the reader may, like Margaret, be sceptical of the spirit world that Selina seems to be in touch with, but gradually as Margaret comes to believe Selina's story, the reader is similarly seduced and blinded.

The storylines of the two novels present some similarities. Woolf's Katharine Hilbery lives in a highly literary family, much like her author's. Katharine is the granddaughter of a famous poet on her mother's side, and her father edits a 'Review'. She spends her days occupied with the genteel duties of an upper-middle-class unmarried woman, pouring tea for various visitors, showing them her grandfather's manuscripts and other memorabilia, and assisting her rather endearingly dithering mother on the biography of Katharine's grandfather, which never seems to get written. Katharine does this work more from filial duty than interest. While occupying the role assigned to her by virtue of her class and her family's connection to literary greatness, she longs to study mathematics – as befits someone so given to abstraction – and to gaze at the stars at night. Upstairs in her Cheyne Walk room:

> she rose early in the morning or sat up late at night to . . . work at mathematics. No force on earth would have made her confess that. Her actions when thus engaged were furtive and secretive, like those of some nocturnal animal. [. . .] It was only at night, indeed, that she felt secure enough from surprise to concentrate her mind to the utmost. (Woolf 1992: 34)

She loves the 'star-like' quality of mathematics and keeps it secret, not only because her interest would be considered 'unwomanly', but also because she is loathe to confess how much she prefers the 'exactitude' of mathematics to the literature that is part of her family tradition (ibid.).

Margaret Prior, in *Affinity*, has been similarly engaged, albeit with much greater interest, in working with her late father, a historian, and she initially draws upon her experience of scholarly work to narrate her experiences. Like Mr Hilbery, Mr Prior is a great authority in his field; and the father who is a great scholar recalls not only Sir Leslie Stephen, but also the dead father in *Aurora Leigh*. Now that Margaret's father has died, Margaret becomes a 'Lady Visitor' to the female inmates at the nearby Millbank prison, modelled on the Benthamite panopticon. Philanthropy among women of the working-class and poor is also a theme in Browning's poem, while in Woolf's novel the social cause is women's suffrage. In both Katharine's and Margaret's cases, the relationship with their mothers is one of obligation, though more benignly so in the former's case. While Katharine feels bound to assist her mother with the biography and also feels the pull of social convention, Margaret increasingly experiences her mother as a tyrant who attempts to force her into 'appropriately' gendered social roles. Mrs Prior ostensibly drugs her daughter into submission by administering the laudanum and chloral prescribed after Margaret's suicide attempt following her beloved Helen's marriage to Stephen, Margaret's brother. Now Mrs Prior is vigilant about her 'deviant' behaviour, and Margaret comes to think of her as a prison warder. (Marian Erle's mother in *Aurora Leigh* is even more sinister as she attempts to sell her into prostitution).

While the plotlines are far from identical, some of the themes of Waters' novel echo Woolf's preoccupations, especially in terms of the desire to find true connection with another soul beyond the bounds of social convention. Indeed, 'affinity' is significant in both novels, albeit in somewhat different configurations. (This is also true in Browning's poem, in which, after Aurora refuses her cousin Romney's proposal, he becomes engaged to Marian Erle, but Lady Waldemar convinces her that the class difference makes the marriage inappropriate; in the end Aurora and Romney recognize their true connection to, and affinity with, one another). In Woolf's novel, which explores the conscious and unconscious and the social and interior lives of its characters, this plays out in Katharine's choice of a husband. At first, she agrees to marry William Rodney, a socially acceptable choice because of his class and family status. Although she is fond of him, there is no real connection. Similarly, Mary Datchet, who works for women's suffrage, and Ralph Denham, first seem drawn to one another. Katharine gradually comes to realize that the lower-middle-class Ralph is the person with whom she feels a true affinity, and their connection is so deep as to risk remaining subterranean. But ultimately Katharine finds in Ralph 'some one [who] shared her loneliness' and her vision of the world (Woolf 1992: 419).

The theme of affinity is obviously central to Waters' novel, which also develops various combinations of lovers, and all is not what it initially seems. Once Margaret meets Selina Dawes, a Millbank inmate, she comes to feel that her earlier love for Helen pales in comparison now that she has met her true kindred spirit – 'that other soul, that has the affinity with her soul', that might be 'kept from her by some false boundary' (Waters 1999: 210). Selina does everything in her power to elicit these feelings in Margaret and to convince her that she feels the same way. In this very cleverly plotted novel, which leaves us wondering until the very end just how much we should suspend our disbelief in favour of accepting the supernatural world, we come to realize that Margaret is not a reliable narrator after all, but that she has been duped and that those who possess true affinity are Selina and her lover on the outside, Ruth Vigers, for whom Selina will go to any length. She concocts an elaborate plan to escape with her lover by drawing in a prison warder and by convincing Margaret that she is able to travel non-corporally through the night and rematerialize at dawn in Cheyne Walk.

In both novels, the search for true affinity, and the freedom to transgress social barriers that is associated with it, are constructed spatially and temporally. Both novels are remarkable for their clear demarcation of spaces that are open or shut to the characters because of their gender, class and sexuality. Indoor and outdoor spaces are clearly marked, and doors, windows and other thresholds are significant in both texts. Both novels are also notable for their specificity in the treatment of London's spaces. *Night and Day* opens in the Hilberys' Cheyne Walk drawing room, when Ralph Denham, a young man from a less distinguished family and class, comes to take tea. The atmosphere of upper-class gentility and the weight of history produce both envy and a contrary response in him. He is attracted to the daughter and main character, Katharine, but at the same time, he pushes her away with socially awkward responses. He arrives just as Katharine has been musing on what impressions would be formed in the mind of someone opening a door to their drawing room on a Sunday evening gathering at teatime. When Ralph does indeed open the door and enter the room, he feels 'as if a thousand softly padded doors had closed between him and the street outside', and he 'cursed himself very sharply for having exchanged the freedom of the street for this sophisticated drawing room' (Woolf 1992: 4).

The constantly mentioned opening and closing of doors delineates the different self-states, as well as associated social spaces, which are often contrasted with the rambling spaces of city streets. Interiors, particularly those of the Hilbery home on Cheyne Walk represent something that Katharine longs to escape. It is 'an orderly place, shapely, controlled – a place where life had been trained to show to the best advantage' (Woolf 1992: 33). Each of the other main characters – Ralph Denham, William Rodney and Mary Datchet – have clearly defined interior spaces. While Ralph lives in Highgate, other characters are located in Bloomsbury, and Mary works in Russell Square. Rooms represent the boundaries of the psyche and are more or less porous at different moments of being, allowing entry and egress to others to varying degrees. For instance, early in the novel, Ralph goes into his room in the rather cramped family house in Highgate and places a 'do not disturb' sign on his door. Even so, he wants his sister to come in. Mary allows a range of people into her rooms for cultural and political activities. Yet, rooms are also confined places from which their inhabitants must escape, and thus they enter restlessly into the streets of London. When they need a moment's reflection, they often repair to the Embankment.

As in Woolf's fiction, 'In Waters's novels, buildings never serve as setting only', and the rarefied atmosphere of a Cheyne Walk drawing room is something with which Margaret Prior in *Affinity* is also familiar (Boehm 2011: 241). This would set her apart from Selina, even if the latter were not in prison and had not previously acquired, through her spiritualist clientele, a degree of social mobility which allows her to take on an air of gentility: 'Her accent is good' (Waters 1999: 45). Even more than Katharine, Margaret finds the social constraints of the drawing room and polite society a strain, especially because of her sexuality. As in Woolf's novel, social stricture is constantly expressed through metaphors of doors and other barriers in *Affinity*, not only with the ways that social convention restrains Margaret, but also more obviously with the metaphor of the prison that runs through so much of Waters' work. For instance, in *The Night Watch* (2006), two of the characters are in prison during the war; in *Tipping the Velvet* (1998), the main character is imprisoned by her sadomasochistic lover. In *Fingersmith* (2002), the insane asylum stands in for the prison, and the gallows is always in view, while in *The Little Stranger* (2009), the house itself becomes a prison. *Affinity* opens with Selina's journal, just before her actual imprisonment when something has gone terribly wrong during a séance. She writes, 'they have locked the door on me' (Waters 1999: 1). When she first meets the man in charge of the prison, Margaret thinks 'I was glad that Mr Shillitoe knew nothing of my history [. . .] that will keep that history in its place. I imagined them fastening my own past shut, with a strap and a buckle' (Waters 1999: 29); she is thinking not only of her attempted suicide, but her love for another woman. Selina's surname, Dawes, sounds very much like *doors*. That Margaret's brother misremembers Dawes' name as 'Gates' (Waters 1999: 97; see also Armitt and Gamble 2006: 149) emphasizes this allusion to spatial barriers and thresholds, as do other names: Mrs Brink (Selina's client who dies) and Mr Locke (the prosecutor in Selina's trial). Throughout the novel, doors that are expected to remain locked actually open portals to transgression, the implication being, perhaps, that lesbian desire will out.

Indoor spaces dominate in Waters' novel as so much of it takes place either in Millbank where Selina is imprisoned or in the family home on Cheyne Walk, which Margaret experiences as carceral. Margaret's narrative opens with a description of her first view of the prison and its 'many gates and twisting passages' (Waters 1999: 7). As in so much of her fiction, here Waters sees society in Foucauldian terms with surveillance inside and outside of the prison controlling lesbians in particular (Foucault 1995). In *Affinity*, Selina's need for duplicity is a reaction to surveillance. That is, the panopticon is important not only for the design of Millbank, but also for the notion of seeing that the plot depends upon, particularly for its final ironic twist. As a spiritualist or medium, Selina is meant to be clairvoyant, and indeed she sees much more clearly than Margaret, even though Margaret seems at first to have the advantage as she looks surreptitiously upon her through the peephole – called *'the eye'* – to her cell (Waters 1999: 23). As Llewellyn points out, 'Margaret's higher social status allows her to occupy both the role of observed and observer, and displace her punishment onto others, voyeuristically examining Selina through the cell door' (2004: 211). Yet Margaret is also scrutinized not only by her mother, but ultimately by the warders at Millbank who watch the way she watches Selina, and of course by her maid Ruth Vigers. Looking is also erotically charged and transgressive. Just before she first sets eyes on Selina, and thinks of the other women prisoners, Margaret feels her 'heart beating': 'I imagined how it would be to have that heart drawn from me, and one of those women's coarse organs pressed into the slippery cavity left at my breast . . . I put my hand to my throat then and felt, before my pulsating heart, my *locket*' (Waters 1999: 26, italics mine). In this passage, not only is the act of looking erotic, but also desire is surreptitiously *unlocked* – in one of the significant moments in her seduction of Margaret, Selina uncovers her locket. Margaret writes of the moment when she first sees Selina: 'I put my fingers to the inspection slit, and then my eyes. And then I gazed at the girl in the cell beyond – she was so still, I think I held my breath for fear of startling her' (ibid.). One of the guards warns her not to put her eye up to the peephole as another inmate had jabbed something into another watcher's eye. Later, 'it is no accident that Selina should stab Miss Brewer *"upon the eyes"*' (Llewellyn 2004: 211); this foreshadows the ending and the way that Selina manages, with the help of Ruth Vigers, chloral and laudanum, to distort Margaret's perception and make her believe she sees a different reality.

While indoor spaces predominate in *Affinity* for obvious reasons, outdoor London spaces are significant in both Woolf's and Waters' novels, and both authors situate their characters in specific neighbourhoods, streets or locations. For Woolf's characters, once in the streets, a feverish quality takes over, which represents the ways the characters use the city streets to pace out interior conflicts as their feet lead to paths they had no conscious intention of taking. For example, early in *Night and Day,* drawn by a feeling for Katharine that he doesn't yet understand, Ralph finds himself following her and Rodney who make their way towards the Embankment, just as later he finds himself with his back leaning upon the Embankment wall on Cheyne Walk and looking across the street to Katharine's house. Similarly, towards the end of the book, Katharine's restlessness reaches such a pitch that she rushes into the street, anxious to find Ralph. She finds herself in Mary's rooms not knowing whether she should dash up to Highgate or wander the city streets in search of Ralph. Mary accompanies her home, when Katharine finally finds Ralph and recognizes her connection to him. In these journeys through London's streets the characters discover their true feelings.

In *Affinity,* London spaces are more limited as the main action takes place at either the Cheyne Walk house or at Millbank (although Selina's journal also mentions Holburn and Sydenham). Like Katharine, Margaret also enters other spaces: the British Library, which she used to frequent as a researcher to her father, and the library of spiritualists, where she conducts research to assess whether Selina is a charlatan or a talented, and thus unjustly imprisoned, spiritualist. The two libraries represent different types of knowledge, and the occult is associated with the lesbian: 'Waters deliberately uses spiritualism throughout the novel as a metaphorical cover for the underworld of lesbian sexuality, hence the punning on the more modern meaning of the word "queer" in relation to mesmerists' (Llewellyn 2004: 210). Frequent punning on the word 'queer' underlines this connection; for instance, at Mrs Brink's house in Sydenham, where Selina works as a medium, she uses 'quite a queer sort of room' for the séance (Waters 1999: 119). Alex Owen also sees the séance as 'a transgression and transposition of normative femininity' (Owen 1989: 11); Selina's diary suggests that the young women that she and Ruth Vigers 'train' as spiritualists are actually experiencing lesbian desire. This different way of knowing, represented by the alternative space of the spiritualist library, attracts Margaret.

London's streets also offer Margaret respite from the two punishing options of conformity, denoted by the Cheyne Walk home, or of incarceration, represented by Millbank, which form a continuum of the carceral society. Yet, women's direct access to the streets is often challenged, and in both novels cabs represent a space between social convention and freedom of movement. Although both Katharine and Margaret resist conformity by walking in the city streets, the expectation is that they should take cabs. William Rodney virtually forces

Katharine into a cab on the Embankment at midnight, even though she would rather walk: 'William beckoned, with a despotic gesture, to the cab with one hand, and with the other he brought Katharine to a stand-still' (Woolf 1992: 54). Early in *Affinity*, as Millbank is 'a straight cab's ride from Chelsea', the porter at the prison assumes that Margaret will take a cab home, but she:

> . . . stopped him, and I crossed to the embankment wall [. . .] then I began to walk. I walked the length of the embankment, and only paused again before the house [. . .]. I walked, because I guessed that Mother would still be busy with Pris. When I went home, however, I found that she was not out as I had supposed, but had been back for an hour, and had been watching me. How long was it, she wanted to know, that I had been going about the city on foot? (Waters 1999: 32, 51)

Another time, after the visit during which Selina writes in her book, Margaret does take a cab home. That 'they had shut [her] into the cab' suggests her sense of entrapment (Waters 1999: 116).

As the interior and exterior spaces in both novels represent different aspects of life, so do night and day, and both novels are particular in the ways they delineate time. In Woolf's novel, day and night represent, respectively, the characters' conscious and unconscious lives. Moreover, day symbolizes the pull of social convention, night, the interior life and the possibility of freedom and self-actualization. It is at night that Katharine longs to gaze at the stars and indulges in her 'unwomanly' passion for mathematics, which brings her to a different realm. The novel examines the nature of:

> . . . this perpetual disparity between the thought and the action, between the life of solitude and the life of society, this astonishing precipice on one side of which the soul was active and in broad daylight, on the other side of which it was contemplative and dark as night[.] (Woolf 1992: 288)

Night and day are similarly constructed in Waters' novel, which privileges 'the other side' and is 'contemplative and dark as night', as it promises to open up a world of freedom to its lesbian protagonists. Early on, when she leaves Millbank after a visit, Margaret finds that, '[t]he day, after the closeness of the women's wards, seemed pure to me' (Waters 1999: 51). Despite this 'purity', it is night that seems to offer the possibilities she seeks. Just as Katharine searches out the stars at night, Margaret pursues another realm by imagining the spirit world that Selina fabricates. The night on which Margaret reads the note that Selina writes in her diary is described as 'a harsh one' in which only she – and Vigers – seem awake on all Cheyne Walk (Waters 1999: 116). She is spooked, feeling:

> . . . the night has Millbank in it, with its thick, thick shadows; and in one of those shadows *Selina* is lying – *Selina* – she is making me write the name

> here, she is growing more real, more solid and quick, with every stroking of the nib across the page – *Selina*. In one of those shadows *Selina* is lying. Her eyes are open, and she is looking at me. (Waters 1999: 116–17)

This passage is full of double meanings, which underscore the duplicity of the plot: the stroking of the nib suggests Margaret's desire which makes Selina seem real; Selina is also 'lying' in the sense of being mendacious, and her eyes are indeed open and watching Margaret, while Margaret's are blinded until the end of the novel. Night holds Selina's and Margaret's desire, which is 'furtive and secretive', as Katharine says of her nights. In *Affinity*, night – and the in-between time of dawn – allows transgression, represented in part by chicanery and trickery, to take place. At night, the 'spirit' world – fake though it turns out to be – emerges, and with it the occluded world of lesbianism that it masks. At the same time, night holds out the threat of punishment, and after she attacks one of the warders, Selina is put in 'the darks' of solitary confinement.

In addition to the apparent opposites of day and night, interior and exterior space, both novels present in-between spaces, represented by the Thames. The location on Cheyne Walk of both protagonists' homes already makes the Thames a significant location. Yet for Katharine, Margaret and other characters, the Thames holds particular importance. In *Night and Day*, Woolf uses the Thames to signal a hiatus and a moment of reflection at a crisis point in the characters' lives, particularly in relation to the recognition of loneliness and the desire for affinity which seems unavailable in social settings. (Similarly, in *Street Haunting: A London Adventure*, the river offers the narrator pause for reflection about the significance of her wanderings and her search for creativity and self through London's streets.) When Ralph realizes his feelings for Katharine after hearing that she has accepted William's proposal, his first impulse is to stride 'with extreme swiftness along the Embankment', and he initially feels that he is 'a man with no grasp upon circumstances any longer' (Woolf 1992: 129). As he gazes into the river, its 'swift race of dun-coloured waters seemed the very spirit of futility and oblivion' (Woolf 1992: 130). Feeling it impossible to 'trust [. . .] in men and women [or] in one's dreams about them [. . .] [h]is mind plunged lower and lower' (ibid.). Although he leaves the Embankment unhappy, he re-enters 'a populous and teeming world', for the moment giving up on his dreams (Woolf 1992: 131). Similarly, Mary Datchet goes to the Embankment to reflect upon her feelings for Ralph, whom she loves. Only by the river does she break away from her work for the suffrage movement and the other demands of her life to recognize her loneliness and the longings for an inner life. But for Mary, who commits herself to social change, this moment is brief.

Despite dwelling on Cheyne Walk, Katharine initially spends little time on the Embankment; at one point, she avoids the river which would make her 'think about things that didn't exist' (Woolf 1992: 227). This changes in the middle of the book once Katharine and William come to realize they should not marry. Ralph knocks at the door, and Katharine urges William to 'open the door', symbolic of her initial, yet still submerged, openness to a real connection with Ralph (Woolf 1992: 248). As they go out into the streets, Ralph thinks, 'The Strand was too busy' and he tries to lead Katharine towards the Thames, saying: 'It's quieter by the river' (Woolf 1992: 250, 251). Here he is able to express his feelings: 'I see you everywhere, in the stars, in the river, to me you're everything that exists; the reality of everything' (Woolf 1992: 251). At the river, '[a]s if obeying a common instinct, they both stopped, and bending slightly over the balustrade of the river, looked into the flowing water' (Woolf 1992: 252). The Thames offers a space apart from the constraints of the surface of social life and allows the characters to glimpse the 'reality' of interior life and thus the possibility of connection. Towards the end of the novel, Katharine and Ralph walk to the river. As he accompanies her home, 'Katharine pushed the door half open and stood upon the threshold', and they part for the evening (Woolf 1992: 432). Their 'good nights', which close the book, are significant for the connection they have been able to make to the 'reality' of the interior of life. We see Katharine at the end of the novel, no longer inside, but on a threshold, not only of a new life with Ralph, but more importantly in an in-between place which allows the various parts of life – night and day, interior and exterior – to coalesce. Significantly, she is simultaneously, at the end of the book, at the river, on the street and at home.

For Margaret, in *Affinity*, there is no such happy ending, though Selina and Ruth might tell a different story. But here, too, the Thames is significant. Margaret is willing to sleep just below the maids' quarters 'for the sake of my view of the Thames, which I could not give up' (Waters 1999: 69). The Thames is also important in the novel because Millbank prison is located along another stretch of the river, and when Ruth Vigers comes to work in the house at Cheyne Walk, she says she likes the location because 'she has another friend in another situation near to the river and would like to be near her' (Waters 1999: 68). After Selina hits a warder to ensure her permanence at Millbank prison until she is ready to escape, Margaret walks out into the street because she 'could [not] bear the closeness' of a cab (Waters 1999: 251). Instead, she 'walked home, quickly, through the darkness, without a thought for my own safety. Only at the end of Tite Street [which leads to Thames Embankment] did I slow my step, to turn my face into the breeze, to cool it' (ibid.). Margaret attempts to use this as an in-between space to pull herself together before meeting her mother's gaze.

A third space is particularly important for the masked lesbian world in Waters' novel. As Selena writes in her journal, 'The spirit-medium's proper home is neither this world nor the next, but that vague & debatable land which lies between them' (Waters 1999: 73). Indeed, it is the space between Margaret's home and the prison – along the Thames – that becomes the in-between space promising the arrival of Margaret's 'own *affinity*' (Waters 1999: 275). The 'tokens' from Selina that apparently come via the spirit world, arrive, Margaret believes, 'to make the space between us thick. They make a quivering cord of dark matter, it stretches from Millbank to Cheyne Walk, it is the cord through which she will send me herself' (Waters 1999: 285). The dark rope she imagines recalls the Thames itself, which will be the only thing available to her at the end. As preparations for Selina's arrival near, and Margaret manages to stay alone, with her servant Vigers, at Cheyne Walk, she looks out into the night at the Thames, where 'I should never have guessed that that dark night could have had so many colours in it' (Waters 1999: 298). As the Eve of St Agnes' arrives, the night that Selina should 'travel' to her, she quotes from Keats' poem of that title, which echoes the arrival of the beloved, though perhaps Margaret forgets that St Agnes herself died a virgin and a martyr. Space and time seem to intersect, and this night-time perambulation promises freedom: during the day, Margaret is subject to the demands of others, but at night, or in that in-between time just before dawn, Selina will 'travel' to Margaret. In actuality, under the cover of night she will escape prison and reconnect with her true affinity, Ruth Vigers.

As with Katharine, Margaret's story ends at the river, on the street and at home. But her ending is very different. Having waited all night and through the dawn for Selina to materialize, she rushes to the prison, only to find that Selina has escaped. Fearing that the warders would 'find a way to keep me there, for ever' and away from Selina, Margaret runs 'to the embankment, and then I followed its wall, keeping very close to that one bleak way. I watched the river, that was quicker than I; and I wished I might take a boat, and make my escape like that' (Waters 1999: 328). She stops briefly at Pimlico Pier and then reaches Albert Bridge. Finally she encounters Mrs Jelf, a Millbank matron, who has also been tricked by Selina into helping her escape, and the two return to Margaret's Cheyne Walk home. Once she realizes that *'Selina has taken my life, that she might have a life with* Vigers *in it!'*, Margaret goes to the window overlooking the Thames: 'Before me, London lay perfectly white and still. [. . .] There was the Thames, and there [. . .] the blunted tips of Millbank's towers. [. . .] And [. . .] Cheyne Walk [. . .]' (Waters 1999: 340, 342).

At the end of these novels, both Katharine and Margaret see their worlds and their relations to others differently. After Katharine's frenetic search for Ralph in the streets of London and their mutual declaration of love, there are frequent allusions to her clearer sight, and by the water, she wonders, 'how could she herself have been so blind?' (Woolf 1992: 390). This is a question that Margaret must also ask herself as she realizes, 'There never was a cord of darkness, never a space in which our spirits touched', and she 'know[s] [her]self untouched, unlooked for and alone' (Waters 1999: 348, 349). Ultimately her only connection is with 'the river, which flows on beneath the frigid sky, through its accustomed courses, to the sea. How deep, how black, how thick the water seems tonight! How soft its surface seems to lie. How chill its depths must be' (Waters 1999: 350–1). She sees anew, but as she reflects upon the Thames, there is no future to contemplate, only a cold death by water.

These two novels focus on women's struggle to define their own lives in the face of familial and societal restrictions. In so doing, both explore alternative configurations of space and time as they destabilize gender, sexual and class norms to varying degrees. Katharine Hilbery, in her various perambulations through London, is able to connect to some extent with Mary Datchet, who represents women's professionalism and feminism. Both Katharine and Mary break with conventions for women – Mary by working for the suffrage movement, Katharine by claiming her freedom to walk in the streets, thereby finding both herself and her 'affinity', Ralph, with whom she considers cohabitating rather than marrying. However, as the final night-time twist in Waters' novel suggests, alliances between women that ignore the inequalities of class differences are doomed. In Waters' novel, Margaret attempts to break out of the social strictures in various ways, most spectacularly by planning to run away with Selina to Italy after she is 'spirited' out of the prison. But much more subversive are Selina and Ruth, Selina's lover and Margaret's maid, who manipulate Margaret into providing the means for their life together on the Continent. The much greater class divide in Waters' novel undercuts the sense of 'sisterhood', and it becomes clear that these are two different worlds, in sharp contrast with one another. Woolf's feminist novel focuses on relatively minor class differences, and it is perhaps worth remembering that in Browning's *Aurora Leigh*, which underscores these social conflicts, the aristocratic Lady Waldemar tricks the working-class Marian Erle into leaving her betrothed because she wants to marry him herself. In Waters' novel, the tables are turned, and the working-class Selina and Ruth similarly deceive Margaret. As Kohlke writes, 'Margaret's envisaged Utopia-of-two in Italy is foreclosed by female rivalries and insurmountable class differences that perpetuate patterns of cultural conflict and exploitation' (Kohlke 2004: 162). While Margaret has been given more voice and narrative space, the novel ending with Selina's subversive liberation leaves another 'sister' in the darkness of death and opens the reader's eyes to a desperate resistance to a system rooted in class hierarchy.

CHAPTER TWO

Sexing the Labyrinth: Space and Sexuality in Sarah Waters' *Affinity*

REBECCA POHL

Chapter Summary: This chapter addresses questions of space and sexuality (and their relation) in *Affinity*, routing this discussion through the concept of the labyrinth. Rather than identifying characters in the novel with characters in the labyrinth myth, the chapter examines how practices enacted in the myth reappear in the novel and how key figurations in the myth also figure relations in the novel. Taking the thread as a starting point, it demonstrates how desire is materialized through the repeated practice of walking and how the motion of twisting, a recurrent image in the novel, ties together space and queer sexuality. By considering space through the thread, rather than the perhaps more obvious notion of architecture, a more nuanced understanding not only of space, but of the interrelation between space and sexuality becomes possible, a more precise investigation of how practices of repetition constitute space and sexuality as materiality.

Keywords: *Affinity*, space, sexuality, labyrinth, materiality, queer.

The importance of space to Sarah Waters' fiction has been discussed in a number of studies, especially the texts' engagement with the city of London and with spaces of confinement, be it the home (suburban and middle class), the prison or the asylum. Stefania Ciocia maintains that, 'Waters's atmospheric chronicles of forbidden, and forgotten, passions against the backdrop of the Victorian capital had become the trademark of her fiction' (Ciocia 2007). Lucie Armitt and Sarah Gamble contend that *Affinity*, specifically, 'primarily preoccupies itself with the difficulties of negotiating space' (Armitt and Gamble 2006: 149) and Ciocia argues in turn that Waters' neo-Victorian protagonists are concerned with escaping confining spaces into 'the non-hierarchical pageant of the city streets' (Ciocia 2007). Rather than subscribing to the more conventional public/private dyad, the spaces in Waters' fiction can be considered in terms of degrees of confinement and liberation.[1] *Affinity*, Waters' narrative of the encounter between Margaret Prior, a middle-class spinster and lady visitor to Millbank Prison, and Selina Dawes, a spiritualist medium incarcerated for fraud and assault, affords a particularly interesting avenue into this query because of the centrality of the prison to the narrative. In many readings of *Affinity* the prison has been at the centre of attention, in particular its figuration as a panopticon and the feminist and/or queer politics related to that (Macpherson 2004; Armitt and Gamble 2006; Arias 2009; Braid 2010). The importance of sexuality to Sarah Waters' neo-Victorian fiction has also been argued (Llewellyn 2004; Palmer 2007; Carroll 2007). This essay will further explore this juncture of space and sexuality in *Affinity*, arguing that space and sexuality are (re)produced through social relations and practices, each producing the other: they are relational networks where sexuality is a certain way of inhabiting space. One particular instantiation of this relation between space and sexuality is the labyrinth, a polysemic space characterized by complexity, contradiction and ambiguity, notions which also characterize the representation of sexuality in the novel. A critical reading of materiality will serve as the lens through which this relation, as manifested in the labyrinth, is investigated; more specifically, I argue that the notion of the thread figures desire in this novel and that space and sexuality are produced through following this thread, as well as being troubled by its fragility.

'Selina, you will be in sunlight soon. Your twisting is done – you have the last thread of my heart. I wonder: when the thread grows slack, will you feel it?' (Waters 1999: 351). These are Margaret's final lines in the novel. The lines are intriguing because of their ambiguity: does Margaret commit suicide or not? They are also intriguing, however, because of the way that desire is figured, not only as a connection but also as a thread. I will later look more closely at the language at play here and its relation to the 'labyrinthine' spaces that populate the novel. The labyrinth is often invoked as a metaphor for Millbank prison, viewed as a complicated space that resists intelligibility (Armitt and Gamble 2006; Arias 2009; Braid 2010). I suggest that there is something firmer to the relationship between *Affinity* and the labyrinth than the somewhat neat metaphor often invoked, that the labyrinth is not (only) a convenient image that effectively describes Millbank prison, but that it is a process of spatial becoming through which the space and the social relations at play are produced, are materialized. Along with space and sexuality, materiality is a recurrent concern in Waters scholarship, but instead of focusing on the materiality of language (Brindle 2009/10) or the séances where spirits are invoked and even materialized (Spooner 2007), I would like to pick up on the notion of the thread, a crucial element of labyrinth mythology and a recurrent figure in Waters' novel.

In the myth, it is the thread that enables Theseus to find his way out of the labyrinth. The thread, given to Theseus by Ariadne, represents not only a path, the path back, but it also represents desire and betrayal. Ariadne's motivation for supplying the thread is her love for Theseus, which she chooses over the love or even the duty towards her father and brother, both of whom she is betraying. A similar set of relations occurs in the novel: at the climax of the plot, when Selina is to come to Margaret's bedroom during the night with the help of her spirit friends so that the two of them can elope to Italy, Margaret envisions Selina 'like a thread inside a labyrinth, long and quivering and tight – so tight that, buffeted by rough shadows, she might break!' (Waters 1999: 308). The thread, tension and desire are correlated here, with the addition of the explicit invocation of the labyrinth. Margaret is longing for Selina, she is nervously expecting her appearance which she, against her better knowledge, attributes to the 'spirit friends' and she is about to be betrayed by the one person she has vested all her hopes and desires in.

This scene also offers an intimation of the complex relations of materiality considered in the novel. This very *materially* imagined thread, in the sense that it has physical substance which allows it to have qualitative attributes such as 'quivering' and 'tight', is susceptible to the impact of ostensibly insubstantial entities: the textured 'rough shadows'. The effect of a shadow on an object of physical dimensions cannot correspond with a relation of cause and effect, and yet here it does. Through the material thread the text begins to question common-sense understandings of materiality as grounded in physical substance entirely separate from metaphor, as well as connecting it to issues of sexuality. Given substance through a chain of metaphors the thread has potentially devastating material consequences for Margaret, for whom it is a physical entity closely linked to her (sexual) desire for Selina. The labyrinth is explicitly associated with the thread here and threads are repeated throughout the text, rendering the labyrinth integral to the relations between space and sexuality. It is ultimately through the figure of the thread, as representative of desire, that the prison as a space is produced.

One of the distinctive aspects of the thread in the ancient myth is less that it shows Theseus the way, than that it shows him the way *back*. The classical labyrinth of antiquity was unicursal, that is, it had one path that inevitably lead to the centre which suggests that rather than serving as a navigational tool, the thread serves as a reminder for Theseus to return to Ariadne, the would-be lover waiting on the outside. It is her pull on him, the figuration of her desire, and the necessity of this figuration points towards the precariousness of their situation. Additionally, *un*winding the thread and then *re*winding it figures a process of repetition, it is in fact the thread that allows the repetition of the path – Apollodorus writes, 'Theseus [. . .] made his way out again by pulling back on the thread' (1997: 140), and Ovid has, 'Theseus rewound the thread he had laid, retraced his steps, and found the elusive gateway' (1955: 183). It is through Margaret's repetitive practice of making her way to and through the prison that the particular relation between her and Selina is produced, one characterized by the tension, desire and precariousness that appear in the myth.

'Selina, you will be in sunlight soon. Your twisting is done – you have the last thread of my heart. I wonder: when the thread grows slack, will you feel it?' (Waters 1999: 351). This passage emphasizes the thread by repeating it, thereby suggesting that it is important and appropriate – important because it has material consequences (Margaret's potential suicide) and appropriate as a metaphor for desire. The repetition already invests the thread with power and authority, the authority to represent and the power to effect change. This particular thread signifies a connection between two entities, in this case Selina and Margaret, who appear to be holding either end of it. There is urgency to this connection which tightens the thread, but the connection also appears to be a troubled one: Selina has previously been twisting – perhaps in an attempt to untangle herself from this connection, possibly in an attempt to unwind herself from an undesirable situation. The urgency is exacerbated by the invocation of the heart which suggests that the connection in question is romantic, although it is clear that one party is pulling on the thread, or holding onto it, much more strongly than the other; it is Margaret's pull that tautens the thread, Margaret's release that will render it 'slack'. This is another echo of the labyrinth myth where Ariadne awaits the return of Theseus, with some urgency. She now relies on the Athenian hero to whisk her away to safety from the social formation, both the family and the polity (which she has betrayed), only to be abandoned on an island along the way. The pull is unevenly spread along both threads; both Margaret's and Ariadne's positions are precarious, and both end in despair.

Margaret's final lines in the novel reinforce the notion of 'twisting'. Desire is repeatedly figured via the notion of 'twisting', as well as via an emphasis on longing, so desire enacts a pulling movement (reminiscent of Apollodorus' terms). When Margaret first becomes aware of her own desire for Selina, she writes in her diary: 'Now I can see that my heart has crept across these pages, after all. I can see the crooked passage of it, it grows firmer as the paper turns' (Waters 1999: 241). Margaret is here remarking on the fact that she has failed at writing a journal that does not express her emotions and desires. Notably, the terms she chooses to express this include a personified heart, a heart that moves in an animalistic, even feral fashion. 'Creeping' connotes cunning but also the gradual yet persistent colonization of a territory (as in creeping plants used to cover the facades of houses) – the emphasis is on the processual quality of the movement. This heart is also one that progresses via a 'crooked passage' rather than, the implication seems to be, a straight line. The emphasis is on the practice (of creeping) here, as the heart creeps along the crooked path, deviating from the direct linearity Margaret had hoped to master and pathologizing her in the process. It is, after all, her deviant femininity, both in terms of desire and in terms of ambition, that is the cause of her recent illness, an illness she is now struggling to recover from to reintegrate herself into the structures of heteronormative society.

Sara Ahmed uses the idea of the straight line to figure heterosexuality in her phenomenological study of queer relations where she argues 'how compulsory heterosexuality operates as a straightening device, which rereads signs of queer desire as deviations from the straight line' (Ahmed 2006: 23). The notion of the straight line, which Ahmed develops from Freud's thinking on sexuality as outlined in 'The Psychogenesis of a Case of Homosexuality in a Woman' is central to her argument here and to the operation of heteronormativity. Although he himself problematizes the approach, Freud's method suggests that if he traces the 'chain of events' backwards he will be able to identify the point of sexual deviation which is the moment when lineage is disrupted by homosexual desire (Freud 1955: 167). Once that point has been located, the subject can be re-directed onto the correct, that is straight, path and lineage can be reinstated. The non-normative, the abnormal, the un-straight – the queer, is thus rendered pathological. Ahmed also contends that (queer) desire 'helps generate a lesbian landscape, a ground that is shaped by the paths that we follow in deviating from the straight line' (Ahmed 2006: 20). Her metaphors of queer sexuality are distinctly spatial and describe a practice that is repeated: the path is followed more than once and the deviation is continuous, thus creating a space for desire. It is through the repetition of a spatial practice that sexuality is produced, in this case 'a sexuality that is bent and crooked' (Ahmed 2006: 67), whose 'crooked passage' Margaret makes out on the pages of her diary where she has, through the process of writing, documented her own desire – she must have written similar entries in the past that allow her now to reconstruct that path. Crucially, Margaret turns the pages of her journal as she re-reads old entries, changing the direction of her process of knowing as she becomes retrospectively aware of what has been happening to her. (This backward movement that produces queer desire also begs the question of queer temporality, see Freeman (2007) and Love (2007), for example; Ahmed (2006) also discusses this notion). And it is this re-reading, enabled by *turning* pages and moving backwards along the same path she has previously been moving forwards on, that makes the passage 'grow firmer'. The practice of creeping is repeated, and through this repetition the heart, figuring Margaret's desire, becomes more solid, more 'material' in as much as it enhances the realness of the experience.

A similar repetition of movement that doubles back on itself occurs when Margaret watches the prisoners exercising in the prison yard in 'three great elliptical loops' that soon make it impossible to identify a starting point for any of the 'great wheeling line[s]' (Waters 1999: 13ff). Katharina Boehm points out that it is the 'disciplined bodies' of the women exercising in the yard and reproducing the shape of the prison that constitute the space, rather than bricks and mortar (Boehm 2011: 241). It is through movement, and its repetition, that space is solidified in this scenario, where walking along a given path serves to discipline the bodies of the socially deviant women. However, walking can also be a form of resistance. According to Michel de Certeau, it is through everyday practices, such as walking, that 'users reappropriate the space organized by techniques of sociocultural production' (de Certeau 1984: xiv). In fact, practices – or as de Certeau argues, tactics – not only reappropriate space and change its organization, they can also be a form of resistance (de Certeau 1984: 38). According to this argument, tactics, of which walking is an example, move within the grid of rationalized space but find new relations; walking fragments and disrupts the coherent totality of spatial rationality (de Certeau 1984: 101ff.). Margaret's walking practice, which returns her to Selina again and again, is just such an act of resistance whose repetition materializes her queer desire. Margaret purposefully removes herself from family settings (accompanying her sister to have her portrait painted, joining her mother to visit the newly wed sister at her new home) and instead uses the time to make her way to Millbank. After she has fallen ill, Margaret pretends to write a letter to inform the prison that her visits will cease. Instead, she writes Selina's name over and over again and prepares to visit the prison once her mother has left the house, and she continues to visit Millbank during her mother's absences, resisting the disciplining of her own body, and desire, by her mother (Waters 1999: 264–5, 298). These journeys through London and towards Millbank are often completed on foot, to the implicit chagrin of Mrs Prior: Margaret walks when she thinks her mother is out and 'linger[s] over the paying of the driver, hoping Mother would see it' after taking a carriage home (Waters 1999: 51, 68). Through the practice of walking Margaret appropriates the prison space which is designed to punish Selina and to haunt Margaret as a threat she escaped (not having been imprisoned after her failed suicide attempt). Instead Millbank figures her equally socially deviant desire.

In the aforementioned episode the heart stands in for romantic love and this desire is investigated in conjunction with the labyrinth. This is compounded by the fact that Margaret is also 'twisting' her hands before writing the passage. All this 'twisting' is a productive avenue into the correlations between sexuality, space and materiality as played out in *Affinity*, as well as the importance of the labyrinth as more than a convenient metaphorical convention. In the novel, twisting is directly linked to desire, to matters of the heart. When the announcement is made that Selina is to be moved to a less strict prison, Margaret relates how her 'own heart had given a terrible kind of twist' as she fears the separation from her object of desire (Waters 1999: 245). This movement, attributed to the hitherto abstract heart, physicalizes it and simultaneously locates emotions in the body – Margaret's desire has physical effects and these are 'terrible'. Again desire is correlated with movement. More precisely, desire is correlated with twisting and this queers as well as spatializes it. As Eve Sedgwick points out, the word 'queer' derives from the Indo-German 'twist' and this in turn refers back to a particular mode of moving through space (Sedgwick 1993: xii). In contrast to the twisting discussed earlier, where the motion is attributable to Selina's attempt to extricate herself, this twist implies a moment of recognition and of longing. Margaret recognizes her desire for Selina, her longing for her, at the moment when it is to be made impossible. Even though this moment of recognition produces Margaret's lesbian subjectivity and allows her to acknowledge her desire, it is a painful moment – it is 'terrible' and 'twist[ing]' rather than affirming and enabling. The recognition at play here is not a relief to Margaret, it is terrible, perhaps just as much for its strength as because it can be read as a return of the repressed in as much as she has had to move beyond her desire for her former lover Helen, who has since married Margaret's brother and borne him a child (Palmer 2004: 124). This ambiguity is manifested in the repetition of the twisting motion, even as it is interlocked with the tug of longing. The recognition will be repeated every time Margaret visits Selina in her cell and it is also retrospectively reconstructed as Margaret re-reads her journal and identifies earlier moments of recognition. Through this repetition, the thread of desire between the two women is spun and becomes firm, but the ambiguity in *Affinity* remains, in something akin to Butler's contention that 'recognition takes place neither as an event nor a set of events, but as an ongoing process, one that also poses the psychic risk of destruction' (Butler 2004: 132). Of course, Selina's twisting is not done: at the close of the narrative she, presumably, is living the twist, she is living her queer desire with Ruth while Margaret has indeed suffered psychic destruction.

When Selina says that the spirits revealed to her that the purpose of her incarceration was to meet Margaret, the Lady Visitor exclaims:

> She might have put a knife to me and twisted it: I felt my heart beat hard and, behind the beat, caught another, sharper movement – that *quickening*, grown fiercer than ever. I felt it, and felt an answering twisting in her . . . (Waters 1999: 272)

Now Margaret has recognized not only her own desire but also what she believes to be Selina's longing. The twisting, which expresses pathology, ambiguity and longing, animates her and crucially, it is answered. It is here that Margaret seizes the thread that will tie her to Selina, or that Selina picks up the thread that Margaret is trailing. Margaret is thrown completely off course after Selina's revelation and 'twists' her gloved hands until they burn before leaning 'into the twisting dust to catch' what Selina next says to her (Waters 1999: 273). The winding movement is maintained throughout this crucial scene where Selina first articulates the notion of affinity: 'I was only seeking you out, as you were seeking me. You were seeking me, your own *affinity*' (Waters 1999: 275). The doctrine of affinity was circulated within Spiritualist communities and maintained that every soul has a soul mate to whom there is an insurmountable, nearly primal, attraction – an affinity that transcends the physical realm, including such constraints as marriage.[2] Affinity, then, could be read as a spiritual attraction that is opposed to the realities of the physical world and that is characterized by the strength of the pull it exerts. This pull is translated into the relation between Margaret and Selina when Margaret has to lean forward to hear what the medium is saying to her – through the 'twisting dust' which fills the space between their bodies. It is crucial here to note that by claiming affinity, a spiritual quality, Selina is drawing Margaret's body closer (a dynamic that will be reversed later on as we have already seen). By calling upon affinity Selina is explicitly endangering the social order and Margaret's life.

This danger is manifested in a shaking up of solidity. After the crucial moment of recognition, the acknowledgement of desire, seemingly stable, material objects appear to give way. Selina incants:

> 'Now you know, why you are drawn to me – why your flesh comes creeping to mine, and what it comes for. Let it creep, Aurora. Let it come to me, let it creep . . .' [. . .] I felt the tug of her, then. The lure of her, the grasp of her, I felt myself drawn across the coir-thick air to her whispering mouth. I clutched at her cell wall – but the wall was smooth, and slippery with limewash – I stood against it, but felt it slide from me. (Waters 1999: 276)

Margaret then walks from the cell 'as one might walk, in a terrible torture, gagged and goaded and feeling the flesh ripped from one's bones' (Waters 1999: 277). This scene is built upon a troubling of stability: Margaret's body is disintegrating, her flesh torn from its frame, and the walls of the prison, previously read as impenetrable guarantors of incarceration, dissipate with the realization of her longing. Not at all liberating, the moment of sexual recognition, reverting to bestial terminology (again, the notion of creeping), here elicits feelings of disorientation and a slippage of physical substance. It is as though the wall itself has become mobile, insubstantial. There is nothing reliable for Margaret to lean on and she flees the cell in an ambivalent state of terror. It remains unclear whether she is overcome with desire, is giddy with the prospects now open to her, or is terrified of the consequences her recognition might entail. This compounds the physicalization of desire in the shape of the heart, but it is also interesting to think in terms of the spatial situation: both Selina's and Margaret's bodies are within an enclosed space, a space that Selina cannot leave, and yet Selina routinely transcends these walls through her spirit friends and Margaret finds the brick unreliable.

In her study of prison metaphoricity, Monika Fludernik remarks on the 'corporality of imprisonment' arguing for the idea of an 'enforced corporality' (the doubling of the prison in the materiality of the body) which she couples with the 'myth of carceral transcendence' (Fludernik 1999: 67, 69). Prison imagery, Fludernik contends, emphasizes bodies. In fact, it is precisely the circumstance of incarceration that produces the body in its materiality, a materiality that is determined by the solidity of the prison walls and leads to the figuration of the body as a prison itself. Simultaneously, though, this limiting materiality engenders an ideal of spiritual transcendence, where the prison walls and the limited body can be exceeded by the mind – or by spirit friends.

The notion of being drawn to Selina is repeated throughout the text and the power relations constructed through the thread that connects these two women are (re)produced via the movement that is elicited by the pull of desire. When Margaret requests reassurance about the proceedings of the escape, Selina explains, 'It works through – love; and through wanting. You need only want me, and I will come' (Waters 1999: 287). Then, during the next visit to Millbank, Selina remarks, 'This will draw me to you, through the dark' (Waters 1999: 299). Although Margaret doubts her connection to Selina when she is waiting for her to arrive through the London night, she ultimately places her trust in that thread of desire, concluding her deliberation, 'I know she will come, for she could not feel my reaching thoughts and not be drawn by them' (Waters 1999: 317). The directionality of the pull has changed at this point in the narrative; it is no longer Selina who is pulling Margaret to her cell, but rather Margaret pulling, in vain as it will turn out, Selina to her room. The situation has been reversed and the pull does not exert the same strength in this new direction, reinforcing the unequal power relations between the two women now that Margaret can no longer engage in the practice of walking but must wait, enclosed in her bedroom.

Margaret performs her desire through the practice of walking the corridors of Millbank. This practice not only materializes her desire, it also (re)produces the prison itself. It is through Margaret's repeated passages through the corridors that the prison is (re)constructed and it is through her repeated walks that the relationship between the two women is strengthened and ultimately becomes available for manipulation. It is Margaret who keeps returning to Selina, answering an unspeakable longing and making her way through the twisting passages of Millbank. This repetition of the visit(ation), which re-enacts the earlier visitations by spirits in the séances as well as mirroring the continuing visits of the spirits to Selina's cell, demonstrates the uncertainty attached to the materiality of space, to solidity. Upon her final visit to Millbank prison, just before the carefully tautened desire is about to be fulfilled, Margaret is convinced that her flesh, the flesh that previously was 'streaming' from her body, is tugging at Selina's and that this tugging of the flesh exerts an incontrovertible pull (Waters 1999: 310).

Earlier Selina argues it is their spirits that are attracted to each other beyond the imaginative possibilities of material constraints, so this very physical tugging complicates the idea of affinity as a purely spiritual phenomenon and demonstrates its effects in the material world, specifically on bodies.

The pulling of the thread experienced by Margaret is associated with the power relations constitutive of the relationship between the two women, as well. Later Margaret will remember the above scene as follows:

> I thought she took my life that day. I felt it leap to her! But she had already begun to tug at its threads. I see her now, winding them about her slender fingers, in the shadows of the Millbank night; I feel it still, her careful unravelling. After all, it is a slow and delicate business, losing one's life! and not a thing to happen in a moment. (Waters 1999: 321)

Here the relation between the thread, desire and the threat it poses is explicitly articulated, as is the wielding of the thread and the power this grants. When Margaret finds Selina's infamous velvet collar hidden within the pages of her journal she:

> . . . stood at the glass and fastened it about my throat. It fits, but tightly: I feel it grip, as my heart pulses, as if she holds the thread to which it is fastened and sometimes pulls it, to remind me she is near. (Waters 1999: 294)

Margaret is enacting her submission to Selina here which expresses her desire for her and 'in the shadows of the Millbank night' she can feel the physical effects of Selina's response.

Millbank prison itself is less reliable than it initially appears to be, its walls are less stable and its maps are imprecise to say the least. The limewashed walls that slide away from Margaret are only one instance of the prison's unsettled materiality. When Margaret first takes up her duties as Lady Visitor to the women incarcerated in Millbank, she remarks that it 'is vast, and its lines and angles [. . .] seem only wrong or perverse' (Waters 1999: 8). She can merely see a 'wedge of sky' above the narrow, enclosed path she is led down, where the shadows 'are the colour of bruises', the ground is 'damp' and 'dark', and the air 'smell[s] sour' (ibid.). Her description associates flesh and dampness with the bricks of Millbank prison, associations that are reiterated towards the end of the novel when the porter describes the building as:

> A terrible creature – though I say it, who is her keeper. And she's leaky – did you know that? There were floods, in the old days – oh yes, many times. It is this ground, this wretched ground. Nothing will grow in it, and nothing will sit in it straight – not even a great old, grim beast like Millbank. (Waters 1999: 312)

Again, images of bestiality and the need for control embodied in the figure of the keeper, are combined with the erosion of materiality and stability, in this case even quite literally as the ground is washed away from underneath the walls. The porter also remarks that nothing will go 'straight' suggesting that no object in this setting is or can be reliably orientated in the right direction.

Millbank's unsettled materiality is inextricable from a question of intelligibility. Margaret conducts a considerable amount of research before first visiting Millbank, consulting both volumes of social commentary and architectural drawings of the building; initially the building appears to submit to her knowing gaze. But the space itself, once she experiences it from within, resists recognition, resists knowability, and to a certain degree falsifies its own representation in the form of those structuring architectural drawings that are inadequate when it comes to gauging the space. Margaret cannot get a grip on Millbank and, as Armitt and Gamble have argued, finds it more akin to Piranesi's fantasies than to the building she has previously seen from the master perspective of the top-down, omniscient view (Armitt and Gamble 2006: 144–8). Before her first visit, Margaret finds 'a volume of the prison drawings of Piranesi, and spen[ds] an anxious hour, studying them, thinking of all the dark and terrible scenes [she] might be confronted with' (Waters 1999: 9) and her first impression of the building is informed by this 'anxious hour': 'It is as if the prison had been designed by a man in the grip of a nightmare or a madness' (Waters 1999: 8). Margaret worries especially about the 'dim and complicated path I should never be able to retrace alone' (Waters 1999: 9). Eventually, Millbank's winding corridors will become familiar territory to her, when she will have walked them repeatedly in pursuit of Selina. By the end of the novel, Margaret will even be able to traverse the corridors without a guide, but even then Millbank persists in its ability to disorientate and trouble the subjects within it: when she is first taken to see the 'dark cells' where inmates are sent as punishment, Millbank suddenly becomes 'unfamiliar' again as Margaret is led along 'a passage which wound downwards, via spiralling staircases' which terrifies her (Waters 1999: 179). In other words, although it becomes possible to stabilize Millbank and to make it knowable by a practice of repetitious walking, this stabilization can only ever be provisional, and other practices – in this case a particular form of discipline – reshape or even dematerialize it.

In her theorization of materiality, Judith Butler argues that materiality '[constitutes] an object domain, a field of intelligibility' (Butler 1993: 35) – the stabilization of productive processes, such as walking a labyrinth, creates intelligible, solid objects, objects such as the prison building, and also objects of desire, such as Selina. However, both of these seem to remain unintelligible in Butler's sense where intelligibility is a process of normalization and naturalization (Butler 2004: 3). The key notion underpinning this argument is Butler's conceptualization of materiality. She argues that sex 'is not a simple fact or static condition of a body, but a process whereby regulatory norms materialize "sex" and achieve this materialization through a forcible reiteration of those norms' (Butler 1993: 1–2). Butler is intent on rethinking matter 'not as site or surface, but as *a process of materialization that stabilizes over time to produce the effect of boundary, fixity, and surface we call matter*' (Butler 1993: 9). Important for the present discussion is the emphasis on process and its *effect* of stability. Materialization is conceived as the sedimenting effect of a regulated iterability, it is stability achieved through repetitive citation. Materiality is the dissimulated, productive effect of power that constitutes an object domain or a field of intelligibility; and as a process it operates through practices, in this case regulated and regulating normative practices (Butler 1993: 1). Space, too, is produced through the repetition of practices (de Certeau 1984) and can be conceived as 'the outcome of a series of highly problematic temporary settlements that divide and connect things up in different kinds of collectives which are slowly provided with the means which render them durable and sustainable' (Thrift 2008: 85). Here space is seen as a multiplicity of 'temporary settlements' which, in Butler's schema, would be subsumed under 'materialization', the latter encompassing the provisionality and the repetition, that is the process, invoked to 'produce' the effect – of space or sexuality, where to produce means to 'demarcate, circulate, differentiate' (Butler 1993: 1).

If repetition is seen as the operation of materialization, then both Millbank and Selina appear to defy that process, they remain slippery and unpredictable, refusing to repeat in a way that could enable their stabilization and consequent intelligibility. At the close of the novel, Margaret finally realizes that her connection with Selina was not as strong as she believed:

> I reach for the cord of darkness that once seemed to bind her to me, quivering tight. But the night is too thick, my thoughts falter and are lost, and the cord of darkness – There never was a cord of darkness, never a space in which our spirits touched. There was only my longing – and hers, which so resembled it, it seemed my own. (Waters 1999: 348)

Even at the end, the imagery invoked by Margaret combines ideas of materiality (cord) with immateriality (darkness). This is repeated in the notion of the space where 'spirits touched': if touch is a sensation tied to the body, then spirits cannot touch – unless they have materialized. At the moment of its dissolution, the more vulnerable thread has been replaced by a robust cord that seems to emphasize the strength of the connection between the two women. A cord, after all, is produced by twisting individual threads together to form a sturdier rope. Yet it is here, at the moment of its imagined strength, that Margaret realizes the insubstantiality of the connection, as well as the fact that the thread leading her through the labyrinth never did lead her towards 'a space in which our spirits touched'. The effect of this realization (along with her increasingly drugged state) is that Margaret feels very light, her 'flesh filled with nothing' (ibid.). Suddenly, the metaphor of the 'threads' Margaret has constantly been referring to, is recognized as imaginary: the connection is unreal. The connection has, in fact, been predicated on repetition and practice, among other things, an obsessive twisting. The notion of the labyrinth, then, allows for a specific arrangement of relations, or relational connections, that here tie into questions of sexuality via orientation, possession, power and control as represented by the recurrence of the 'twisting' thread. Millbank, a labyrinth, is an unpredictable space with unpredictable effects produced by the repetition of its paths as well as disrupted by their unforeseen turnings, so that 'all the solid surfaces seemed to shift and bulge and shiver' (Waters 1999: 268). It, along with the relations it produces and is in turn produced by, refuses to be sedimented by regulated iterability. In *Affinity* space is much more than a setting or a backdrop for the queer narrative, it is more even than a metaphor: space *is* desire.

Notes

1 The public/private dichotomy works in some instances, for example *Tipping the Velvet*'s settings of the theatre stage and the city streets as opposed to domestic enclosures (1998). However, the private is by no means necessarily a sheltering space (think of Sue Trinder's Borough home or the private asylum she is sent to) (*Fingersmith* 2002) and often the space opposed to the city is a public institution, for instance Millbank prison.

2 Critics of Spiritualism picked up on this especially to prove the moral degeneracy of the whole movement, claiming the Swedenborgian principle championed promiscuity. For a fuller discussion of this notion from a feminist perspective, see Owen (1989).

CHAPTER THREE

'I know everything. I know nothing': (Re)Reading *Fingersmith*'s Deceptive Doubles

SARAH GAMBLE

Chapter Summary: This essay argues that a recurring characteristic of Sarah Waters' work as a whole is that it is written to be re-read. In *Fingersmith*, this demand surfaces via Water's manipulation of the trope of doubling, presenting the reader with two narrators who both know less than they realize, and whose different versions of the same events resist symmetrical alignment. This is a text obsessed with knowledge, and the recurring question of who knows everything and who knows nothing raises pressing concerns about identity and authenticity that come to preoccupy the characters and their audience. The idea of 'plotting' itself takes on a double meaning in this context, positioning the author herself as adroit a 'double-crosser' as any of the schemers in the narrative itself. The only way for the reader to achieve a secure perspective on the novel is to repeat the experience and become a re-reader, returning to the text with full knowledge of the outcome.

Keywords: *Fingersmith*, dualism, reading, queerness, knowledge, double-crossing.

The reader of Sarah Waters' fiction must always be suspicious and alert, since she is a writer who excels in narrative deception. Although Waters' first novel, *Tipping the Velvet* (1998), was a relatively straightforward *bildungsroman*, her second, *Affinity* (1999), marked the advent of what has become one of Waters' hallmarks – her fondness for sending her audience up narrative blind alleys. Through the use of first-person narrators who themselves are only in possession of half the story, and whose trickery of others frequently stems from their own vulnerability to deception, Waters repeatedly lures readers into following quite the wrong plot; a fact that is invariably only revealed at a later point in the novel. In *Affinity*, the main protagonist is duped by a background character hidden in plain sight all along, while in *The Night Watch* (2006) the act of telling the story backwards gives the protagonists a privileged vantage point denied to the reader – we know how the novel ends, but not how it began. In *The Little Stranger* (2008), the narrator – maybe consciously, maybe not – represses his own crucial role in the events of the text, and we only realize the true significance of Waters' title in the novel's final line. Particularly because she is too inventive and innovative a writer to use the same trick twice, habitual readers will consequently approach each new Sarah Waters novel with a certain frisson of anticipation: certain that the story will contain a catch, but unsure what it will be, or when it will be made apparent.

The specific focus of this essay is Waters' third novel, *Fingersmith*, published in 2002. It is a particularly appropriate text through which to investigate Waters' propensity for narrative trickery, since this intention is signified in its very title. 'Fingersmith', we are informed early on in the story, is underworld slang for 'thief' (Waters 2002: 40), and Waters presides over this tale of multiple deceptions as the most audacious deceiver of them all, carefully constructing her story so as to prevent her reader gaining an overview of the workings of the plot. As I will argue, the questions the text constantly throws up regarding how to distinguish between the authentic and the counterfeit, '[r]eal secrets, and snide' (Waters 2002: 110), come to puzzle the reader as much as the protagonists, giving Waters considerable scope to play her narrative games.

Fingersmith's deceptive effects are founded upon a double first-person narration split between the novel's two principal protagonists, Sue Trinder and Maud Lilly. The first section is told in the voice of Sue, daughter of a woman hanged for murder, and inhabitant of a Dickensian den of thieves presided over by the baby-farmer Mrs Sucksby, whom she regards as a substitute mother-figure. Through the machinations of a regular visitor to the house, Gentleman, Sue becomes a participant in an elaborate con-trick designed (or so she thinks) to cheat Maud Lilly out of her inheritance. Maud, who lives in a country house outside London with her uncle, is an heiress who will only gain access to her money on marriage. Sue masquerades as Maud's maid while her partner-in-crime, Gentleman, becomes Maud's art instructor. In this position, he intends to court Maud, marry her, then have her declared insane and thrown into an asylum, taking her fortune for himself. However, after the covert marriage has taken place Sue discovers that she has herself been the dupe all along, manipulated into playing the part of a substitute for Maud and becoming incarcerated in her stead.

When the narrative perspective subsequently switches to Maud, the events already related by Sue are replayed from her point of view, revealing that she is far from the naïve and inexperienced girl depicted in Sue's section of the novel. In fact, it appears that Maud and Gentleman schemed together to use Sue as a pawn in order to achieve their joint objective of financial gain and – on Maud's part – freedom from the rule of her tyrannical uncle, a collector and cataloguer of pornographic texts.

Yet even this is not the definitive revelation it appears to be, for there is another layer of deception that has yet to be uncovered. After Maud herself is hoodwinked by Gentlemen, becoming a virtual prisoner in Mrs Sucksby's house, we learn that the true architect of the plot in which both young women have been caught is Mrs Sucksby herself, who is in fact Maud's true mother. The real heir to the Lilly fortune is Sue, who was swapped for Maud as a baby by her mother, Mr Lilly's sister, who died shortly after her birth.

What this brief plot summary demonstrates is the way in which *Fingersmith* is constructed around multiple disclosures which periodically force the novel's audience to radically reformulate their interpretation of characters and events, and this has a particularly destabilizing effect upon the first-time reader. This aspect of the text is readily described through recourse to metaphors of spatial disorientation since, as Adam Mars-Jones writes in his review of the novel in the *Observer* newspaper, 'Serpentine plotting of the sort that Sarah Waters practices so well often leads to moments of vertigo, when the reader no longer knows which way is up, who knows what, who wants what and why' (Mars-Jones 2002).

Waters herself appears to anticipate this sense of narrative vertigo when she has Sue Trinder, early on in her narration, recall a visit to the Cremorne Gardens in Chelsea where she sees 'the French girl cross the river on a wire [. . .] and almost drop – *that* was something' (Waters 2002: 33). Although this 'French girl' is unnamed in the novel, she is identifiable as the tightrope walker Madame Genevieve – also known as 'the Female Blondin' – who attempted to cross the Thames on a tightrope strung between Cremorne and Battersea in August 1861. The events obliquely alluded to by Sue Trinder are described in detail by W. S. Scott in his book *Bygone Pleasures of London* (1948):

> The tightrope was raised on trestles from Cremorne to the opposite shore. The female Blondin started from Battersea, but when about only six hundred feet from the end of her journey she stopped, and there was a long pause while attendants tried to tighten the remaining portion of the rope, which was sagging too much to make it possible for Madame Genevieve to continue her journey. The rope was tightened and she began to move forward, but as she moved the rope began to swing to and fro, and it was discovered that some unspeakable rogue had cut the guy ropes in order to steal the lead weights. It was of course impossible to proceed, and with the greatest presence of mind the girl threw away her balancing pole, bent down and caught the rope with both hands, swung herself down onto one

> of the sway ropes, and slid down into the river, where she was picked up by a boat. (Scott 1948)

While Madame Genevieve achieved her Thames crossing a few days later, it is significant that Waters has her character witness the tightrope walker's failure, not her success, making this account a sly warning to the novel's audience about the perils and pleasures of the narrative on which they are about to embark. The first reading of *Fingersmith* is indeed a vertiginous experience, as the reader follows a disorientating series of confidence tricks and narrative reversals in the process of uncovering multiple revelations concerning maternal origin and inheritance. Throughout the novel, Waters deprives the reader of the security of a reliable narration, as what we think we know is consistently proved to be false supposition. Waters' use of first-person narration ensures that we are forced to rely on the perspectives of characters who often know far less than they suppose; moreover, her use of doubled first-person narrators frequently confuses, rather than assists, our attempt to understand the wider implications of the events we witness. Sue's and Maud's separate voices often compete with one another for possession of 'definitive' meaning – and even when one account does potentially elucidate the other, the time that must elapse between our reading of the two versions means that the novel's audience can only make such connections belatedly. It is for this reason that we are drawn into following in the footsteps of the female Blondin and repeating the attempt. But while the act may be the same, the outcome is not, for to return to *Fingersmith* as a *re*-reader is an entirely different experience. Matai Calinescu characterizes re-reading as inducing a sense of 'meaningful and gratifying repetition' in the reader (Galef 1998: 52), but Waters, I would argue, deliberately embeds information in the novel that can only be appreciated in the light of one's awareness of how it ends. Such foreknowledge allows the reader to recognize the subtle ironies encoded within Sue's and Maud's narratives, and to both anticipate and relish Waters' methods of authorial misdirection. Thus one moves from being Waters' dupe to an accomplice who is appreciative – and fully cognizant – of her trickery.

To read *Fingersmith* for the second time, therefore, is a distinctly different experience from the first, and provides a pleasure beyond mere repetition, conforming to what Roland Barthes defines as a 'plural' reading. In *S/Z*, while Barthes does allow that the act of venturing 'behind the transparency of suspense' allows the re-reader to gain pleasure from 'the anticipated knowledge of what is to come in the story', he also upholds the value of re-reading as an act that 'multiplies' the text 'in its variety and its plurality' (Barthes 1990: 15, 165). Thus, a re-read text is also a double(d) text; what Barthes describes as 'a plural text: the same and new' (Barthes 1990: 15).

Waters' commitment to plurality is woven through the novel: the figure of the female tightrope walker, herself in the most literal of terms a 'double-crosser', prefigures *Fingersmith*'s preoccupation with narrative double crossings, both literal and figurative. As an exercise in deceit, double-crossing works by luring the victim into a false sense of security and exploiting their trust (something all the characters in the novel attempt, with varying degrees of success), but this novel also requires a literal 'double-crossing' in the form of a second encounter with the text. A study of doubleness in *Fingersmith* reveals that Waters does not ever allow us to gain privileged access to superior knowledge except through re-reading: there is always more than one version of the same story, and no single character has access to all the different epistemologies circulating in the novel.

The Self-regarding other: Chiasmus, Chirality and Mirror-images

Waters evokes this notion of doubleness on a formal and symbolic level through the use of a roughly chiastic structure that places the two narratives – and their narrators – in an inverted parallel relationship. Within this novel, dualism is not only synonymous with repetition but also mirror-imaging, underlined by the way in which Waters frequently positions Sue and Maud face-to-face as if staring at their own reflections in a looking-glass. One might expect her repeated deployment of this trope to situate the two women even more firmly as each other's inverted doubles, but, as will be explained, it actually provides Waters with considerable scope for generating a sense of ambiguity which resists any attempt to impose such neat and tidy distinctions upon her text.

Even before the two women meet in person they are placed opposite each other in a way that invites the reader to see them as contrasting opposites. When Sue Trinder first arrives at Briar, the Lilly mansion, and is shown to her bedroom, she notices that '[n]ear the head of the bed there was another door, shut quite tight and with no key in it' (Waters 2002: 60). On being told that this door leads to Maud's room, Sue imagines what lies on the other side:

> I wondered what I would see, if I went and bent and looked – and who can think a thing like that, and not go and do it? But when I did go, on tiptoe and stoop to the lock, I saw a dim light, a shadow – nothing clearer than that, no sign of any kind of sleeping or wakeful or fretful girl, or anything. (Waters 2002: 62)

When Sue puts her 'ear flat to the door', she hears nothing more than 'my heart-beat [. . .] the roaring of my blood' and 'a small tight sound, that must have been the creeping of a worm or a beetle in the wood'

(Waters 2002: 62). It is not until Maud takes over the narration that we learn that she has echoed Sue's actions on the other side of the door:

> I must lie, hearing her step and murmur, my eyes upon the door – an inch or two of desiccated wood! – that lies between her chamber and mine.
>
> Once I rise and go stealthily to it, and put my ear to the panels; but hear nothing. (Waters 2002: 241)

However, neither protagonist discerns the closeness of their physical proximity because the solidity of the locked door obstructs both sight and sound; and the reader's view of this incident is similarly baffled, for two reasons. First, we are not made privy to Maud's presence on the other side of the door until we have access to her part of the narrative; and, secondly, it is not clear whether the women are literally acting in synchronicity or if there is a time-lag between their actions.

This episode is thus a good example of the complexity involved in Waters' use of doubling in *Fingersmith*, in that the sense of symmetry it evokes is always imperfect because the two halves of the double can never quite be mapped onto each other with any degree of exactitude. The exact parallel reversal required of a strictly chiastic narrative structure can only be taken so far, because even at those moments when Sue and Maud do physically mimic one another their accounts reveal a complicated layering of knowledge and ignorance that disrupts any attempt to achieve an exact correspondence between the two. This is neatly illustrated in an episode that occurs the morning after Sue's arrival at Briar when, on entering the library in which Maud is working with her uncle, she is taken aback by Mr Lilly's dramatic reaction:

> I looked at Maud, who stood, still fumbling with the fastening of her glove; and I took a step, meaning to help her. But when he saw me do that, the old man jerked like Mr Punch in the puppet-show, and out came his black tongue.
>
> 'The finger, girl!' he cried. 'The finger! The finger!' (Waters 2002: 76)

As Sue falters in confusion, it is Maud who approaches her in order to indicate the 'flat brass hand with a pointing finger' set into the floor, which demarcates the point beyond which servants are not permitted to pass (Waters 2002: 76). Thus, the image of the two girls standing on either side of a locked door is superseded by that of them standing on either side of the brass hand. As before, it is as if they are contemplating their own mirror reflection, but they are still far from being straightforward copies of each other; an asymmetry revealed in their separate narratives. While Sue and Maud are united in regarding the hand as demarcating the boundary between innocence and knowledge, a comparison of their contrasting descriptions of this event reveals its ultimate inability to act in this capacity.

In her account, Sue views Maud as sheltered, naïve and vulnerable to deception, and herself, in 'helping to make' Maud's fate, in possession of the real truth of their situation (Waters 2002: 96). But she is unaware of the secret from which she is barred by the image of the pointing hand – the fact that what the prohibited room houses is a library of pornography. Maud has been trained from childhood to aid her uncle in compiling a definitive catalogue of erotic texts, and is thus far from the unworldly ingénue Sue believes her to be. From Maud's point of view, the perspective is reversed: 'the bounds of innocence' lie on the other side of the pointing brass finger, and it is Sue who 'in her innocence does not see it, and tries to cross it' (Waters 2002: 245–6).

There is a gleeful play on the repeated iteration of the word 'innocence' here, since it relates both to the machinations of the plot which both women believe they control, and to the kind of specifically sexual knowledge to which Maud has access, and Sue has not. The hand's inability to act as an absolute dividing line between the two is further reinforced by an image with which it is closely associated; that of gloves, which Maud's uncle forces her to wear both night and day with an almost fetishistic persistence. Made of white kid, they are both pale and absorbent, and thus vulnerable to stains and splashes. Consequently, they showcase rather than disguise the corrupting substances with which they come into contact, such as ink, blood and food. Whereas one might expect that gloves would be worn to handle Mr Lilly's treasured books and taken off outside the library, in this novel the opposite is the case, as the library is the only place in which Maud is permitted to leave her hands bare.

In *Fingersmith*, therefore, the hand is a permeable boundary: simultaneously a guardian of innocence *and* the gateway to knowledge, which is often of a sexual kind. When Maud enters puberty, her gloves, as the housekeeper euphemistically observes, serve to 'keep her from [. . .] mischief' (Waters 2002: 201), but they are removed when she handles pornography, giving her a physical connection to the explicit texts her uncle makes her read. Furthermore, hands later become the means by which a specifically lesbian desire is satisfied, for when Maud and Sue become lovers it is hands and fingers that form the erotic point of connection between them: 'When her hand moves again, her fingers no longer flutter: they have grown wet, and slide' (Waters 2002: 282). Although Maud cannot help but relate sexuality to its pornographic literary depictions, her belief that this encounter will conform to the crude dualism portrayed in her uncle's books – 'two girls, one wise and one unknowing' (Waters 2002: 281) – is unsustainable, since wisdom and knowledge cannot be so easily partitioned. For her part, Sue sees herself as the instigator of their sexual encounter: led on by Maud's feigned ignorance, she is the one who 'must show her how to do it' (Waters 2002: 142).

The image of the hand, so central to *Fingersmith*, hints at another way of understanding Waters' presentation of duality and doubling in this novel. In the terminology of molecular chemistry, duplicate images that are non-superimposable mirror-images are labelled 'chiral'. This word was coined by the nineteenth-century physicist Lord Kelvin, who asserted in his Baltimore lectures of 1884 that: 'I call any geometrical figure, or groups of points, *chiral*, and say that it has chirality, if its image in a plane mirror, ideally realized, cannot be brought to coincide with itself' (McManus 2004: 125). The etymological root of the word 'chiral' is *'kheir'*, the Greek word for 'hand', and as Chris McManus observes, 'right and left hands are chiral objects, since a right hand in a mirror cannot be brought into exact register with itself' (ibid.). I would argue that chirality provides us with a valuable way of understanding how the relationship between Sue and Maud prefigures the value of this text to a re-reader. Sue and Maud relate to each other not as duplicates or straightforwardly chiastic parallels, but as right hand to left; a fact that is foregrounded when Sue appropriates one of Maud's gloves before they leave Briar, 'to remind me of her' (Waters 2002: 148). After the workings of Maud's plot have been revealed and Sue is incarcerated in the lunatic asylum in her place, she finds she still has 'the crumpled white hand' (Waters 2002: 401) concealed in her dress, marking her as Maud's chiral opposite. A right-handed glove will not fit a left hand, and this becomes a metaphor for the act of re-reading, which creates a parallel version of the text for the reader which is both absolutely the same as the original encounter, and yet absolutely different.

(Re)reading the Fictional Subject

This vacillation between similarity and difference comes to define the very identities of Sue and Maud, who are constantly on the move between the two subject positions. They may frequently be presented as mirror images, but the question of who is viewing whom, of which is the original and which the reflection, is persistent and disorientating. Both women begin their stories similarly, in a way that appears to assert their separate identities and origins, but which in fact continues the process of blurring the boundaries that divide them. Constructing their narratives in the form of an autobiography, they start by relating the tales they have been told of their birth, as exemplified by Sue:

> My name, in those days, was Susan Trinder. People called me Sue. I know the year I was born in, but for many years I did not know the date, and took my birthday at Christmas. I believe I am an orphan. My mother I know is dead. But I never saw her, she was nothing to me. I was Mrs Sucksby's child, if I was anyone's. (Waters 2002: 3)

Yet it is clear from the outset that Sue's account does not fully *account for* her, since its vacillation between speculation and fact simultaneously validates her life story and places it in doubt. The opening of Maud's narrative, while more graphic and dramatic, demonstrates many similarities to Sue's. Beyond the fact that they both believe themselves to be the daughters of dead mothers, Maud, too, has an autobiography that is founded on a great deal of supposition:

> The start, I think I know too well. It is the first of my mistakes.
>
> I imagine a table, slick with blood. The blood is my mother's. There is too much of it. My mother is mad. The table has straps upon it to keep her from plunging to the floor; another strap separates her jaws [. . .] another keeps apart her legs [. . .]. When I am born, the straps remain: the women fear she will tear me in two! They put me upon her bosom and my mouth finds out her breast. I suck, and the house falls silent about me. There is only, still, that falling blood [. . .] the beat telling off the first few minutes of my life, the last of hers. (Waters 2002: 179–80)

There are similarities here that invite the reader to position the two narrators of *Fingersmith* in a parallel relationship, yet it is important to note that the similarity between their two accounts is not so much based on knowledge, but on the lack of it. They share a lineage delineated by loss (of the mother) and absence (of the father), and their origins are similarly indeterminate, the openings of both their stories foregrounding the way in which gaps in what they know are filled in with conjecture. With no knowledge of the precise date on which she was born, Sue invents a birthday for herself; possessing no information about her father, she characterizes herself as an orphan. Maud similarly exercises her imagination in constructing a graphic account of her birth which deliberately utilizes many literary devices, such as the onomatopoeic '*drip drop*! *drip drop*!' of her mother's blood upon the floor beneath the delivery table (Waters 2002: 180). Maud's opening sentence, 'The start, I think I know too well', signals that this is a quite deliberate move on Maud's part which opens up the same dialogue between fact and imagination the reader has already witnessed in the opening of Sue's narrative (ibid.). Both girls are aware that 'knowledge' is not necessarily the same as 'fact', and that identities can be constructed out of fictions and lies.

As the novel progresses and the plot gets underway, the pure supposition on which both these accounts are based becomes gradually apparent, as 'Maud' and 'Sue' become subject positions that can apparently be occupied by either girl. Maud dresses Sue in her own clothes in order to ensure that she can be mistaken for 'quite a lady' (Waters 2002: 155), while Maud herself plays the part of the maid; a swap that allows Sue to take Maud's place in the asylum. What neither knows at this point in the text is that Maud really is Sue, and Sue Maud, meaning that in retrospect this branch of the plot gains a warped sense of authenticity. As Gentleman explains to Maud: 'One baby becomes another. Your mother was not your mother, your uncle not your uncle. Your life was not the life that you were meant to live, but Sue's and Sue lived yours . . .' (Waters 2002: 335, ellipses in original). Incarcerated in the asylum, isolated and abused, Sue too begins to experience one identity dissolving into the other, finding that 'it seemed to me I *must* be Maud, since so many people said I was' (Waters 2002: 445).

Fingersmith is accordingly a text obsessed with knowledge; and in particular (to paraphrase the quotation that forms part of this essay's title) with the question of who knows everything, and who knows nothing. The words 'I know everything. I know nothing' are Maud's, but this is only one variant on an oft-repeated refrain yoking together these two antonymous pronouns (Waters 2002: 203). 'I thought I knew all about her. Of course, I knew nothing', says Sue of Maud, and only a few pages further on she reiterates that she finds it difficult to look at Maud, 'knowing what I knew, pretending I knew nothing' (Waters 2002: 82, 103). Trapped in the asylum, she realizes that 'I still knew nothing. Nothing at all': but she escapes and makes her way back to Mrs Sucksby's house only to discover that 'nothing was as I had thought it would be' (Waters 2002: 437, 493). When the two women, now both aware that they are, in effect, each other, reunite, the question of knowledge continues to obsess and perplex them: '"When did you know?" I said. "When did you know everything, about us, about – Did you know at the start?"' (Waters 2002: 542).

What is at stake here for Sue and Maud is their sense of an authentic identity. Their origin stories have been revealed as imaginary, fictions mistaken for fact, so as far as they are concerned, to know 'everything' means learning where they came from and who they 'really' are. Conversely, to know 'nothing' is to be bereft of any sense of authentic self. In particular, the distinction that both characters draw between 'everything' and 'nothing' throughout the novel suggests that they are haunted by the fear that if one of them is proved real, then the other must be fake, for they share a view of themselves as frighteningly malleable beings. Sue has been brought up in a house in which '[e]verything that came in [. . .] looking like one sort of thing was made to leave it again looking quite another', so is well versed in the mechanics of forgery and transmutation (Waters 2002: 10). As she says, she herself is the 'only [. . .] thing [. . .] that had come and got stuck', but what she comes eventually to realize is that she *is already* not the 'thing' she was (Waters 2002: 11). In Briar, Maud is locked in a fearful solitude, but is also threatened by a persistent phobia that she is a mere shadow or reflection of those around her. She believes her uncle has moulded her into a reproduction of his group of pornographic connoisseurs, telling Gentleman that he 'has made me like them': a statement later echoed and contradicted by Gentleman, who gleefully informs her that '[y]ou are like me' (Waters 2002: 225, 302).

Such pressing issues of identity and authenticity become a means by which the reader is drawn into direct participation in the text. Sue's question, 'When did you know? [. . .] Did you know at the start?' may be directed at Maud, but it could also be asked of us, as an appeal to the audience for a validation of her subjecthood. What answer we give will depend on whether this is our first or second experience of the novel. If the former is the case, the answer will be no; but if we have a prior familiarity with the text we do, of course, start it knowing everything. Thus we, too, are drawn into the construction of these characters' identities, and, as re-readers, given the power to tell them who they are.

Reading and Epistemology

Fingersmith is therefore deeply concerned with epistemological questions regarding the reliability of what we know, how we know it and where that knowledge comes from. To read Waters' novel is to be required to navigate a criss-crossing, double-crossing narrative in which knowledge does not necessarily lead to understanding and dual identities cannot be neatly resolved. This is because knowledge, like anything else, can be forged; the information circulating in this novel is both real and 'counterfeit' (Waters 2002: 264). Not even the characters can easily discern the difference between the two, for, as Sue says, the narrative contains '[t]oo many [secrets] to count. When I try now to sort out who knew what and who knew nothing, who knew everything and who was a fraud, I have to stop and give it up, it makes my head spin' (Waters 2002: 110). The repercussions of this confusion for the subject are expressed by Maud, who reaches the point where the workings of the plot have become so labyrinthine that 'I can no longer say with certainty which of my actions – which of my feelings, even – are true ones, which are sham' (Waters 2002: 271).

What is made clear from the outset is that reading is not a reliable means of attaining authentic knowledge, and warnings to this effect are scattered throughout the book. 'Believe me', cautions Gentlemen, himself never averse to '[t]elling you half of a story and making out you had it all', 'I have some knowledge of the time that may be misspent, clinging to fictions and supposing them truths' (Waters 2002: 42, 225). No character is better positioned to appreciate this than Maud, a trained bibliographer who has read about every permutation of the sexual act, but who finds the actual bodily experience to be entirely different: 'Is this desire? How queer that I, of all people, should not know!' (Waters 2002: 277). When she is small, she 'suppose[s] all printed words to be true ones' (Waters 2002: 186), but what the novel so graphically demonstrates to both characters and readers is that words lie, can be erased and misread – and, in the hands of a capable author, can also be designed to mislead. For Mr Lilly the power of literary pornography is that: 'words [. . .] seduce us in darkness, and the mind clothes and fleshes them to fashions of its own' (Waters 2002: 216). In other words, a successful author must also be an astute plotter who seduces the reader into 'putting on the things she sees the constructions she expects to find there' (Waters 2002: 227).

Fingersmith's assertion that words are inherently tricksy and slippery things, creating fictions that masquerade as reality and lure the reader away from discovery of the truth, is counteracted by a faith in the fidelity of what *cannot* be said. The central role played by hands in the novel suggests that it is through touch and sensation that the characters really come to discover each other; and thus, by extension, themselves. Knowledge is attained not by reading, but through desire. This is, of course, the ultimate aim of literary pornography, a form that seeks to link both reading *and* desire. Mr Lilly's associate Mr Hawtrey keenly champions the cause of erotic photography, which he sees as possessing the potential to circumvent the limitations of language in order to attain 'a thing beyond words, and beyond the mouths that speak them' (Waters 2002: 215); but *Fingersmith* concludes that no simulacrum of desire, be it linguistic or imagistic, is any substitute for the physical ability to touch and love another being. The novel can be regarded as an endorsement in fiction of Angela Carter's view that pornography 'has the power to arouse, but not, in itself, to assuage desire', since sexuality 'is a quality made manifest [only] in being' (Carter 1979: 14, 15).

This has particular implications for Waters' portrayal of lesbian desire, a form of sexuality in which, as Mandy Merck says, the hand plays a particular role 'as an instrument of sexual contact' (Merck 2000: 127). An adjective that echoes through the novel is 'queer', and although it is used by the characters in its original sense of 'odd' or 'strange', for a contemporary reader – particularly in the context of Waters' fiction – the word cannot help but also evoke its contemporary meaning of 'non-heterosexual'. When Gentleman describes Maud as 'a queer sort of girl', or Maud sees Sue's face in the mirror as 'queer in reflection', they activate a hidden counter-narrative of sexuality located outside heteronormativity (Waters 2002: 26, 284). *Fingersmith*'s portrayal of lesbian desire participates in the novel's obsession with doubleness and duality, in that in Mr Lilly's house it is portrayed as heterosexuality's outlawed 'other', acceptable only when framed as a titillating performance for a male observer. However, the distance Waters maps between the kind of male-authored representations of lesbianism with which Maud is familiar and the lesbian sexual act as it is actually experienced serves to establish the queer as a distinct identity with its own potentialities. Lesbianism is not a parody or inferior imitation of the (hetero)sexual act any more than Sue is a forgery of Maud or Maud of Sue. In Waters' novel, the hand that blurs rather than demarcates boundaries is a 'lesbian hand' (Merck 2000: 127) possessing the ability to 'put back [. . .] flesh' (Waters 2002: 283) in order to 'know' the authentic queer desiring self beneath.

Conclusion

Fingersmith's final twist, however, is that despite all its warnings to the audience about the untrustworthiness of words, it remains implicated in both their production and transmission. Not only does Maud herself become a writer of pornographic texts, but she and Sue together become the fictional producers of the novel we are reading – a novel which, as this essay has discussed, takes full advantage of the deceptive power of the word. One must always bear in mind when reading this text that the credulity of the narrators is recollected and reconstructed, and that the voices telling the story are in full possession of the knowledge they so deliberately withhold from the reader. This foreknowledge surfaces in deliberately performative declarations that often take the form of provocatively direct address: 'You are waiting for me to start my story. Perhaps I was waiting then. But my story had already started – I was only like you, and didn't know it' (Waters 2002: 14). 'You must remember this, in what follows. You must remember what I cannot do, what I have not seen' (Waters 2002: 203). As I have argued throughout this essay, the only way to avoid becoming the 'pigeon' (Waters 2002: 175) in this narrative double-cross is to take on the implicit challenge to re-read the text again. While, like Madame Genevieve, we may make our first crossing with any security cut out from beneath our feet by the deft manoeuverings of these literary fingersmiths, our second foray has every chance of success, since this time we share the privileged perspective of the novel's fictional authors and their sympathy for their – and our – gullible former selves.

Nevertheless, the inherent plurality of *Fingersmith* should not be ignored: it ends with a suggestion that, particularly when situated within a distinctively queer context, it may be possible for words to act as vehicles for authentic knowledge. The final key to the secret of Sue's and Maud's origins, after all, is a letter written by Sue's real mother that settles the question of their true identities, and establishes them as equals rather than uneasy halves of an unsettled and unstable dualism. In their final discovery of the truth, the two narrators reach a symmetrical resolution: Maud, the working-class girl raised as a 'gentlewoman' and Sue, the daughter of an heiress raised as a working-class girl, each have possession of half of the Lilly fortune and inhabit Briar together (Waters 2002: 532).

It is also highly significant that when Maud and Sue are reunited, it is in the library, in a scene that both replicates and transforms their earlier encounter on Sue's first morning in the house. With Mr Lilly's prohibiting brass finger now 'prised from the floor', Sue is free to cross the room and see the books housed within it, which constitutes the final move in her journey from ignorance to knowledge (Waters 2002: 541). As has already been discussed, 'knowledge' in *Fingersmith* is strongly associated with sexuality, as is made clear in Sue's accusation to Maud that:

> 'You knew it all [. . .]. That's the first thing I thought. 'You said that you knew nothing, when all the time – '
> 'I did know nothing,' she said.
>
> 'You knew it all! You made me kiss you!' (Waters 2002: 545)

Here, the issue is not the plot, but the fact that Maud feigned sexual ignorance when they became lovers. In teaching Sue to read, and in using pornographic texts as primers, Maud is giving her more than access to literacy, and also the deceptive power of the text. This time, however, it is a text that has been authenticated by lived desire, rather than salaciously imagined by a male author. Maud's lament that 'There are no girls like me' is clearly no longer true, for she learns, through both words and actions, that she is not alone, and that doubles do not have to be deceptive (Waters 2002: 547). Instead, pornography becomes Maud's unambiguous love-letter, in which she tells Sue 'all the words for how I want you' (ibid.).

CHAPTER FOUR

'Something New and a Bit Startling': Sarah Waters and the Historical Novel

JEROME DE GROOT

Chapter Summary: This chapter argues that Sarah Waters' work as an historical novelist is clearly influenced by her own scholarship on the genre. In reading her critical work – particularly her doctoral thesis and a chapter on lesbian historical fiction – we can comprehend how her novels intervene in, contribute to, and develop, debates on the form, meaning and purpose of the historical novel. Waters manipulates her chosen genre to great effect, for clear political reasons, and this is demonstrated in the chapter by a consideration of three key elements: her use of the word 'queer', her attention to the possibilities of objects in historical rendering, and her sense of the utopic possibilities of the historical novel.

Keywords: *Tipping the Velvet*, *The Night Watch*, queer, historical novel, objects, utopia, genre.

The trend since 1990 for British literary fiction authors to write what are recognizably historical novels has been demonstrated by the great success of Hilary Mantel, Rose Tremain, Ian McEwan and Sarah Waters. Hitherto a devalued genre, where once the historical mode – as a 'straight' representation of the past, rather than the complex reordering of history and identity that might be found in Salman Rushdie's *Midnight's Children* (1981) or Jeanette Winterson's *Sexing the Cherry* (1989) – was considered pulpy, marginal and tired as a format, novelists began to embrace it (see Keen 2006; Bentley 2008: 128–60; Tew 2008: 124–58). Now the genre is generally reviewed in newspapers, magazines and on television; there are literary prizes for historical fiction, and it is increasingly seen as a standalone genre. Furthermore, literary historical fiction has begun to infect the popular imagination through television adaptation – Waters,

Alan Hollinghurst (*The Line of Beauty*) and Michel Faber (*The Crimson Petal and the White*) have all seen their work translated to the small screen. Key, though, to this brief narrative of (re-)assimilation is the fact that these novelists were hailed as literary as much as popular, were short-listed (and won) major prizes and surrounded themselves with all the armoury of literary fiction. Waters' own status as a writer has been augmented by the various prizes she has won or been shortlisted for, her endorsement by various important critical institutions, and her swift acceptance by the academic establishment. Waters' critical work on the historical novel demonstrates her engagement with the mode before becoming a fiction writer. Of the high-profile writers that are generally thought to have kick-started the move to the mainstreaming of the historical novel – Mantel, McEwan, Tremain, David Mitchell and Kazuo Ishiguro – she is the only one who works solely within the historical framework, the only one who might identify herself as an historical novelist rather than a novelist working by chance in this representational medium of history.

The marginalization of the historical novel since 1930 or so (and its reinvention as a 'female' genre) demonstrates literary prejudice quite clearly (see Wallace 2005). It might be argued that the post-1990 reclamation by literary fiction writers of a form that once was considered marginal at best, and the injection of gravitas given impetus by prize-winning and audience figures, is merely a belated recognition of something that was always there. From Scott onwards writers have understood that the historical novel is a genre that allows for great complexity and is more challenging than readers realize. Historical fiction has always been innovative and thoughtful as a mode of writing. Fiction undermines the totalizing effects of historical representation and points out that what is known is always partial, always a representation. Historical novelists seek solace in authenticity and fiction simultaneously – citing their extreme research at the same time that they distance themselves from 'reality'. The historical novel therefore sits at a peculiar angle to its creator, who seemingly disavows its realism while asserting its diegetic wholeness and truth.

As a form, the historical novel raises significant questions about representation, and the choices made by both author and reader in interrogating and understanding the world. Historical novels force the reader into a temporal disjuncture. They demand a shifting of imaginative time and, most particularly, a recognition of temporal otherness. The strategies inherent in knowing, enacting and constructing official versions of history are laid bare by the effects of historical novels, which attempt to hold within them the actuality and the authority of history but are conscious that they are fabrications. Historical novels critique the hegemonic structure of a totalizing, explaining past. The past as presented in historical fiction is a re-enactment, a recreation, a performance of pastness; it is a mimicking of a dominant discourse that enables the consideration of other multiplicities of identity and behaviour. To write (and read) historical fiction therefore is to engage in an ethical mediation and demands an aesthetic and epistemological sophistication that is often missed by critics of the genre. The disjunction between 'real' and 'fictional' history allows for an exploration of the ethics of representation and the ways that history has sought to repress and discipline the other (see Southgate 2009). If the past is other, artificially located in a binary relationship with now, its representation – particularly its fictional recreation – invokes numerous ethical issues. The translation of the past into a recognizable, readable present demands a set of procedures and assumptions that are particularly disconcerting, accruing around the illusion of authenticity.

This chapter considers Sarah Waters as an historical novelist and in particular looks at the ways in which her practice as a writer has been influenced by her own critical work on the genre. The first section outlines her own critical work on the historical novel, and argues that her fiction mirrors her scholarly interventions; in reading her critical work we can comprehend her novels in more depth, particularly their politicized engagement with the representation of the past. Waters makes a clear historiographic intervention in her work, but this is largely expressed through her engagement with the possibilities of the historical novel genre. This contention is then demonstrated through consideration of three key elements: Waters' use of the word 'queer' as a multifaceted term allowing for a traversal of the space between then, 'now', past and 'history'; the way in which, similarly, particular objects are used in Waters' fiction to critique the wroughtness of 'history'; and a final consideration of the way in which utopic thinking in Waters' early novels might provide an alternative space to that provided elsewhere in 'history'.

Before she was an historical novelist, she was a critic of the genre, and her scholarship enables us to comprehend her practice in more depth. Waters wrote a PhD thesis on historical fiction that was passed in 1995. Her purpose in her critical work was both reclamatory and revelatory: reclamatory, insofar as she looked 'beyond the historical canon, into middle-brow fiction and popular culture', and sought on occasion to trace those pasts that were not articulated by gay writers, that path not taken, the identities not expressed (Waters 1995: 12); revelatory, in her account of 'homosexual histories' as challenges to and interrogations of mainstream, heteronormative historiography (as reflected in critical work on the genre as much as that genre itself). Waters' early work on historical fictions is quite tentative, and prescriptive. Her doctoral work is interested in the figuring of homosexuality, particularly within some form of historicizing/fictionalizing content. It argues that fictional historical representation of sexuality demonstrates clearly the concerns of the moment it is written in more than a clear communication of 'historical' identities. She is stridently articulate about the way that the genre itself allows space for experimentation and complexity of expression: 'It is precisely the historical novel's capacity for *interference* with literary and cultural models that I am interested in exploring' (Waters 1995: 145). The clear sense of the way in which the historical novel somehow falls between discourses while challenging and interrogating them is important for Waters' later fictional work. Her own novels manipulate this mongrel quality of the genre (on the one hand, site of the most celebrated of European writings – *War and Peace, The Red & the Black, Middlemarch* – on the other, a pulpy, recondite, marginal genre written by Catherine Cookson, Jean Plaidy, Margaret Irwin) (see Light 1989). Yet despite her interest in *'interference'* her early critical work is not yet quite 'queer', more tentatively sketching out the space that queer might possibly work out of. It is not until her first published piece of academic writing, discussed below, that a more recognizably 'queer' critical model is propounded. As her critical standpoint develops and matures, so her writing and her historiographical engagement similarly change (see Boehm 2011).

Scholarship on the historical novel form has long been interested in questions of definition, rather than more complex notions of aesthetics, formal innovation or implication (see Fleishman 1972; de Groot 2009; Maxwell 2010). Waters herself points out that, 'preoccupation with the *form* of the historical novel, however, has obstructed analysis of its content' (Waters 1995: 11). Critics have spent so long arguing about what it *is* that they have had precious little time to think about what it might do, and what it might contain. Waters' critical work, to an extent, participates in a wider critical shift towards engaging with the historical novel as a complex and important form; her creative work most definitely contributes to a contemporary reinvigorating (possibly even reinventing) of the form through the perception of its protean quality and breadth of reference. Her fiction seeks to reflect this critical development and complication, as her novels address complex issues rather than simply debating the logic of representing the past.

Waters admits that her critical work on the form directly contributed to her beginning to write fiction:

> I started [to write] for two reasons: one, because I was reading a lot of historical novels and really enjoying the genre (there seemed to be a burst of interesting historical fiction around in the late '80s/early '90s: *The Name of the Rose, Nights at the Circus, Possession, Oscar and Lucinda . . .*); two, because in 1991 I started work on a PhD thesis looking specifically at lesbian and gay historical fiction, and I ended up wanting to write a lesbian historical novel of my own. I've never lost the basic excitement I felt then, at taking on a very familiar area of history ('Victorian Britain') and a very familiar style of writing ('the nineteenth-century novel') and making it do something new and a bit startling. (Waters 2006c)

The novels she mentions clearly situate her own style of writing – literate, thoughtful, challenging texts that articulate a new way of thinking about historical fiction as a genre. Waters is happy here to ascribe generic definition both to her own work ('a lesbian historical novel') and to that of writers (particularly Angela Carter and Peter Carey) who might not be thought of as historical novelists. She underlines the sense that there was a 'burst' of writing at the turn of the 1990s, placing herself in that move towards a more sophisticated version of the genre. What is key here furthermore is the sense of newness, of bringing a new perspective to familiar styles and contexts. She is clearly engaging with the practices of the 'nineteenth-century novel' and with the imaginative construction of 'Victorian Britain' (both are cited in quotation marks). In particular she links the sexual inclination of the new type of 'startling' writing she is presenting with the interrogation of 'familiarity'. This conscious reinvention of the form, the exciting reconfiguration and re-imagination of something hitherto 'recognizable', is evident in all of her work.

Waters' work has been seen by literary critics as part of a 'Neo-Victorian' movement, a turn throughout contemporary culture to engage critically with and represent the nineteenth century (see Heilmann and Llewellyn 2010; Mitchell 2010). Such novels, for Kate Mitchell, 'struggle [. . .] with the issue of what is involved in this re-creation of history, what it means to fashion the past for consumption in the present [. . .] can these novels recreate the past in a meaningful way or are they playing nineteenth-century dress-up?' (Mitchell 2010: 3). Neo-Victorian novels work at an interface of cultural representation, social nostalgia, postmodernism and collective memory, engaging with the historical imaginary in complex and challenging fashion. Key to this, though, is their status *as* historical novels, and the self-consciousness of this form, as suggested earlier, enables the Neo-Victorian text to work. Mitchell's work, particularly, seeks to reorient understanding of Neo-Victorian writing by providing a counter to Linda Hutcheon's influential model of postmodern 'historiographic metafiction'. This latter form is seen to complicate historical representation intentionally so that it might demonstrate the problems inherent in conventional historiography and epistemology. Mitchell argues that the historical novel has always 'been invested in historical recollection *and* aware of the partial, provisional nature of such representations' (Mitchell 2010: 4, italics original). This tension between authenticity and provisionality is key to Waters' work, particularly expressed linguistically and through the use of objects, as discussed below. The peculiar status of the historical novel as something which can both negotiate the ways in which pastness is resourced and represented, *and* seem to (or attempt to) communicate something particular, specific, revelatory or actual *about* that past, enables the writer to create something exceptionally complex while appearing to cleave to a steady, straightforward (even old-fashioned) genre. In many ways, and particularly through her use of and critical engagement with the historical novel as a genre, Waters offers an extremely complex version of pastness.

In 2000, Waters wrote a book chapter with the prominent queer critic Laura Doan about lesbian historical fiction (Doan and Waters 2000). Again, this concern with broader, more abstruse issues demonstrates Waters' academic credentials as a theorist of the historical novel and her commitment to exploring the implications and definitions of the form. She had already published two novels (*Tipping the Velvet* and *Affinity*), and was well known as a writer of historical fiction, but, more importantly, of 'lesbian' historical fiction. Her scholarly intervention with Doan, then, is a key moment in the development of her public persona as an historical novelist, and it allows us to contrast her own practices with the theorizing they undertake. Her development as a critic of the genre mirrors the increasing sophistication of her fiction.

Doan and Waters outline the 'quest for historical precedent' undertaken by lesbians and gay men, and argue that this is reflected in a desire for a past that finds its articulation in historical fiction (Doan and Waters 2000: 12). Finding a 'tradition' has proven particularly difficult for lesbians, while the 'male homosexual tradition [. . .] is often indistinguishable from patriarchal accounts of cultural reproduction more generally' (ibid.). In order to circumvent this and attempt to provide a discursive account of what might be possible (or preferable), they offer a reading of several writers and novels in order to understand more fully 'how [. . .] the past [is] negotiated in lesbian literary production' (Doan and Waters 2000: 13). They dispense with writing that mimics standard structures or seems to offer little in terms of 'new' identity; writing that seeks a genealogical connection to a past that clearly cannot – and, politically, ought not to – have a bearing on the present.

David Halperin's famous formulation suggests that queer is a kind of refusal to be part of a binary:

> Queer is by definition *whatever* is at odds with the normal, the legitimate, the dominant. *There is nothing in particular to which it necessarily refers.* It is an identity without an essence. 'Queer' then, demarcates not a positivity but a positionality *vis-à-vis* the normative [. . .]. [Queer] describes a horizon of possibility whose precise extent and heterogeneous scope cannot in principle be delimited in advance. (Halperin 1995: 62)

Oftentimes this is taken to mean a dissident, transgressive identity formulation. However, in the work of Doan and Waters, queer becomes something more complex and profound. Rather than celebrate work that simply seeks to mimic heteronormative genealogical linearity they look to the work of Jeanette Winterson as someone who reveals 'the lure of history in lesbian writing, but also its limits' (Doan and Waters 2000: 13). Doan and Waters find that more traditional, older, lesbian historical fiction tended to reinscribe the historical, linear, teleological patterns of heteronormativity, rendering lesbian identity a product of 'not historicism so much as nostalgia' (ibid.). 'Nostalgia' here seems to be shorthand for uninflected, apolitical, non-reflective work and the term relies heavily on Fredric Jameson's (and after him, Linda Hutcheon's) critique of the way nostalgia allows the tropes of history to become mere pastiche (Jameson 1991; Hutcheon 1998). In contrast, Winterson's 'more inventive use of history' allows 'an affirmation of female agency and autonomy grounded not in history but in a metafictional utopian space, a space bound neither by temporality nor by limiting paradigms' (Doan and Waters 2000: 24). Winterson's work refuses to be in thrall to history, instead demonstrating the wroughtness of such a limiting and narrativizing (and constricting) discourse. 'Like a ghost', they argue, 'the lesbian past grows increasingly insubstantial the nearer one draws to it', concluding:

> The relevance of historical fiction for 'lesbian life in the late twentieth century' may lie most fully in its capacity for illuminating the queer identities and acts against which modern lesbian narratives have defined themselves and which they perhaps continue to occlude. (Doan and Waters 2000: 25)

Waters' own novelistic practice, then, needs to be seen within this critical framework. The argument of the essay written with Doan affirms that her novels are not simply filling in the gaps, refocusing attention on the previously marginalized. They work backwards and forwards, commenting upon contemporary lesbian identity and the workings of sexuality in modernity. They articulate Halperin's 'horizon of possibility', refusing to articulate a well-defined 'otherness', instead inflecting the form of the historical novel with their explorations of potentiality. While Waters' work is far less experimental than Winterson's, it still attains a level of self-consciousness and formal innovation (from Nan's point-of-view account in *Tipping the Velvet* to the inverted chronology of *The Night Watch*). Her critical practice, then, allows us to reflect upon her fiction and look anew at some of her techniques. Waters is extremely conscious of the limits, demands and potentialities of her chosen form, and she is alive to the possibilities that the historical novel affords the writer to make a historiographical and political intervention.

A central example of Waters' queer versioning of the historical novel form is the use in her fiction of the word 'queer' itself. The term is used throughout her novels. It most obviously connotes authenticity, being a word that is diegetically, contemporaneously, correct.[1] Simultaneously, though, it is a contemporary word relating to sexual identity, dissidence, challenge, otherness. Waters' use of the word seems a minor wink to the reader, but, like the objects discussed later, it inflects the text. It reaches out, explicitly brokering a relationship between the historically authentic and the contemporary. Waters uses the word 'queer' 43 times in *Tipping the Velvet*, which in itself is quite a substantial incidence for a term rarely heard in contemporary speech. Throughout her corpus the word is repeated with astonishing frequency: *Fingersmith* (68 uses); *Affinity* (40); *The Little Stranger* (37); *The Night Watch* (26).[2] While it is a flexible term, used in a multiplicity of ways (its protean quality itself is interesting), it seems undeniable that Waters is embedding it consciously. So, for instance, in *Fingersmith* the terms of Maud's inheritance – that she will only inherit if she marries – are described as 'a queer condition' (Waters 2002: 24). This early narrative conceit of the novel seemingly revolves around a kind of queering of marriage (and tying it to economic status). The duality of the word 'queer', being both diegetically accurate and also contemporaneously significant, renders this moment something that reflects upon its own fictiveness while also attempting to persuade the reader of its authenticity.

The following are some moments from *Tipping the Velvet* when Waters' use of the word seems particularly acute:

> 'My view of her now, of course, was side-on and rather queer'. (Waters 1998: 17)
>
> 'For the oyster, you see, is what you might call a real queer fish – now a he, now a she, as quite takes its fancy. A regular morphodite, in fact!' (Waters 1998: 49)
>
> 'You must know too that I can never be happy while your friendship with that woman is so wrong and queer'. (Waters 1998: 134)
>
> 'The man had looked like Walter; I had pleasured him, in some queer way, for Kitty's sake; and the act had made me sicken'. (Waters 1998: 199–200)

The first quotation is Nan's initial view of her future lover Kitty, the second Nan's father's account of a transgressive physiological interspace (a challenging of gender identities), the third a direct criticism by Nan's sister of their relationship (both labelling and not, describing while also shirking taxonomy). The final quotation presents us with what is both a seemingly homosexual act (although the reader knows it is not) and a 'queer' act, a moment of alterity that is also linked to a transgressive sexual encounter. It makes Nan feel ill. 'Queer', then, is productive and authentic, referential and strange, there and not there. It traverses the boundaries of past/now that historical fiction itself happily shifts between, and, in its sheer oddness as a term (and its obviousness), it demonstrates to the reader what is happening (while, clearly, realistically, pointing out that this cannot be happening). 'Queer' makes odd, but it also makes 'historical'; the term brokers the relationship between then and now through its indistinctness/materiality. It both is and isn't, insofar as it both achieves historical effect (it is authentic) and contemporary resonance. It creates a discursive space between allegedly fixed 'contemporary' identities and the 'past' (and its representations).

Hence the reader's relation to the 'queered' text might be conceived of as similar to the woman who interrupts Kay and Helen in *The Night Watch*: 'She must have glimpsed the end of their embrace, but was doubtful: puzzled and embarrassed' (Waters 2006a: 322). Queer is something that might but might not be, apart from definition, something that challenges and confuses the normative. This illustrates Middleton and Woods' relation of the 'distance between epistemology and ontology' (Middleton and Woods 2000: 78), that is, the way that the historical novel can explore – *must* explore – the hinterland and the relationship between experiential comprehension and (textually) formulated knowing. This might also be formulated as the relationship between history and the body, again something that Waters' use of the world 'queer' negotiates elegantly.

As can be seen from the example of the word 'queer', Waters is able to innovate by ensuring reflection upon contemporary sexual identity, while also using the word to illustrate the complex negotiation between realist authenticity and scepticism that the historical novel has always held within it. She therefore yokes her critical practice with her fiction here, submitting her form and the discourse of history to scrutiny. Similarly *The Night Watch* formally challenges heteronormative linearity to provide another set of narrations and to reflect upon the ethics of historical representation. By its simple inversion of linearity *The Night Watch* demonstrates to the reader how the act of engaging with an historical product is inherently insightful and hence powerful. The position of the reader is that they *know*, and therefore have an ethical conflict when engaging with the text. The strength, and awful power, of that knowledge – that the character will die, will be in pain, will suffer loss – is often hidden by linear, positivist, realist fictions that invite the suspension of this historical othering in the service of comfort. Time-slip fictions have long allowed a meditation such as this, as the protagonists (those who fall through time) are left to reflect upon their ethical relation to those in the past, and the value and status of their knowledge. The temporal dislocation that all fiction demands on the part of the reader, an imaginative movement between there and wherever, is brought into focus by the historical novel. These iterations of the novel show in relief key concerns of all writing: death, knowledge, identity. The reader is not only empowered in relation to the text through this 'foreknowledge' but also forced to think about their ethical relation to both text and historical event.

The Night Watch undertakes this kind of work, but, further, demonstrates to the reader how all historical fiction is time-slip of a type, with the reader themselves in the problematic ethical position in relation to the text. 'We might all be dead tomorrow' says Viv, and, of course, they are (Waters 2006a: 298); they never lived, but people like them did, and their manifestation in the past is over; they are 'dead' to the contemporary. Waters' formal innovation in *The Night Watch* is to elegantly render the novel's deconstruction of linearity as part of the fragmentation of identity and selfhood that are its themes. The unravelling of self that is undertaken in the plot, and in the workings of the narrative, reflects the concomitant fragmentation of meaning and infects the historiography of the text, ensuring that the novel's version of the past itself is contingent and insubstantial.

The text demonstrates this through its concern with an object, a ring. Kay gives Viv a ring when she is in her most extreme pain, a moment of comfort and anonymous connection. The ring allows Viv to pass as married, so it works to concretize her heteronormative identity (performatively, rather than in actuality, given that she is not *actually* married). This is ironized by the fact that the ring has been given to her by a queer character. It is a metonym and a material actuality, and this doubleness – both presence and absence, freighted with imaginary meaning and composed of something simple and elegant – informs the entire text retrospectively. The physical itself is invoked as a way of linking together disparate people through time, as Viv thinks to herself:

> She caught the dusty, nasty smell of the hotel carpet; she pictured all the men and women who might have embraced on it before, or who might be lying like this, now, in other rooms, in other houses – strangers to her, just as she and Reggie were strangers to them [. . .] The idea was lovely to her, suddenly. (Waters 2006a: 188)

This affective connection figures the material bodies in the novel as imaginatively conjoined with others (as in the case of Duncan and Fraser, or the laying on of hands of Mr Leonard). Such sympathy and synchronicity are illusory, of course, but they create an imagined connection that works through the conceptualization of the physical. The ring has a similar ability at once to connect and articulate difference, its invocation of physicality (the finger) seeming to link both Viv and Kay. Viv's restoration of the ring is one of the first things to occur in the novel, and it works to return Kay to the evening she gave it away and her life fell apart. It is, therefore, an object that allows for conceptual, imaginative, memorial work to be done both by the character and, later, by the reader. It renders Viv's happiness and Kay's tragic loneliness simultaneously. It stands for a physical link between the two women – and their personal histories – while demonstrating quite how far apart they are. As an object that suggests connection, it also signifies fragmentation and disconnection.

The ring describes an absence (both geometrically and conceptually). It is both specific and common, gathering meaning from its physicality and its imaginative iteration. It needs the warm body of an individual to give it significance, but that meaning itself is prey to change or misinterpretation (malicious or otherwise, given Viv's use of it). *The Night Watch* is a novel that is interested in the plodding banality of some objects, and their sudden transformation into, for instance, things that might kill (razors) or allow time-travelling (Kay's ring). Material objects and things in texts allow a reflection of 'not just the physical determinants of our imaginative life but also the congealed facts and fantasies of a culture, the surface phenomena that disclose the logic and illogic of industrial society' (Brown 2003: 4). Kay's ring is diegetic and authentic, something with physical heft that clearly is only imaginatively/fictively constructed by the text (it does not *actually* exist). The concern with the physical object renders the text in thrall to materiality while it points out its unreality; like the ring, it is substantial and empty. Kay's ring is an echo, a spectre, a trace of the past diegetically in the present. It is an object fetishized and given value and meaning. It is also a clue, something the reader looks for throughout the subsequent narrative due to the inverted chronology of the novel. It provokes a range of interpretations but at the same time is simply a ring, a band of metal, without inherent 'value' or meaning.

The absences/presences inherent in the ring, the physical emptiness it enacts as an object, serve as a motif for *The Night Watch*'s intense interest in ghostliness and memory, and, more, how these issues interact with 'history'. The novel is obsessed with the gaps between solid objects, particularly in its concern with ruins and the way that the destruction of the urban landscape fosters new, innovative relationships: 'She supposed that houses, after all – like the lives that were lived in them – were mostly made of space. It was the spaces, in fact, which counted, rather than the bricks' (Waters 2006a: 195). That which is physical *means* only in relation (and not outwith relation) to the spaces in between, the echoing, dusty, lonely places. Objects – bricks – only have significance in social/spatial relation, only describe meaning (rather than geometrical shape) in dynamic interaction. The ring, again, stands for a motif that inflects the whole book's conceptualization of the space between people (diegetically and in terms of the audience's response to these other lives, these 'dead' characters). It is real and it is false, empty and full, and this ability to broker an interrelationship between such states demonstrates inherently the power of the historical novel not simply to dislocate history but also to provoke new ways of thinking about the past, to construct new relationships and possibilities.

Julia says at one point of her work surveying the bombed buildings of the city, 'We're recording ghosts, you see, really' (Waters 2006a: 269). This quite physical sense of the lost, the way that 'ghosts' can be recorded and archived and taxonomized, but still never really understood or comprehended, is key to Waters' practice as a historiographer. The insubstantiality of the historical revenant, or the ghostliness of the referent, and its near-rational (but not quite) link with the reality of modernity is her subject through the Spiritualism of *Affinity*, the performativity-illusions of *Tipping the Velvet*, to the actuality of haunting explored in *The Little Stranger*. Things, ghosts and the spaces between, then, are central concerns for Waters' fiction and elements that enable the works to reflect upon their own fictiveness. This self-consciousness, an interrogation of historicity imbibed via gender theory and the last vestiges of the aesthetics of postmodernism (see the list of novels Waters cites as inspiration – Carter, Byatt, Eco), enables the articulation of a dissident sensibility at the same time that her work cleaves to authenticity, realist tropes and the modes of a form long thought conservative. The ring motif – empty and material, object/fiction, real and ghostly, remembered and textualized – stands for the ways in which Waters is concerned with brokering the relationship between the real and the fictive.

This duality – the doubleness at the heart of all historical fiction – is both trope and purpose for Waters. The queer multiplicity of 'queer' and the complicating physicality of objects both contribute to a historiography which is essentially utopic, insofar as it seeks to enable a new, undefined space of identity. *Tipping the Velvet* concludes in Victoria Park, in a celebration of working-class life: '"Some wretched scheme," I said, "dreamed up by all the guilds and unions of East London, to fill Victoria Park with socialists –" "A demonstration," interrupted Florence. "A wonderful thing, if it works"' (Waters 1998: 439). The event itself is a celebration of socialism and community, an idealized space of equality and hope. Nan arrives at Victoria Park to find it 'transformed' with:

> Speakers and exhibitions [. . .] for every queer or philanthropic society and cause you could imagine – trade unionists and suffragists, Christian Scientists, Christian Socialists, Jewish Socialists, Irish Socialists, anarchists, vegetarians [. . .] 'Ain't this marvellous?' I heard as I walked, from friends and strangers alike. 'Did you ever see a sight like this?' (Waters 1998: 443, 444)

The park has become a place of marvel, of wonder. In a novel that has dwelt upon the illusions and temptations of performance for most of its pages, and reminded the reader of contemporary fascination with the Victorian music-hall (a fascination that Nan shares, only to find it corrupt and empty), this move to end in a 'real' political locus is striking (see Wilson 2006; Jeremiah 2007). The same audiences that would visit the music hall for empty entertainment (or, moreover, the Great Exhibition) are here being given speeches on 'Why Socialism?' (Ralph's speech that Nan gives him tips on – bringing her West End skills to bear on political oratory) (see Auerbach 1999). The descriptions – 'marvellous', 'transformed', 'wonderful' – are deliberately deployed to remind the reader of the awestruck responses of audiences to theatrical performance. As much as the theatre, this is the performance of life in Victorian London, and the identities – queer, anarchist, socialist – it might offer are in many ways more 'real' than those suggested by the other performative spaces Nan inhabits (as an actor, Diana's prostitute, rent-boy). Yet there is an inherent melancholia in this celebration. The space of leftwing possibility that Victoria Park represents here, and the life free from strain and prejudice it seems to allow Nan and Florence, seems to be an ideal, a fantasy, something that never existed and, seemingly, never will. This utopic conclusion is predicated upon the reader knowing that it is just that, idealized, potential rather than real, desired but never achieved.

However, this idealistic space seems a challenge, an upsetting of the standard view of Victorian Britain. Certainly the space allows for the final coming together of Nan (who rejects the name Kitty gives her, choosing 'Nancy') and Florence as concrete, honest, solid lovers: 'careless of whether anybody watched or not – I leaned and kissed her' (Waters 1998: 472). The novel ends at this point with 'a rising ripple of applause' from the speakers' tent, a diegetically realistic salute to the power of the political oratory within and a slightly ironized comment upon the transformative, revelatory identities articulated without (ibid.). Their love is framed as the only 'real' performance worthy of applauding, framed by a political sense of the transformative possibilities of the future. The nineteenth century, rather than being the incipient engine of capitalism, empire, expansion, industrialization, is a place where new worlds were thought of and conceptualized. Just because they never materialized does not mean that the imaginative leaps undertaken to speculate upon them were worthless – in fact, such dreaming might be more important than the concrete, proper 'reality'. The account of the idealistic, utopic space here is a challenge to rationalist histories – a provocation to dream better futures, based in political commitment and individual liberty. The new, strange, relationships of the end of the novel – queer, cross-familial (both with Ralph and the child Cyril), eschewing patriarchy and hierarchy – suggest a possible world outside of the taxonomies of class, sexuality, gender. This might be the 'utopian space, a space not bound by temporality nor by limiting paradigms' that Doan and Waters see in Winterson's work (Doan and Waters 2000: 24). Thus a book which had suggested the freedoms of theatrical and sexual/gendered performance goes further than this by presenting a potential space of unlimited possibility; but this is a space of real communal, committed, collectivist relationships. The utopic space thus is a locus that offers an alternative to the narratives of history, an invitation to step outside of the rational, linear, positivist modes of knowing the past and to dream a better future through the conception of an alternative history. This is, then, the model of *'interference'* Waters identified in her critical work.

As this chapter has demonstrated, Sarah Waters approaches the historical novel carefully and thoughtfully in order to ensure that it is not merely uninteresting 'nostalgia' but something more profoundly challenging. Her work inflects the form as much as the form itself enables the subversion of her writing. The protean potentialities of the historical novel enable Waters to make a clear political intervention, to suggest and contest in order to query and queer the ways that history attempts to constrain and control. As she argues about her own work:

> I think that to focus on what you might think of as the lost or marginalised voices of history inevitably gives your books a political resonance; your novels are effectively making the statement: 'These people are worth writing and reading about; these people are worth paying attention to'. It's an implicit rather than an explicit political agenda. (Waters 2006c)

This sense of implicit political meaning, the meaning suggested by historiographical or fictional strategies, goes to the heart of Waters' practice. The novels are correctives rather than attacks, utilizing the ambiguous tropes of the historical novel in order to posit new and revelatory relationships between people. They seek to disrupt (to 'queer') the smooth running of history, to interrogate and fragment, to reveal the ethical complications of representation in order to articulate a new space of possibility.

Notes

1 The first citing of this meaning of the word in the *OED* is 1513, but it is a word that seems particularly to accrue meaning and usage from around 1850–1950.

2 By way of contrast, the word occurs in the following comparable texts: Ian McEwan, *Atonement* (0 uses); A. S. Byatt, *Possession* (1); Sebastian Faulks, *Birdsong* (0); Pat Barker, the *Regeneration* trilogy (0).

CHAPTER FIVE

'Possibility, Pleasure and Peril':[1] *The Night Watch* as a Very Literary History

NATASHA ALDEN

Chapter Summary: The desire to 'fill in the blanks' of lost or occluded lesbian history is apparent in each of Sarah Waters' first four novels. In their different ways, each of these works resists the suggestion that the past can be recovered reliably. Instead, they illustrate the maxim/truism that representations of the past reflect the concerns of the present as much as those of the era they seek to recreate. Arguing that Waters' fiction aims to create an affective community of readers, this chapter explores how *The Night Watch* uses some of the techniques of historiographic metafiction to create a self-reflexive pastiche of fiction of the war, which reworks literary mannerisms of both mainstream and gay fiction of the period.

Keywords: Memory, historical fiction, empathic unsettlement, war fiction, gay history.

In Waters' 1996 article 'Wolfskins and togas: Maude Meagher's *The Green Scamander* and the lesbian historical novel', she identifies an intense need among lesbian authors and readers for representations of a lesbian past (Waters 1996). Waters and Laura Doan, in a co-authored article on lesbian historical fiction, subsequently argue that the roots of this desire lie in a sense of historical disconnection, or lack of continuity: 'If, as Foucault suggests, the homosexual was "born" out of the conjunction of particular cultural factors, at a distinct historical moment, then s/he was born yearning for a genealogy with which to transcend that moment' (Doan and Waters 2000: 12). *The Night Watch*, which, through its fragmentariness and complex, incomplete narrative structure, stands as an extended metonymic fragment, allows Waters to offer a playful reinscription of a possible lesbian past which uses many of the techniques common to historiographic metafiction to make the reader aware of the constructed nature of the text. It also allows her to circumvent what Halperin describes as 'cultural chauvinism' leading to 'homosexual essentialism', that is, assuming a simple continuity of lesbian identity from the 1940s till today, while not relinquishing her attempt to offer some kind of glimpse into a potential lesbian past (Halperin 2004: 14, 16). She deliberately engenders what LaCapra has called 'empathic unsettlement', which allows an affective bond to develop between a witness to trauma and their audience, but which limits the audience's objectification of the witness, preventing them from over-identifying and forgetting the 'otherness', or alterity, of that witness (LaCapra 2001: 41). In *The Night Watch*, while the reader (especially the gay reader) is able to read the text as genealogy, we are constantly reminded, by the metafictional nature of the text, of the otherness of the 1940s. While this, like Waters' other novels, is carefully researched, examining how this novel relates to the literary context Waters draws from, and the historical context it is set in, allows us to see how she encourages a double-consciousness in the reader.

Historical material on lesbian life during the war is hard to come by, but Waters was able to access some material, primarily recent studies of lesbian life, oral histories and recently published diaries and memoirs, such as Barbara Bell's autobiography, *Just Take Your Frock Off* (1999). Bell provides a detailed account of the opportunities wartime offered her. As Waters observes, although gay novels of the period make 'conducting a same-sex relationship seem like a grave and daunting business', Barbara Bell's autobiography suggests that 'the war gave many lesbians a licence to do things they had always enjoyed doing but which, until then, they'd had to do more or less illicitly – such as cutting their hair, wearing ties and trousers, driving cars' (Waters 2006b). Bell, as Waters notes, was able to take advantage of being a police officer to approach women who were on their own, and to enter 'London's sexual underworlds' (ibid.). Bell also notes the sense of freedom she felt, and excitement at the possibilities the war had opened up for her: 'You were living on another plane. I can't say it wasn't exciting [. . .]. It was the whirl and swarm of wartime. The immediate future was unknown' (Bell 1999: 79).

Bell was able to have numerous relationships and shorter flings with other police women, and women she met on the beat (one chapter on her wartime experience is gleefully titled 'On the Prowl'). She met women in clubs in Mayfair, on the underground and on the streets, and although she had to be discreet, and pass herself and her partner off as flatmates, they were able to live together without being asked the kind of questions two apparently single women might have faced in peace time. Subtle references to historical lesbians allow Waters to 'situate [her] lesbian stories in something bigger, like an echo chamber. There are hints at other lesbian texts or traditions of representation – but that's something that most of [her] readers won't necessarily pick up on' (Armitt 2007: 117). Two such 'hints' are references to friends of Radclyffe Hall's. The name of Kay's mechanic friend, Mickey echoes Naomi Jacob's nickname directly; another of Hall's friends, Marion Barbara Carstairs (known as Joe) started an all-women chauffeuring service called 'The X Garage' after returning from driving ambulances in the First World War. These glancing allusions are easily missed – the reader would have to know a reasonable amount about the circle of lesbian friends Hall moved in to recognize them – but to a reader who does recognize them, the effect is, indeed, to situate this story in a bigger context of lesbian history, and to give it added weight as a re-imagining of what might have been.

Another useful source on lesbian life in wartime was the diary of Joan Wyndham, published in the 1980s as *Love Lessons* (1985) and *Love is Blue* (1986). Although Wyndham was heterosexual, her observations, first of gay men and women in London clubs, and later of lesbians in the WAAF (Women's Auxiliary Air Force), provide not only a useful insight into how openly gay people could behave in the late 1930s and war years, but also of the censure they still faced. Wyndham, extremely open-minded herself, had to report lesbian relationships to her superiors, with the effect that the women were split up: despite the relaxation in sexual mores wartime brought, as we see in *The Night Watch,* caution was still necessary. Waters' emphasis in *The Night Watch* is not so much on caution during wartime as afterwards; in 1947, Kay and Mickey make no attempt to hide their sexuality (and suffer for it), but the more conventional Julia and Helen are paranoid about their neighbours realizing they are a couple, going to great lengths to put up a facade of a 'normal' relationship even after it is clear that the neighbours have guessed. Wartime offers a contrast here: Kay and Mickey are often mistaken for boys or men while on shift driving ambulances, but no one much cares, accepting them, in the circumstances, as 'honorary men'. The relaxation of social mores that is so apparent in Wyndham's account of her own sex life, and relaxed attitude to taking drugs (especially Benzedrine), is at odds with the fear and shame that runs through much gay fiction of the time, such as *Winter Love* (Suyin 1962) and *The Charioteer* (Renault 1959). Thus Waters does what she does in her earlier fiction, and appropriates a highly researched, intensely detailed landscape for a re-visioning of the gay past.

Writing about the more recent past was a new challenge for Waters, who was used to using the Victorian period as her backdrop:

> The big change for me with this book was the volume and variety of materials I could potentially consult: film, photos, sound recordings, as well as all the wartime ephemera which is still floating around. (None of this sort of thing, apart from photos, had been available to me for the Victorian-set novels, where I relied almost exclusively on books from and about the nineteenth century.) I used the [London Metropolitan Archives] to call up photographs

> of specific bomb-damaged streets, and to look at maps of the damage. I visited Westminster and Camden local archives to look at a few things: civil defence pamphlets at Westminster, and info on Hampstead Heath in wartime at Camden. I spent a day or two in the Imperial War Museum reading room looking at call-up papers and pocket diaries and one or two other things. I also spent a day at the Ambulance Museum, looking at vintage ambulances and first-aid stuff. As far as archives go, I think that was about it [. . .]. My biggest resources were diaries, novels and films. (Waters 2010)

Waters felt that she had a responsibility to get 'concrete' details right, according to the historical record. But she is less interested in the details of specific events in themselves than in the fictional events she projects onto them; the historical details she researches serve merely as a backdrop to the main drama of the characters' lives at various moments of the war. Her use of this material is, therefore, generally unremarkable in itself. It is thus unsurprising that while Waters feels a responsibility to represent the details of the places and events accurately, the inaccuracy – or to be less pejorative, the re-imagining – we find comes in relation to the characters' personal lives. Specifically, their language and their understanding and (generally) relaxed acceptance of their sexuality are updated to various degrees.

Waters' characters might live against a backdrop that any 1940s lesbian would recognize, but their emotional and sex lives are conducted in a way that is significantly different to the way in which gay and lesbian lives were depicted in the fiction of the period, which forms the other part of the source material Waters used. While it seems from Barbara Bell's memoir, at least, that some gay women were unblighted by crippling self-hatred and fear, in the very few novels depicting gay life of the time, this seems to be a universal condition.

Why does how fiction of the period depicts gayness matter in relation to this? Mainly because it helps us understand what this text is – pastiche? Homage? Metafictional intervention into the historical record? The significant differences between literary representations of lesbian life from the time, and Waters' twenty-first century take on this, suggest that this is certainly not pastiche. Having gone to some trouble to recreate the tone of 1940s fiction, the atmosphere in general, and specifically in the 1944 Blitz, she deviates significantly from her literary source material. Waters does not want to echo the apparent misery that being gay brings in fiction of the period, but to show an alternative which, while not always happy, does allow her characters the possibility of not ending the novel dead, alone, or in a heterosexual marriage, the chief options on offer in fiction of the time.

Waters' use of literary source material is complex, drawing on different aspects of different types of novel. While she uses researched details of the physical landscape of wartime London, these details are all selected to build an atmosphere which is heavily influenced by

Elizabeth Bowen and Henry Green. The literature of the time Waters has read provides the model, or template, into which the physical detail she takes from diaries, historical accounts, memoirs and films is fitted. Rod Mengham, writing on Green, suggests that the narrative complexity of *Caught* could function as a way of resisting tidying wartime experience into a readily understandable 'package' (Mengham 1982: 96–8); this is arguably what Waters is doing with her reverse chronology and partial withholding of key information. As Patrick Deer suggests, Mengham follows Eric Fromm in arguing that 'glossification, or rationalizing, is the terminus of a process in which the self is governed by the promise of meaning after the event' (Deer 2009: 268). It's this kind of narrative 'rounding-off' which Waters pointedly refuses at the end of her novel (unlike the television adaptation), as both the reader and the characters are left in the limbo the characters have inhabited since the end of the war. The reverse chronology of the novel means that we understand more of the characters' lives than they do in some respects; reading from 1947 back to 1941, we know their futures. But we're not given some key pieces of information (such as Julia's having been in love with Kay, not vice versa) until late in the narrative, if at all. We never see how Kay and Helen's relationship developed after their first meeting, for example, and thus miss out on Helen's coming out story, a dominant element of much lesbian fiction, yet entirely missing from this novel.

Waters, like Green, sees the opportunities for illicit eroticism that the war, especially the blackout, provided. Like him, Waters uses the blackout as a plot device (Julia and Helen's affair begins during a walk in a blacked-out city). Her depiction of the sudden, intoxicating sexual encounter which begins Helen's relationship with Julia reminds us of the kissing couple Roe, the fireman, comes across in a shelter in the aftermath of a raid, whose embrace has somehow locked them away from the rest of the world:

> In the near corner a girl stood between a soldier's legs. He had been kissing her mouth, so that it was now a blotch of red. He held on to her hips, had leant his head back across the white painted brick. Hair came down and trembled over his closed eyes with the trembling of the wall. Man and girl were motionless, forgotten, as though they had been drugged in order to forget, as though he had turned over a stone and climbed down stairs revealed in the echoing desert, those two were so alone. (Green 1943: 95–6)

This passage bears a clear resemblance to the tone, setting and events of Julia and Helen's night-time walk; their sense of being totally alone in this *unheimlich* landscape, empty yet full of the living and the homes of the dead, their sense of freedom and the shrinking of their world to awareness only of the other all echo Green's narrative technique. This focus allows Helen to act on her feelings, but it is clear that she is able to do so in part because of the frenzy in her that she has caught from this 'mad, impossible landscape' (Waters 2006a: 363).

Waters' description of the bombed city as a surreal, otherworldly and entirely new and familiar-yet-unfamiliar place owes much to both Bowen and Green. As Bowen puts it:

> Walking in the darkness of the nights of six years (darkness which transformed a capital city into a network of inscrutable canyons) one developed new bare alert senses, with their own savage warnings and notations. And by day one was always making one's own new maps of a landscape always convulsed by some new change. (Bowen 1999: 99)

In her short story 'Mysterious Kor', Bowen creates a similar conflation of place and mood, as a young couple wander through the streets in bright moonlight. The girl suggests that the bombing has blown something savage open, that civilization has faltered. Bowen creates a similar effect in *The Heat of The Day* (1949) in her description of London as a living city, which sighs, and where the sense of unease, of being watched, that the characters feel is deepened and echoed by their new awareness of the fragility of solid buildings, which might be there when one went into a bomb shelter but not when one emerged. The conflation and collapse of interior and exterior boundaries – as though things having been blown apart by the bombing opens possibilities in people's emotional lives as much as it does in the fabric of their houses – is borrowed directly from Bowen, as Waters explained in an interview with Lucie Armitt:

> Elizabeth Bowen [wrote] amazing short stories about how the city is transformed by darkness and transformed by the moon. Just imagine a full moon in a blacked out city! People talked about the new details you saw because of the blackout, the silhouettes that you didn't notice by day. I just got excited about that and, yes, did use the landscape in this way. It's a city in which all sorts of clandestine things could go on in the shadows. People did seem to be having sex in the blackout all the time: gay sex, straight sex. It was a city newly born through darkness, really. (Armitt 2007: 123)

Being outside during a raid gives Helen and Julia a sense of wild excitement, and they leave the comparative safety of the public shelter to slip behind a baffle wall covering the entrance to a public building, 'a deep [space], jute-scented, impossibly dark' (Waters 2006a: 374). Waters directly links the darkness, and Julia's observation that they're invisible again, to Helen's ability to confess her feelings; their kiss is described in terms which evoke the incendiary bombs falling on London, 'like a fire, [which] drew [and] took hold' (ibid.). Their clothes make 'a second baffle wall, darker than the first' (ibid.), and, as in Green's description, their focus narrows sharply to the only sensation in the darkness, the contact of their bodies.

Waters' text owes much to Green, Bowen, Neville Shute and other novelists and filmmakers of the time in terms of its subdued, emotionally restrained tone and use of language. It uses a prose style that, unlike Waters' other works, employs the third person, popular in the period, to evoke a slightly drier, more detached tone than the first person narrators of Waters' earlier works created:

> There is a sadness, a bleakness – often, a bitterness – to many of the novels of the period; think of Bowen's moody *The Heat of the Day*, Greene's furious *The End of the Affair*. I had not guessed, when I first took the 1940s on, how much the feel of these novels would begin to dictate the mood and shape of my own book. I was used to writing in a lush, gothic style, and somehow thought that I could import all those wonderful Victorian flourishes into the wartime setting, without a jar. Instead I found it more natural, more apt, and more interesting to let the lushness slip away. I submitted to the 'drying out' that had so troubled me at the start, and watched my prose become slightly pared down, my tone more quiet, my focus more interior. The 40s [. . .] emerged increasingly for me as a time of bleak passions tucked firmly away behind façades of understatement and good manners. The challenge, then, was to absorb its own restrained style and suggest a depth of feeling behind the apparently lightly placed word. (Waters 2006b)

Waters' mimicry of the language and literary conventions of the time is particularly indebted to Neville Shute's *Requiem For A Wren* (1955). This text is also about a woman left bereft of purpose and without her lover after the end of the war, and it also has a reverse chronology, albeit a less obviously experimental one. The main character, Alan Duncan, returns from Europe to his parents' Australian sheep farm a few years after the war, arriving just after their housekeeper, a young English woman, has committed suicide. Alan tries to find out more about her, but no one knows much more than her name; it's not until he finds a hidden suitcase full of her things that he realizes that she was the girlfriend of his brother, Bill, who was killed in the war. Alan had tried at length to trace her, to offer to take her back to Australia with his family after the war ended, but found that she had vanished. We discover her identity at the same time as he does, but are then taken through Janet's life story through her diaries, learning, in chronological order, about her 'good war', her love for Bill, her guilt at possibly having killed allied soldiers in error and – most importantly for Waters – her deep sense of loss, loneliness and hopelessness after Bill's death and the end of her career in the Wrens. Like Kay, at the end of the war, Janet has lost her job (and with it her community and sense of purpose), as well as her lover. Like Kay, she becomes a kind of ghost, vanishing completely from her old life, and maintaining almost complete anonymity in her new job abroad. The tone of the novel is unsurprisingly subdued and the language controlled and muted; Alan's attempts to build a new life after his injury in the war, placed alongside the unfolding tragedy of Bill and Janet, colour the narrative with regret.

Waters' new, hybrid form merges elements of contemporary war fiction with literary conventions (such as the reverse narration, or narrative self-consciousness) that are very much of the early twenty-first century. This form is – unsurprisingly – able to do much that contemporary fiction cannot in its depiction of gay life and sexuality, while also owing much to gay fiction of the period. However, the novel should not be read as straightforward pastiche; Waters' concern that the 'battered' design of the UK book jacket would make it appear to be uncomplicated pastiche attests to her desire that we should read this self-conscious re-creation of the period critically and with an awareness of what it tells us about our contemporary concerns. This is most evident when considering what the novel does that gay and lesbian texts of the period were not able to do, in print, at least (compare, e.g. Mary Renault's 1944 novel, *The Friendly Young Ladies*, which spoils her positive depiction of a lesbian relationship somewhat by having one of them leave the other for a man).

Waters echoes other lesbian stories, placing *The Night Watch* in a continuum of lesbian experience. For example, Radclyffe Hall's short story 'Miss Ogilvy Finds Herself' (1934) features a woman, older than Kay but otherwise very similar, who spends the First World War as an ambulance driver. The war, Hall observes, has set many 'Miss Ogilvies' free to cut their hair, to dress mannishly and to take up active, traditionally male roles: 'it was really surprising [. . .] how many Miss Ogilvies, losing their shyness, had come forward asserting their right to serve, asserting their claim to attention' (Hall 1934: 11–12). The beginning of *The Night Watch*, where Kay is standing, passively, simply watching from her bedsit window, exactly mirrors the beginning of Hall's story, where Miss Ogilvy stands, equally passively and mutely, watching as her army car is hoisted aboard ship to make the journey to England. Her unit is being disbanded and she is, suddenly, not only without occupation but also without purpose and company, returned to suspicion and isolation in a female world that neither understands nor much likes her. She simply has no place in this new post-war world, and the story ends in a quasi-mystical slip into a Stone Age past life regression, or dream, in which Miss Ogilvy is the strong man she wishes she was. We never find out whether Miss Ogilvy is truly in her own past, dreaming or hallucinating; she is found dead at the end of the story, at the edge of the cave in which she made love to her girl friend – as a man – for the first time. Kay's fate is more prosaic: like Shute's Janet, she is simply left over, suffering both from the loss of her lover and her place in wartime society.

Loss and regret also feature strongly in another lesbian text which Waters has described as playing a role in inspiring *The Night Watch*, Han Suyin's 1962 novel *Winter Love*. Suyin, a bisexual who had wartime affairs with men and women, describes a wartime lesbian relationship between two trainee nurses, told from the point of view of the woman, Red, who ended the relationship. Looking back from her middle age, where she is married with a child, she describes with regret how she drove her lover Mara away, never quite acknowledging to herself that she did this deliberately, nor understanding why. There are a number of structural and plot echoes of *Winter Love* in *The Night Watch*, which shares its setting, London during the 1944 Blitz, and similarly links the emotional intensity of enduring those very severe raids to the breaking apart of social norms and the subsequent possibility of sexual relationships between women.

What is more significant, however, is what Waters leaves out, that we might find in the original texts. The omissions here not only tell us a great deal about social change between the periods of the setting and the composition, but they also make the informed reader very much more aware of the ways in which this novel is dramatically different to its wartime predecessors, as a gay text. Waters herself has observed that gay novels of the 1940s and 1950s paint a grim picture 'and yet the 1940s was a fantastically exciting period for many lesbians and gay men' (Waters 2006b). In fact, what Waters does in *The Night Watch* is to emphasize the excitement and possibilities found by gay people in this period. Her characters' experiences of new possibilities, and delight in them, owe much to historical works on gay history (such as *You, You and You* (Grafton 1981) and *From The Closet to the Screen: A History of the Gateways Club* (Gardiner 2003)) and to memoirs, such as Barbara Bell's, which illustrate just how life changed for gay people. As Radclyffe Hall and Bell relate, life in wartime could be extremely enjoyable for gay women, who were able to wear mannish clothes, mix freely in all-women environments and take on active, physical and useful jobs that were otherwise denied to them. They could enjoy a sense of romantic, personal and professional fulfilment not available in peacetime. But beyond this, Waters also deliberately edits out some of the most frequent and powerful elements of gay fiction of the period, chiefly the misery of having to live in secret, the shame and self-loathing many gay characters in contemporary fiction were shown to feel, and the frequent recourse to sexology, or to Freudian analysis of how they had been 'warped' into perversity. Unlike *The Night Watch*, where the issue is unimportant, there is no free and easy acceptance of sexual orientation for characters such as Red in *Winter Love*, or Laurie Odell in Mary Renault's *The Charioteer*. While Waters has spoken of her desire to 'appropriate' the landscape of films about erotic longing, loss and desire, such as *Brief Encounter*, she also brings a wholly modern consciousness to her appropriation (Waters 2010). By contrast Neil Bartlett describes the 1950s novel *The Heart In Exile* as containing a great deal of 'barely digested sociological and psychological "theory" concerning the "problem"', typically of the genre: the gay character needs special pleading, to be excused their fault (Garland 1995, unpaginated). They do not choose this life, but cannot live it publicly or, on the whole, happily, as it places such stringent limits on when and with whom they can be themselves. Alec, the sympathetic character who is defiant of society's disapproval in *The Charioteer*, and says he will not accept being labelled a criminal, cannot escape from the seedier element of the wartime gay world in London despite loathing it, simply because it is the only gay world there is (Renault 2003). He is repeatedly drawn back there by needing to be with people he can be open with, even though he despises them. Waters' novel exhibits far more recent sexual mores, and this is in part an effort by Waters to encourage her readers to recognize that this is a metafictional text – she is trying to encourage a double-consciousness in her readers, as Rachel Carroll has argued that she does with her emphatic use of the word 'queer' in this and other texts, to remind us of the differences between then and now, and to see how this period setting is shaped by our contemporary concerns (Carroll 2006: 145).

Waters is, obviously, able to be far more sexually explicit than authors writing before gay liberation; neither Suyin nor Mallet-Joris, whose novel *The Illusionist* (1951) depicts an obsessive relationship between a girl and her father's mistress, dare to go far beyond Radclyffe Hall's infamously elliptical 'and that night they were not divided' (Hall 1999: 316). Waters does take this opportunity – as in her fairly graphic description of the beginning of Helen and Julia's love-making in the bombing raid, in the 1944 section – but this is a far more restrained account than the joyful, carnivalesque scenes of *Tipping the Velvet* or *Fingersmith*. *The Night Watch* is designed to resemble the fiction of the period, in terms of tone; it does so, here, but in a qualified way which again reminds the reader of the constructed, hybrid nature of what they are reading.

Waters also omits the hand-wringing and careful 'excusing away' that forms an inevitable part of published gay texts of the time. Kay is very like Miss Ogilvy, in her physical mannishness, her alienation from wider society, her delight in having an active, purposeful role in wartime, and her despair at losing it. But while she is clearly a close relation of Miss Ogilvy in these respects, her conception of her sexuality and gender, and their relation to each other, is wholly different. As has been discussed elsewhere, Hall's lesbian fiction is strongly influenced by models taken from contemporary sexology, particularly the work of Richard von Krafft-Ebing and Havelock Ellis' model of sexual inversion (see Bauer 2009). Miss Ogilvy is a typological prefiguration of Stephen Gordon, the tragic protagonist of *The Well of Loneliness*. She voices her wish that she had been born a man, and her sense that having a woman's body leaves her 'deeply defrauded', explicitly (Hall 1934: 10). (Leo, the butch lesbian character in Mary Renault's novel *The Friendly Young Ladies* (1944) feels similarly, that she 'contains' both a man and a woman; the man part of her has to die, metaphorically, at the end of the book when she unexpectedly falls in love with her male friend Joe, and leaves her girlfriend for him). The concept of inversion no longer shapes our understanding of homosexuality; Kay, although she dresses in men's clothes, can pass as a man, wishes to have the kind of active job traditionally restricted to men and sleeps with women, does not view herself as inverted, and never alludes to such a model. Kay, and most of the other lesbian characters in *The Night Watch* are, however, more like Miss Ogilvy in their emotional restraint (with the exception of Helen, whose emotional volatility threatens to wreck her relationship with Julia). This is an interesting move away from the extreme emotional intensity of the characters and drama of lesbian novels such as *The Illusionist* (Mallet-Joris 1951) and *Winter Love* (Suyin 1962), which feature intense and arguably histrionic protagonists wreaking emotional havoc. Waters is more interested in the more prosaic daily lives of her characters, and focuses on how they react to wartime conditions, or the effect of the bleakness of life after the war. In this respect the text owes far more to Shute and Green than to the gay tradition.

Similarly, the discourse of intense shame, self-loathing and theorizing about psychological retardation that dominated psychoanalytical thinking about homosexuality in this period is particularly notable by its absence (compare Rees 1955 or Schofield 1952). As discussed above, Bartlett's introductory essay on *The Heart in Exile* notes the large volume of pseudo-scientific musing on the causes of homosexuality in the novel, pointing out that in providing this, Garland is hoping to offer a pre-emptive defence of the hapless gender-normative homosexual, who cannot help his condition, would wish to change, and recoils from the more deviant parts of gay identity. Male effeminacy is reviled in both *The Heart in Exile* and *The Charioteer*, and in both the heroes are seen in gay social settings – parties and gay pubs – where their difference from the effete, histrionic homosexual man, and their horror at such men (which, it is heavily implied, the reader surely shares) is strongly emphasized. Duncan, the gay male character in *The Night Watch*, does not analyse his feelings explicitly, but is overwhelmed by a sense of shame linked to his having been in prison, as well as to his unverbalized sexual difference. He sees himself as 'a kind of oddity or fraud' (Waters 2006a: 95), and has retreated from the world into a job created for the war-handicapped, and a quasi-paedophilic relationship with his former prison warder, Mr Mundy. What Duncan feels is, however, markedly different in kind to the shame that dominates *The Charioteer*. Duncan's sense of shame and worthlessness is an all-pervasive part of his personality which only relates in part to his sexuality. Waters doesn't use Duncan's sense of shame to try to 'excuse' his sexuality; in fact, despite the similarities between Laurie Odell and Duncan, Waters' refusal to dwell on Duncan's sexuality distances him from Laurie, whose sense of shame results specifically from his sexual identity.

Renault, unlike Waters, knows she must protect her characters from a hostile readership and thus deploys shame as a defence. She is very careful to offer a detailed vindication of the happy ending Laurie and his partner Ralph reach; the novel begins with Laurie's father walking out on him and his mother, and depicts the intense relationship that then forms between the sensitive son and overbearing, needy mother. In *Winter Love,* Suyin's narrator explains that she was seduced into lesbianism by an emotionally unstable older woman, but once 'converted' could not go back, no matter how much she wished she could. Ralph too believes that his sexuality is a direct result of an incident in his childhood, but nonetheless has tried hard to have relationships with women and abstain from gay sex; Renault thus presents him as both blameless and heroic. Ralph and Laurie are hardy, brave, resourceful and tough: they are, Renault clearly implies, the opposite of some of the other gay men she depicts who are effeminate, manipulative, selfish and childish. Laurie does not fit into this group, and clearly does not want to; his longing to be accepted by society prevents him from accepting his sexuality for nearly the entire duration of the book. He does not question that he cannot expect to be accepted if he is known to be gay, concentrating instead on his anguish at how the world would see him if he joined 'nous autres' (Renault 2003: 305). To be reduced to the sum of his deviant sexuality, and the loss of innocence and respect that goes with this propels Laurie into rejecting the idea of trying to live happily as a gay man: 'we sign the warrant for our own exile. Self pity and alibis come after' (Renault 2003: 308). Waters' text is entirely free of this type of anguish; the characters' sadness and alienation comes from what has happened in their relationships, rather than the fact that they are homosexual. When Helen and Julia discuss 'the whole grisly "L" business' (Waters 2006a: 274), it's clear that Julia finds her lesbianism difficult or distressing enough to want to avoid naming it, but Helen's response betrays none of the self-loathing or obsessive self-analysis that we see in *The Charioteer* or *Winter Love.* Helen's analysis of her first lesbian relationship is remarkably devoid of anxiety, other than for a slight frisson of self-consciousness about how her description of Kay must sound to Julia, and a 'slight shudder' (ibid.) as she remembers being bombed. When Julia pushes her, asking what she'll do when life goes back to normal after the war, Helen's pragmatism is spelt out: '. . . well, I'd never want to advertise it. I'd never dream, for example, of telling my mother! But, why should I? It's a thing between Kay and me. And we're two grown women. Who does it harm?' As Julia sarcastically observes, Helen '[*is*] well adjusted' (Waters 2006a: 275) (about this, at least); she has arrived at a conclusion which takes Mary Renault's heroes in *The Charioteer* the best part of an entire novel, a number of tragic partings and a narrowly avoided suicide attempt. Waters thus alludes to the possibility of not being well-adjusted about one's sexuality, but contains it, taking it no further.

Similarly, when Binkie complains about 'the life we lead' (Waters 2006a: 258) during the party on Mickey's boat, she isn't talking about being abject, but about being single: 'it's all very well [for you]', she says to Kay, 'with your dear little Helen [. . .] But your sort of story is awfully rare' (ibid.). Binkie's problem seems to be the intensity of lesbian relationships, as she describes them, and her desire to 'settle down' (Waters 2006a: 259). It is, of course, because she is gay that the secrecy Binkie must maintain in her relationships intensifies them, and that she can't easily settle down or have children (another of her points – though this relates specifically to not having someone to look after her in her old age rather than to any thwarted maternal longings). But again, Waters doesn't include any hint of self-loathing, or distress at anything other than their circumstances. For these women, being gay is not the personal catastrophe it is for Renault's characters, or Suyin's.

The first draft of *The Night Watch* featured a party scene which 'recalled the horrible gay party in Renault's novel' (Waters 2010). The omission of this episode from the final version is significant in relation to the characters' perception of themselves as lesbians, because it means that we never see them in the context of a wider gay community. There are some suggestions of a scene, such as Ursula's party or the drinks on Mickey's boat, but they're either glossed over or only involve small groups of close friends. The party scene in *The Charioteer* – his first tentative attempt to publicly acknowledge and explore his sexuality – is a pivotal moment for Laurie. The seediness, the overt sexuality and high campness of some of the men there both frighten and disgust him; Renault uses the party, in fact, to further establish a distinction between the 'good gays', the otherwise 'normal' Laurie and Ralph, and the 'bad gays' who, far from trying to correct their deviance, express and enjoy it. Waters' depiction of her version of the 'horrible party' might, perhaps, have resembled Diana Lethaby's parties for her less-than-likable circle of lesbian friends, but this novel, focused so tightly on the interior lives of its main characters, doesn't extend our view of the gay subculture of the time beyond its reach into their individual lives. Waters does not need to construct the kind of elaborate defences of her gay characters that Renault does. Her focus can lie on individual characters, and their lives. Waters writes about lesbians because, as she has said, she wants to appropriate this landscape and reclaim this section of an obscured lesbian past, but she is able to focus on individual women's emotional experiences in their private lives and in reaction to the war, without having to focus on the issue of their sexuality in the way that Renault does. *The Charioteer* is the story of Laurie's progress towards entering a relationship with a man; *The Night Watch* is the story of individual women for whom sexual orientation is only one part of their identity. Waters not only creates a fictional world that attempts to recapture a history which has been vigorously suppressed, but also a world that we can recognize as being related to our own. The empathic unsettlement the text generates prevents simplified over-identifications, but reveals the true harm done to people such as Kay and Duncan, who are forced to live in the shadows because of their sexuality and their inability to 'fight back' when in situations they either cannot, or choose not to, control. This text is a palimpsest of different literary forms, different literary sources and different times; Waters seeks to reclaim lost or silenced history, using history, self-consciously and often humorously, to teasingly reassemble a literary simulacrum of a lost archive.

Note

1 Sarah Waters, 'Romance Among the Ruins', *The Guardian*, 28 January 2006.

CHAPTER SIX

'What does it feel like to be an anachronism?': Time in *The Night Watch*

KAYE MITCHELL

Chapter Summary: This chapter offers a reading of *The Night Watch* in relation to various conceptions of anachronistic, subjective and queer temporality, by examining both the treatment of time as a topic *within* the novel and the nature and effects of the backward narration *of* the novel. In this way it seeks to move on from discussions of lesbianism's 'invisibility', and to develop Annamarie Jagose's analysis of lesbianism as a 'problem' of sequence and derivation. The chapter considers the importance of the historical setting – the atemporal *ennui* of wartime – and examines the drag of the past upon the various characters and the foregrounding of their subjective experiences of wartime, industrial time, family time and time served in prison. In concluding, the chapter assesses the affective and political force of these experiences of asynchrony, the extent to which they might, paradoxically, complicate or challenge a view of homosexuality as backwardness.

Keywords: *The Night Watch*, queer time, anachrony, backwards narration, wartime, history.

Introduction: Telling the Time

From its opening lines, Sarah Waters' 2006 novel *The Night Watch* evinces a keen preoccupation with time and with the extent to which its characters inhabit – or escape, frustrate or refuse – orthodox and official temporal structures:

> *So this,* said Kay to herself, *is the sort of person you've become: a person whose clocks and wristwatches have stopped, and who tells the time, instead, by the particular kind of cripple arriving at her landlord's door.* (Waters 2006a: 3)

Kay is outside regulated, (hetero)normative time, operating instead within a temporality based on reflection and experience, and complicated by the pull of the past. This is a much more subjective, idiosyncratic conception of time but one that also, paradoxically, threatens her stability and substance as a subject. Thus the boy who visits Mr Leonard for treatment appears afraid of her, and Kay thinks 'He must have supposed she haunted the attic floor like a ghost or a lunatic. [. . .] And then it seemed to her that she might really be a ghost, that she might be becoming part of the faded fabric of the house, dissolving into the gloom which gathered, like dust, in its crazy angles' (Waters 2006a: 4).

This 'ghostliness' can be read in various ways. It suggests that Kay – unmarried, childless, queer, jobless, presumably possessed of a private income of some kind – cannot be contained by the routines, the strictures, that bind other people. It expresses how, at various points in the novel, she haunts the streets, a restless flâneuse – in limbo, in thrall to a past that will not let her go (that haunts her, in turn), and unaware of time passing: 'her day was a blank, like all of her days. She might have been inventing the ground she walked on, laboriously, with every step' (Waters 2006a: 6). She is, literally, *not present*, she refuses the lure of the present, still more the lure of the future. Kay's ghostliness also evokes the invisibility of the lesbian – as contrasted with the *unspeakability* of male homosexuality – whose history here becomes part of the 'gloom' and 'dust', overlooked and neglected. Annamarie Jagose notes the 'commonplace, rehearsed in homophobic and antihomophobic discourses alike, that the cultural lot of lesbianism is invisibility' (Jagose 2002: 1) and cites Terry Castle's famous description of the lesbian as 'a kind of "ghost effect" in the cinema world of modern life: elusive, vaporous, difficult to spot – even when she is there, in plain view, mortal and magnificent, at the center of the screen' (Castle 1994: 2).

In one of *The Night Watch*'s more strikingly self-conscious moments, Kay reads a passage from *The Invisible Man* 'at random', while waiting for her friend Mickey to serve a customer at the petrol station where she works:

> 'But you begin to realise now,' said the Invisible Man, 'the full disadvantage of my condition. I had no shelter – no covering – to get clothing was to forgo all my advantage, to make of myself a strange and terrible thing. I was fasting; for to eat, to fill myself with unassimilated matter, would be to become grotesquely visible again.' (Waters 2006a: 102)

In her mannish clothing Kay is, at times, 'grotesquely visible', a subject of mockery in the years after the war as the tolerance for such gender deviance wanes: 'the best thing to do was brazen it out, throw back your head, walk with a swagger, make a "character" of yourself. It was tiring, sometimes, when you hadn't the energy for it; that's all' (Waters 2006a:

100). Yet even this 'brazening' is a kind of invisibility, for she is also, in her suffering, invisible, unable to share with the wider world a loss – of her relationship with Helen – that is both illicit and inappropriate in the face of loss on a grander scale; Helen is not dead, after all.[1]

However, I want to suggest that it is primarily through the exploration of *temporal* oddness – rather than through structures of visuality/visibility – that *The Night Watch* delineates the 'queerness' of its characters. For, as Jagose proceeds to show, 'lesbian visibility' and 'lesbian invisibility' are part of the same logic/schema; both are 'symptomatic of the derivation and secondariness that mark the emergence of lesbianism as a culturally available category' (Jagose 2002: 7). On the basis of this claim, Jagose asserts that:

> The politically efficacious task is less to determine under what conditions the lesbian *can be seen* than to consider the implications of the fact that, invisible or visible, lesbianism depends for its figuration on *derivation*, and not as a mark of its inadequacy but as the condition of its possibility. (ibid., *my emphasis*)

I want to argue, therefore, that her ghostliness also places Kay outside the structures and systems – or, more crucially, the *sequences* – of heteronormative society, gifting her an unrecorded existence that may not even count as a life. As Elizabeth Freeman notes, after setting out the idea of a 'state-sponsored timeline' of birth, marriage and death – and even military service – 'in the eyes of the state, this sequence of socioeconomically "productive" moments is what it means to have a life at all' (Freeman 2010: 4–5).

If this temporal oddness is most marked for Kay, it applies to a lesser degree to Helen and Julia – and Mickey, Binkie, et al. – lesbians whose lives are lived out alongside and across heteronormative narratives of romance, marriage and childbearing. Yet the lesbian characters are not alone in this – arguably all the characters in the novel are 'outside' time to the extent that they are 'outside' the usual regulative frameworks of society: Duncan due to his marked effeminacy and vulnerability, his (implied) homosexuality, his attempt at suicide and the boyishness that seems to keep him in the past (he too is described as a 'ghost' (Waters 2006a: 166)); Fraser as a conscientious objector refusing the more conventional heroisms of wartime and therefore left out of official war narratives; Viv, the mistress whose back street abortion places her at odds with (even hostile to) reproductive/familial time. This 'queer' temporality, then, does not apply only to the homosexual characters, but extends to other non-normative ways of being; indeed, it could be suggested that war is sufficiently disruptive of normative temporalities (in putting the characters into some perpetual present, denied the ability to make plans for some nominal future) that queer temporalities prevail in wartime. It is to this extent that lesbianism is figured as paradigmatic in this text rather than being presented in its more usual form as 'a second-order sexuality' (Jagose 2002: 23).

In addition, the 'backwards' structure of the novel – which is divided into three sections and moves from 1947 to 1944 to 1941 – forces a reflection on ideas of historical progress, the fragility of the future in wartime, and the drag of the past upon characters, each of whom is defined by some past loss or trauma. Building on her comments on 'state-sanctioned' temporalities, Freeman notes that 'having a life' may entail 'the ability to narrate it [. . .] in a novelistic framework: as event-centered, goal-oriented, intentional, and culminating in epiphanies or major transformations' (Freeman 2010: 5). Waters' subversion (or rather, *inversion*) of that novelistic framework does not eschew transformation or epiphany, but it does show how a 'goal-oriented', 'intentional' life is complicated for her various characters and it may, in turn, work to trouble the very logics of derivation and inconsequence out of which the category of lesbianism emerges. Indeed, there is something bold about a lesbian novel that so embraces the movement of regression, given homosexuality's own persistent representation 'as a problem of sequence – that is, as a problem both of origin and outcome and primacy and secondariness', a 'problem' whose very pathologization is utterly imbricated with its figuration as 'backwards', infantile, either as a kind of inversion (the sexological term for homosexuality) or as a fixation preventing growth or forwards momentum (Jagose 2002: 31).

This chapter, then, offers a reading of *The Night Watch* in relation to various conceptions of anachronistic, subjective and queer temporality by examining both the treatment of time as a topic *within* the novel and the nature and effects of the 'backward narration' *of* the novel, considering the particular disjunctions and forms of queerness produced by this narrative examination/strategy of anachrony. In a recent article, Carolyn Dinshaw asks, 'What does it feel like to be an anachronism?' and she proceeds to describe Medieval mystic Margery Kempe as 'a creature in another time altogether – with another time *in* her, as it were', before going on to discuss the *queerness* of such asynchronies (Dinshaw 2009: 107, 108). Anachronism is derived from the Greek *anakhronismos*, from *ana* (backward) and *khronos* (time), so queerness is here conceived of as being out of time (and place) to some extent, while historical queer fiction might be viewed as an attempt to extend the moment of queer contemporaneity backwards. Do queer subjects inhabit time differently? Is their 'queerness' in fact most marked by their being temporally 'out of joint'? What are the ramifications of *Night Watch*'s tacit refusal of closure and progress for the characters who find themselves with 'no future' and no way of moving forward? And what are the effects of the extension of this temporal oddness to characters who are not, in fact, identified as queer (in the sense of being homosexual)?

Finally, I will consider this characteristic foray of Waters into historical fiction as a way of disrupting more linear, chronological conceptions of historical and temporal progression and relationship. Dinshaw suggests that queer temporality allows for 'the possibility of touching across time, collapsing time through affective contact between marginalized people now and then', and claims that, 'with such queer historical touches we could form communities across time' (Dinshaw 2006: 178); this then, might help us see the (queer) political potential of the temporal disruptions of a novel such as *The Night Watch* in modelling new forms of relationality and community as well as new conceptions of history and historical fiction.

Time and History

The Night Watch, I suggest, in its preoccupation with time – and particularly with the *non-naturalness* of time, with time as a social and cultural construction – is an historical novel very much of its *own* time (the early twenty-first century), a time when, thanks to time–space compression, 'the present is all there is' (Harvey 1990: 240). *The Night Watch* brings this self-consciousness about time, an attitude that we might see as dominant following the influential work of theorists like David Harvey and Fredric Jameson – to bear upon an earlier period, in a manner that might be described as anachronistic; and yet, as Ursula Heise asserts, the 'seemingly implausible' claim that 'time is obsolete. History has ended [. . .] has haunted theories of European and American culture since World War II', (Heise 1997: 11). Furthermore, this very 'anachronism' is made possible (and its political potential underlined) by the more critical, interrogative and flexible conception of time now current so *The Night Watch* could thereby be read as a typical 'postmodern novel' in its offering of an 'aesthetic response' to 'an altered culture of time' (Currie 2007: 80). (I should add that I think it is much *more* than a 'typical postmodern novel', whatever a 'typical' postmodern novel might be). Part of this alteration in the 'culture of time' includes an awareness of the *regulative* character of temporal frameworks and an awareness of the 'culture of time' *as a culture*, and therefore as culturally specific or relative, as (to some extent) arbitrary and ideological. As Harvey insists:

> Space and time are basic categories of human existence. Yet we rarely debate their meanings; we tend to take them for granted, and give them common-sense or self-evident attributions. We record the passage of time in seconds, minutes, hours, days, months, years, decades, centuries and eras, as if everything has its place upon a single objective time scale. (Harvey 1990: 201)

Rather than treating time as 'a fact of nature', novels such as *The Night Watch* are alert to the ideological manipulations of 'family time' ('the time implicit in raising children and transferring knowledge and assets between generations through kinship networks') and '"industrial time" which allocates and reallocates labour to tasks according to powerful rhythms of technological and locational change forged out of the restless search for capital accumulation' (Harvey 1990: 202–3). Both 'family time' and 'industrial time' undergo some alteration in wartime and both are problematized in *The Night Watch* which troubles, at each stage, this notion of a 'single objective time scale'.

The particular historical setting of *The Night Watch* facilitates its engagement with, and representation of, an extended present and allows also for that insertion of 'lesbian romance in the interstices of historical narrative' of which Waters is so fond (Waters 1996: 177). Despite the relative abundance of contemporary novels devoted to the depiction of WWII, it remains a challenging and unusual setting for fiction; it allows for a focus on the home front, domestic arrangements, the lives of those left out of the usual accounts of heroism and for the exploration of experiences of *waiting*, surviving, persisting, which seem at odds with narrative demands for tension, dramatic reversal and action. Indeed, by beginning with Kay's experience of restlessness, purposelessness and dispossession in the period after the end of the war, and only subsequently moving backwards in time to scenes of action and heroism during the Blitz of early 1941, Waters foregrounds this sense of atemporal ennui and subverts more jingoistic and action-packed accounts of wartime. Instead, she favours a more perspicacious account of a war characterized by 'frenetic interludes and prolonged lulls' (the latter are crucial, here), whose longer term consequences – the Cold War, the nuclear age, political advancement *and* political retrenchment – militate against conventional temporal and historical logics of progress, emancipation and closure (Waters 2006b).

In addition to the wartime setting making possible the kinds of gender and sexual deviance (e.g. cross-dressing, 'masculine' forms of employment for women), the alternative life narratives (e.g. same-sex relationships), favoured by Waters' lesbian characters – as Helen explains to Julia, 'so many impossible things were becoming ordinary, just then' (Waters 2006a: 274) – it also communicates a sense of the future being put on hold. So, when Julia asks Helen: 'And when the war's over? And everything goes back to normal?', Helen replies: '"It's pointless thinking about that, isn't it?" It was what everybody said, to all sorts of questions. "We might get blown to bits tomorrow"' (Waters 2006a: 275). The future cannot be conceived of in wartime and in some ways this is an advantage for these characters – as Binkie proclaims, 'Thank God for the war is what I say! The thought of peace starting up again, I don't mind telling you, fills me with horror' (Waters 2006a: 259). Thus, when the war does end, their lives become even more difficult, and they find themselves 'stuck', unable to move forwards, but also caught in a nostalgic longing for what has gone before.

In a recent article, Katharina Boehm argues that *The Night Watch* and *The Little Stranger* 'move away from a mode of historiographic metafiction that is centred on history's textuality and towards an approach that concentrates on the affective and disruptive ways in which tactile encounters with architectural places and material objects shape our investments in the past' (Boehm 2011: 238). While this posits, to my mind, a problematic view of historiographic metafiction as utterly unconcerned with material culture (and a view of textuality as something *other* than a material question), it is possible to read *The Night Watch*'s insistence on the materiality of history – its attention (as Boehm notes) to the *object* as a temporal marker of history (and what reviewers praise as its sensory awareness, lush period detail, etc.) – as bound up with its attention to time. Time, then, is presented in this 'novel rich in objects' as something embodied in material objects, such as the odd bits of china that Duncan collects (Boehm 2011: 244). While he is delighted by these relics from the past, Viv finds them disturbing: 'She could never help thinking of the mouths that had touched the china, the grubby hands and sweating heads that had rubbed the cushions bald' (Waters 2006a: 27). The past, here, becomes something tangible and the gap between past and present collapses in that trace of past bodies in/on these material relics – and in the visceral nature of Viv's affective, bodily response, her disgust.

Subjective Time or, How Time Feels

Throughout *The Night Watch*, the characters' subjective experience of time is highlighted, privileged over more 'official' and (allegedly) objective structures and frameworks of marking time and progress. Thus, Viv complains to Helen about time passing too quickly during their cigarette and tea break at the dating agency: '"God! There's ten minutes gone already. Why does time never go so quickly when we've got the clients in?" "They must work on the clocks," said Helen. "Like magnets"' (Waters 2006a: 16). Beyond expressing a familiar reluctance to return to work and describing the mundane drag of work-time, this presents the tea break as a time of feminine intimacy, a brief but defiant refusal of the tyranny of (masculinized) clock time, in which Viv and Helen sit in the sun, unwind, smoke – and come close to letting down personal guards. The return to work, by contrast, is a return to formality, to structure and sequence, to the binds of time and the exclusion of what really matters: 'they pulled on their shoes, dusted down their skirts, climbed back over the window-sill', Viv reapplies 'the old war-paint', and Helen thinks 'how awful it was to be here, while everything that was important to you, everything that was real, had meaning, was somewhere else, out of reach' (Waters 2006a: 20). The 'real', here, exists elsewhere, not only in another place, but also on another temporal plane altogether.

This tyranny of what Harvey might term 'industrial time' is evident too as Duncan leaves the factory at the end of work on a Saturday: 'The sun was sinking in the sky, and he had a vague, unhappy sense that time had passed – real time, proper time, not factory time – and he had missed out on it' (Waters 2006a: 81). 'Factory time' works in conflict here with 'real time', this clash of temporalities signalling Duncan's continued powerlessness. Subsequently, the intense anxiety and self-consciousness he feels, waiting for Fraser to return from the bar, distorts his apprehension of time: 'in what might have been five minutes more – or what might easily have been 10 or even 20 – Fraser came back' (Waters 2006a: 96). Yet this temporal distortion which serves as the primary indicator of Duncan's 'oddness' – his being out of sync with other people – is as nothing compared to his experience of prison. In prison, 'a month [. . .] was an age. A month in prison was like a street with a fog in it: you could see the things that were near to you clearly enough, but the rest was grey, blank, depthless' (Waters 2006a: 216). As in the descriptions of Kay's wanderings around the city, time is figured in terms of space, vision, perspective; it must be navigated, negotiated. Time is also, here, something that continually eludes the grasp of the prisoner, despite his attempts to master it: lying awake in the silent prison, hearing the warden pass every 60 minutes (marking another 60 minutes of prison time served), Duncan thinks, 'if he were the only man awake and knowing, then those sixty minutes, he felt, belonged exclusively to him: they went into his account, with a slither and a chink, like coins in the back of a china pig' (Waters 2006a: 218–19). Yet he concludes, in due course, that prison is 'not a china pig after all' – a rather cosy, childlike image – 'but a great, slow machine, for the grinding up of time. Your life went into it, and was crushed to a powder' (Waters 2006a: 219). This machine imagery dehumanizes time, figuring it as brutal and systematic.

While Kay seems to inhabit the time of the lacuna, a space (or time–space, perhaps?) of emptiness and aimlessness, Duncan is punishingly subject to time and the temporal metaphors used in relation to him continually emphasize his imprisonment and powerlessness. He is bound by the restrictive, suffocating temporalities of prison time, factory time and, finally, the false familial time of Mr Mundy's house, both refuge and prison after he finishes his official sentence. As Viv notices, time seems to move particularly slowly in Mr Mundy's house:

> The room seemed quiet and dreadfully airless, the gas-lamps hissing, a grandfather clock in the corner giving a steady *tick-tick*. It sounded laboured, she thought – as though its works had got stiff, like Mr Mundy's; or else, as if it felt weighted down by the old-fashioned atmosphere, like her. She checked the face of it against her wrist-watch. Twenty to eight . . . How slowly the time ran here. (Waters 2006a: 29)

This temporal queerness expresses the peculiarity of Duncan's relationship with his former prison warden ('Uncle Horace'), its stifling quality and its effect of keeping Duncan infantile, halting any progress he might make. In escaping the oppressive temporality of Mr Mundy's house in order to see his friend, Fraser, Duncan (despite the stark determinism of his predictive claim that, 'People said, "You'll do all right." But I knew I never would' (Waters 2006a: 98)), leaves by the back door and climbs in, finally, through Fraser's window, tentatively opening up for himself the possibility of a brighter future.

Backwards Time

The meditations on time performed within *The Night Watch* are extended and abetted via the very structure of the novel. As Mark Currie comments, the novel form is ideally suited to the *enactment* of a meditation on time due to the 'temporal resources of narrative fiction' which serve 'as a complement to the resources of reasoned argument', and allow the novel to be 'constative and performative at the same time' (Currie 2007: 89–90). *The Night Watch*'s reverse chronology is such that the 'end' of the narrative (fabula) really comes on p. 171 (i.e. at the end of the 1947 section): Kay returns home, having just had the ring returned to her by Viv, after spending hours walking around London aimlessly (again, time is marked out through motion, through Kay's ceaseless perambulations) – she is thinking about the past, still caught in it. She is stopped in the hallway by Mr Leonard (the Christian Scientist), who describes her as 'one of those [unevolved] spirits [. . .] searching, but held in thrall' – as before, she is figured as a kind of ghost (Waters 2006a: 169). It is the past that keeps Kay 'in thrall', and as she sits in the silence of her apartment, she pictures Mr Leonard, in his room downstairs, 'bathed in indigo electric light, hunched and watchful, sending out his fierce benediction into the fragility of the night', the novel (or rather, the fabula) thereby leaving us with a decidedly ambiguous image of redemption and healing (Waters 2006a: 171).

Meanwhile, the 'end' of the novel (szujet) really comes at a much earlier point in the fabula, in 1941, detailing Kay's hopeful, romantic meeting with Helen, the former amazed 'that something so fresh and so unmarked could have emerged from so much chaos' (Waters 2006a: 503). This is an ending that is also a beginning; an image of 'birth' – the girl emerging from the rubble, 'fresh' and 'unmarked', with Kay the midwife/rescuer – that cannot but be complicated by all that we have already learned about the outcomes of this relationship and its successor. If Helen is 'fresh' and 'unmarked' here, we know that by 1947 she will have skin 'like pressed meat', a cheek and arm 'marked red and white, as if in little weals, from where she'd lain upon the carpet' in expression of her bitter unhappiness, and will turn to cutting herself with a razor blade, desirous of a burn or cut that could be 'a miserable kind of emblem' for the jealous imaginings that torment her in her relationship with Julia (Waters 2006a: 46, 153). The optimism of the 'ending', then – the novel's final few lines – is already irrevocably compromised and sullied and its position in the story is such that it cannot offer us closure of any kind.

In an oft-quoted passage of *Reading for the Plot*, Peter Brooks ponders that, 'perhaps we would do best to speak of the anticipation of retrospection as our chief tool in making sense of narrative, the master trope of its strange logic' (Brooks 1984: 23). Is *The Night Watch*'s structure an attempt to offer a different kind of 'strange logic', one that does not offer the possible consolation of the 'anticipation of retrospection', but rather the experience of being 'stuck' and having only retrospection? Certainly it can be read as communicating the experience of having no future, or rather being unable to speculate about the future, suppressing any possible future; but it seems also an attempt to resist endings, and the closure and meaningfulness they apparently confer. Of course, the reader still goes through the process of 'the anticipation of retrospection', but does this by 'making sense' of the characters' respective present(s) by learning about their past(s). The backwards-movement is, perhaps, archaeological, revelatory, (as backwards glances often are) but what revelations there are here – Viv's abortion, Alec's suicide, Kay's meeting with Helen – are not the product of the perhaps more typical narrative tool of analepsis. *The Night Watch*, then, offers a disjunction between the fabula and the sjuzet in order to draw attention to questions of history, memory, the belief in or hope for a future, and to challenge the too-facile acceptance of objective time and of narratives of progress.

Waters herself has commented on the decision to structure the novel in three sections, told in reverse chronology:

> Soon, the novel began to languish, and I struggled. I wanted colour, life, pace, but every time I tried to move my characters forwards, I met resistance. I began to realise that the very things which had led me to the post-war scene in the first place – the blighted landscape, the austerity, the sense of inertia, the reticence – were weighing my writing down, or drying it out. 'Don't let's talk about the war', my characters were muttering to each other, authentically; but the fact was, they had nothing else to talk about, no events to live through that were half as vivid as the experiences I imagined they'd had in the previous six years. At last I saw there was no getting away from it. It was not my characters' futures that would make them interesting to me; it was their pasts. [. . .] I saw that the novel might work best if I put its action in reverse – if I kept its opening in the post-war setting of 1947, but then plunged back into the trauma and excitement of the war itself. (Waters 2006b)

That 'inertia' of the immediate postwar period – our knowledge of how things will turn out for Kay, Helen, Duncan et al. – is hard to dispel, however, as the novel gradually unfolds the events that preceded it. This is not a criticism of the novel, but instead a suggestion that its true objects are precisely the experiences of inertia, aimlessness, deferral, retrospection, rather than 'trauma and excitement', and that its investigation of the drag of the past is decidedly ambivalent. Waters' point about the ineluctable lure of the past is reiterated by Kay within the novel, when she tells Mickey of her trips to the cinema, 'Sometimes I sit through the films twice over. Sometimes I go in half-way through, and watch the second half first. I almost prefer them that way – people's pasts, you know, being so much more interesting than their futures' (Waters 2006a: 105–6). This encodes a subtle pessimism – if 'interest' is always a backwards movement, then what of hope, progress, development? Maria Margaronis reads the backwards narration as a self-conscious device, used to reflect on the author's position in the present, looking backwards, claiming that, 'Martin Amis in *Time's Arrow* (1991) and Sarah Waters in *The Night Watch* (2006) use the device of time running backwards to acknowledge their own position with respect to the events they describe' (Margaronis 2008: 140). Yet this is misleading – not least because time does not 'run backwards' in *The Night Watch* as it does in *Time's Arrow*, it is merely that the three sections of the novel are arranged out of order – and it fails to account for the full affective force of the backwards movement.

According to Currie, the novelistic treatment of time frequently rejects or problematizes linearity. While we might imagine that 'the analepses and prolepses of contemporary fiction [. . .] reflect a valorization of mind time, an experience of time which subordinates the cosmological to the phenomenological' – and the examples of the subjective experience of time given earlier in this chapter seem to support such a reading – yet Currie maintains that 'this is not a satisfactory account' (Currie 2007: 97). In Currie's view, the contemporary novel, distinct from its modernist forebears, 'has been preoccupied with narrative anachrony of a more traditional kind', not in the service of 'a rejection of chronology', but rather in order 'that the gap between the forward motion of life and the backwards motion of explanation are articulated to each other' (ibid.). If that seems to dim the radical potential of a backwards narrative such as *The Night Watch*, then such potential might, I suggest, be reintroduced by reading the novel in dialogue with various theories of queer temporality.

Queer Times

Carolyn Dinshaw is not alone among queer theorists in turning her attention to questions of temporality and to the elaboration of a notion of 'queer time' in recent years. Queer time amounts, in the various accounts of it, to: the refusal of 'reproductive futurism' (Edelman 2004:

2); a turn away from the 'narrative coherence' of the hetero life script in favour of the production of 'alternative temporalities' (Halberstam 2005: 182); the experience or feeling of asynchrony, along with new possibilities of relationality across time (Dinshaw 1999; 2009); instances of temporal multiplicity; and forms of 'temporal drag' which bind us to certain pasts (Freeman 2010). Freeman notes how 'the appearance of sexual identity as a field of knowledge and self-description' in the late nineteenth century formed part of 'the reification of both space and time [. . .] that began with industrial capitalism', yet adds that 'sexual dissidents have also in many ways been produced by, or at least emerged in tandem with, a sense of "modern" temporality', which she characterizes as 'fractured', 'flickering', 'always already wounded' (Freeman 2010: 7). The use of anachrony, as a narrative device, has a particular pertinacity, then, in relation to the representation, historicization and understanding of queer lives.

Furthermore, AIDS contributes to the idea of queer time the notion of a 'constantly diminishing future' and, as a consequence, 'a new emphasis on the here, the present, the now', giving rise to 'an urgency of being' which 'expands the potential of the moment' (Halberstam 2005: 2). Such an understanding of queer time, developed out of the experience of AIDS in the late twentieth century, might yet be used anachronistically to read the experiences of Waters' wartime characters; the very structure of the novel, along with its queer conception of history, seems to legitimate such anachronistic readings. Yet, if queerness is re-thought as 'an outcome of strange temporalities' (Halberstam 2005: 1), then this allows for a reading of *The Night Watch* as 'queer' due to its presentation of time, *not only and not primarily* because of its representation of lesbian characters; indeed, as I hope I've shown, the novel reveals a consistent preoccupation with time, with the frustration of temporal progress and the abandonment of conventional temporal markers, with the subjective distortion and affective force of time versus the tyranny of 'objective' and institutional time. It is a novel about living in queer times. Dinshaw favours the 'reworking' of 'linear temporality', in an attempt to 'apprehend an expanded range of temporal experiences – experiences not regulated by "clock" time or by a conceptualization of the present as singular and fleeting; experiences not narrowed by the idea that time moves steadily forward, that it is scarce, that we live on only one temporal plane' (Dinshaw et al. 2006: 185). As the preceding reading demonstrates, this 'expanded range of temporal experiences' is evident in *The Night Watch.*

But what are the politics of the drag of the past and, relatedly, the *past as drag* (as enacted by the historical novel)? At first glance this appears to be the politics of negativity, at best an empty nostalgia, at worst a melancholic formation; certainly it is no coincidence that certain of the theorizations of queer time (notably Edelman's) form part of what has been viewed as a rejection of the social and an embrace of negativity within queer politics. When Kay breaks down while with Mickey, she explains her own boundness to a traumatic past thus:

> I – I can't get over it, Mickey. I can't get over it. [. . .] What a funny phrase that is! As if one's grief is a fallen house, and one has to pick one's way over the rubble to the ground on the other side . . . I've got lost in my rubble, Mickey. I can't seem to find my way across it. I don't think I *want* to cross it, that's the thing. The rubble has all my life in it still – (Waters 2006a: 108)

Although figured spatially here, the issue is that Kay cannot move on, move forwards *in time* – but also that she doesn't want to, and this attachment (even dedication) to the past is seen as perverse in a culture so focused on productivity and futurity. If the echo of Mr Leonard's benediction with which we leave Kay at the end of the 1947 section is supposed to signal a distant hope of healing, then it does so equivocally at best; the past cannot be overcome so easily, nor should it be – it weighs on us, as it weighs on Kay.

Similarly, when Fraser and Viv talk about Duncan, Fraser avers that:

> He's not even a boy any more, is he? And yet it's impossible to think of him as anything else. He might have got stuck. I think he has got stuck. I think he's made himself be stuck, as a way of – of punishing himself for all that happened, years ago, all that he did and didn't do . . . I think Mr Mundy is taking very good care to keep him stuck; and – if you don't mind my saying so – after seeing the way you were with him on Tuesday night, I don't think anyone else is doing anything to, as it were, unstick him. All that fascination of his with things from the past, for instance. (Waters 2006a: 126–7)

Duncan, like Kay is 'stuck', unable to move forwards – in time, in his life. Viv too remains – for the time being, at least – bound to Reggie, the horror of the abortion binding them together more firmly than any baby would have done, it seems.

Yet we might read this backwardness more productively in relation to Freeman's notion of 'temporal drag', a phrase she uses to suggest both 'drag' in the sense of performance, putting on the clothes of the past ('sartorial recalcitrance') and 'drag' in its associations with 'retrogression, delay, and the pull of the past on the present' (Freeman 2010: 61, 62). A 'bind', in Freeman's explanation of it, is decidedly ambivalent, suggesting 'both a problem and an attachment', and it is a vital part of her eschewal of 'chrononormativity: causality, sequence, forward-moving agency' (Freeman 2010: 62, 64). As she goes on to claim, 'if identity is always in temporal drag, constituted and haunted by the failed love-project that precedes it, then perhaps the shared culture making we call "movements" might do well to feel the tug backward as a potentially transformative part of movement itself' (Freeman 2010: 93). The very conception of a political 'movement' is premised on forward momentum, yet Freeman stresses both the necessity of backwardness for 'movement', and the transformative power of the *feeling* of temporal drag.

For the drag of the past is, as Waters too shows us, all about feeling – especially with what Dinshaw labels 'the *felt experience* of asynchrony.' (Dinshaw et al. 2006: 190, *my emphasis*) – and although the predominant affect of *The Night Watch* might seem to be melancholy (that most retrogressive of affects), its constitutive power is such that Kay in particular doesn't want to move beyond it: 'the rubble has all my life in it still'. If *The Night Watch* dramatizes the feelings that bind us to the past, it also, in turn, infuses the historical past with feeling in a way that brings it to life for us, as readers, collapsing the gap between past and present in a way that is queerly historical, and *remembering* (literally peopling, embodying and infusing with emotion) moments of queer history that pre-date, complicate, yet also make possible subsequent future-oriented 'movements' of liberation.

This feeling that Dinshaw is interested in, of 'simultaneous belonging to one's own time as well as to other times, the balance between contemporaneity and difference, connection and distance', might also be useful for thinking through Waters' use of historical fiction to bring together the hidden queer histories of the past and the queer desires and longings of the present (Dinshaw 2009: 119). Furthermore, this queering of time and history – particularly viewed as a *feeling* – may open up new possibilities of community. Thus, Christopher Nealon notes that, 'In writing about "time" and "history" we're definitely (though often implicitly) writing about the possible forms and destinies of queer community' and Freeman follows this up with the comment that 'the rubric of time at least seems to offer the possibility of unmaking the forms of relationality we think we know' – and, presumably, making new ones (Dinshaw et al. 2006: 187, 188). In *The Night Watch*, in addition to the predictable alliances (e.g. between Kay, Mickey and Binkie), more unlikely, transient yet transformative allegiances are formed between these characters whose different experiences of asynchrony may yet serve to bind them, bring them together: Duncan and Fraser (in the enforced intimacy of prison), Viv and Kay (in the exchange of the ring), Viv and Fraser (in their shared concern for Duncan), Helen and Viv (in the temporary intimacies of their working day).

Is this queering of time necessarily radical? Jagose warns that we should, 'question the reification of queer temporality, the credentialing of asynchrony, multi-temporality, and nonlinearity as if they were automatically in the service of queer political projects and aspirations' (Dinshaw et al. 2006: 191). Yet, the consequences of secondariness are generally punitive, as Jagose points out elsewhere, noting that, 'one of the strategic effects of the representation of homosexuality as derivative is to secure the originality and primacy of a heterosexual culture from whose entitlements the former is debarred' (Jagose 2002: 35). In challenging this 'secondariness', in presenting a situation in which the temporal oddness of the lesbian becomes paradigmatic, expressive of the experience of numerous characters (straight and gay) in wartime, Waters makes her own 'strategic' and subtle argument for the 'primacy' of lesbianism and challenges the originary character of heterosexuality. In *The Night Watch* she thwarts the identification of lesbianism as backwardness through the adoption of a backwards structure that is, thus, rendered truly queer – as it deploys moments of romantic optimism, suggests new possibilities of relationality and initiates affective 'touches across time', while exploring the *longue durée* of melancholy and refusing the consolation of too facile a futurity.

Note

1 See also Palmer 2008 for a fuller discussion of the treatment of lesbian visibility/invisibility in *The Night Watch*.

CHAPTER SEVEN

The Country House Revisited: Sarah Waters' *The Little Stranger*

EMMA PARKER

Chapter Summary: Reading *The Little Stranger* (2009) against a contemporary preoccupation with the country house and the conservative tradition of country house literature, this essay contends that Waters' fifth novel opposes the class and gender politics of texts such as Evelyn Waugh's *Brideshead Revisited* (1945), the adaptation of which helped to inaugurate the English heritage industry. In contrast to the nostalgia and idealization that typically characterizes representations of the country house, Waters' portrayal of a middle-class doctor's relationship to Hundreds Hall and its inhabitants in the years following the Second World War exposes the mystification of class oppression, questions the seductive charm of the country house set and stresses the destructive consequences of envy and anger ignited by social inequality. By also highlighting the repressive effects of the country house as a heteropatriarchal sphere, *The Little Stranger* subverts its reputation as a 'happy rural seat' (Alexander Pope) and a 'great good place' (Henry James).

Keywords: *The Little Stranger*, country house, class, gender, sexuality, *Brideshead Revisited*.

Although described as a 'ghost story' (Boehm 2011: 249), and discussed in terms of the Gothic (Armitt 2009), *The Little Stranger* (2009) is also a country house novel. As such, Sarah Waters' fifth book responds to the conservative class and gender politics that characterize both the tradition of country house literature and the English heritage industry. As illustrated by films such as *Gosford Park* (2001), *Pride and Prejudice* (2005) and *Brideshead Revisited* (2008), television dramas like *Servants* (2003) and *Downton Abbey* (2010), and documentaries including *The Edwardian Country House* (2002), *Restoration* (2003) and *Country House Rescue* (2008), the first decade of the new millennium was characterized by a cultural preoccupation with the country house, the 'flagship' of heritage tourism (Smith 2009: 37). According to Robert Hewison, the country house not only represents a nostalgic desire to preserve the past but also actively reinforces and legitimizes the values of the aristocracy in the present (Hewison 1987: 53). Illustrating this, the rising popularity of the country house in the noughties, coupled with the increasing demonization of the working-class (Jones 2011), reflects resistance to New Labour's attempts to establish greater social equality during its period in government (1997–2010), and belies the myth that Britain had become a classless society.

Set just after the end of the Second World War and the election of Clement Attlee, Britain's first Labour Prime Minister to serve a full Parliamentary term, *The Little Stranger* explores a period of social and political transformation similar to that promised by New Labour. Waters has identified Josephine Tey's *The Franchise Affair* (1948) as an inspiration, a crime novel inspired by a real historical event, which is set in a decrepit country house and exhibits a 'strong vein of conservatism' (Waters 2009b). According to Waters, the novel articulates post-war anxiety about changes in gender, sexuality, and social status through the hostility it directs at Betty, a working-class young woman who represents 'everything that's wrong with postwar life' from an upper-middle-class perspective (ibid.).[1] Appalled by its 'bilious, bigoted vision', Waters initially planned to retell Tey's story from Betty's point of view (ibid.). While elements of *The Franchise Affair* endure in *The Little Stranger* (they are both set in Warwickshire and feature working-class characters called Betty), her novel developed into more than a simple revision of Tey's. Although Ann Heilmann notes the significance of multiple literary allusions in *The Little Stranger* (2012), this essay proposes that an examination of Waters' engagement with the tradition of country house literature makes clear her desire to contest the attitudes to class and gender that characterize *The Franchise Affair.* A key intertext in this regard is Evelyn Waugh's *Brideshead Revisited* (1945), a novel revived in 1981 by a lavish and highly successful television adaptation, which helped to inaugurate the heritage industry and lent support to the materialistic and acquisitive excesses of the Thatcherite 1980s. Indeed, the pace of *The Little Stranger* evokes the small screen version of *Brideshead,* notable for its slowness (Cardwell 2002: 111), an indication that Waters is preoccupied with the ways in which the past is read through and informs the present. Waters' concern with the country house also reflects her interest in how space and place 'confine and construct us, how they get imbued with public and private meanings; and how sometimes those meanings can be subverted' (Waters 2011). Illustrating this, *The Little Stranger* revisits the tradition of country house literature in order to highlight and resist the ways in which it continues to uphold heteropatriarchy as well as class hegemony.

There are numerous links between *The Little Stranger* and *Brideshead Revisited*: both are narrated (unreliably) by a middle-aged, middle-class man looking back on his life and connection to a charismatic upper-class family. Like Charles Ryder, Faraday is an outsider who becomes besotted with a family's country house and inveigles his way into their home. His relationship with siblings Roderick and Caroline Ayres parallels Charles' connection to Sebastian and Julia Flyte. Mirroring Charles, who plans to marry Julia, Faraday becomes engaged to Caroline, but in both novels the wedding is called off by the wife-to-be, and the protagonist ultimately remains shut out from the world of privilege he covets. Despite these links, *The Little Stranger* is deeply at odds with *Brideshead*, a novel that – as Raymond Williams notes – is 'consciously reactionary' in its idealization of the aristocratic values symbolized by the Marchmains' ancestral home (Williams 1973: 249). As Waugh's 'Preface' makes clear, his novel bids a loving farewell to 'the splendours of the recent past' and laments the decline of the country house, which he feared would be 'doomed to decay and spoilation' in a more egalitarian post-war world (Waugh 1959: ix, x). By setting *The Little Stranger* just after the end of the war, rather than in the 1920s and '30s, Waters rejects Waugh's 'conservative nostalgia' (Brannigan 2003: 29). Indeed, unlike *Brideshead*, which contrasts the glorious past with a despoiled present, *The Little Stranger* highlights the benefits of post-war change to ordinary people. Faraday explains that new council houses built on land formerly owned by the Ayres are 'badly needed in the area' and will improve living conditions for his poorer patients (Waters 2009a: 150). Further, the closure of Hundreds Hall at the end of the novel enables Betty to take 'the sort of job she wanted, in a bicycle factory', which she enjoys significantly more than working as a maid: factory work may be dull but her co-workers are 'a laugh', and she is able to go 'dancing' at the weekends (Waters 2009a: 496).

Since Hundreds Hall is neither what Richard Gill, borrowing from Alexander Pope, terms a 'happy rural seat' (1972), nor what Malcolm Kelsall, drawing on Henry James, calls 'the great good place' (1993), Waters clearly resists Waugh's idealization of the country house class and its way of life. Where the country house is traditionally characterized by beauty and fecundity, Hundreds is in 'decline' (Waters 2009a: 7). In contrast to his first childhood visit to the 'lovely' house, when he returns as an adult, Faraday finds 'decay' everywhere, the furnishings 'ripped' and the features 'chipped or cracked' (Waters 2009a: 1, 5, 18, 19). The house thus functions not as a monument to its owners' magnificence but a symbolic reflection of the declining power of their class.

Waters' resistance to the idealization of the country house is further evident in her subversion of a literary tradition that obfuscates inequality and oppression. While the novel invokes *The Franchise Affair* by making the date of Hundreds Hall (1733) the year of birth of Elizabeth Canning (the historical figure at the centre of the case that inspired Tey's novel), it also situates the house in the context of the British Empire. Likewise, the 'Empire Day fête', Mrs Baker-Hyde's 'slave bracelets' and the 'little

Indian monkey' owned by Mrs Ayres' Aunt Dodo (Waters 2009a: 1, 90, 242) link the wealth of the country house set to slavery and imperialism. These links remain merely implicit in most country house novels and, as Laurajane Smith notes, largely invisible in country houses open to the public today (Smith 2009: 45). According to Smith, in its construction and maintenance, the country house relied on the 'semi-feudal' exploitation of servants and estate workers as well as slaves (Smith 2009: 43). In *The Little Stranger,* a resilient 'feudal spirit' is embodied by Roderick, who looks 'very much the young country squire', and reflected in the respectful and affectionate response of locals to Mrs Ayres' demise: Lidcote is 'crowded' with men 'removing their hats and caps' and women 'crying' on the day of her funeral (Waters 2009a: 149, 424).

In the semi-feudal world of the country house set, class inequality is obscured through a process of 'mystification' (Williams 1973: 31). Like the 'spacious' and ornate 'painted parlour' in *Brideshead* (Waugh 2000: 69), the room that the Ayres call 'the little parlour' is actually 'thirty feet deep and twenty wide' and, despite owning a 'Rolls-Royce', Roderick sees himself as an 'ordinary hard-working Englishman' (Waters 2009a: 18, 150, 152). Likewise, just as Mr Samgrass in *Brideshead* describes the drunk driving that lands Sebastian in jail as a 'little escapade' (Waugh 1959: 113), Mr Rossiter's fond reminiscence about the theft of the schoolmaster's car dismisses a criminal act as 'one of Roderick's youthful adventures' (Waters 2009a: 96). Despite their position of privilege, the Ayres claim oppression: Roderick complains that servants 'get better treatment than us', and Caroline protests that Betty is 'better off' than members of her family (Waters 2009a: 6, 16). Caroline's response to Faraday's revelation that his parents, a nursery maid and grocer's boy, had a 'back-door romance' at the house demonstrates that the Ayres underplay the oppression of others as well as their own privilege: 'What fun' (Waters 2009a: 28). However, the novel exposes rather than participates in this process of mystification. Caroline's story about her cruel childhood trick that landed a 'dim' servant in 'dreadful trouble', and Faraday's recollections of the humiliations suffered by his mother, who regularly had her fingernails inspected and personal belongings searched by the lady of the house, illustrate that being a servant at Hundreds was far from fun (Waters 2009a: 27).

Another means by which Waters challenges the mystification of class relations is through resistance to 'the magical extraction of the curse of labour' (Williams 1973: 45). In *The Little Stranger* harvesters work 'until gone eleven', farm labourers start 'at seven', and the novel spotlights the domestic work that makes possible the Ayres' privileged life: 'They both sat comfortably in their chairs, enjoying the tea and the cake that Betty had prepared for them, then awkwardly carried for them, then cut and served for them, from plates and cups which, at the ring of a bell, she would soon remove and wash' (Waters 2009a: 43, 73, 124). *Brideshead* offers no insights into the lives of servants, who are often referred to by role rather than name: 'a footman came with tea and bread and butter' (Waugh 2000: 124). The anonymity of servants is foregrounded when neither Mrs Ayres nor Faraday can identify his mother with certainty in an old photograph of the Hall's once sizeable staff. Behind the woman Faraday thinks may be his mother, he sees 'another servant, also fair haired, and in an identical gown and cap' (Waters 2009a: 29).

In contrast to the anonymity and marginality of servants in *Brideshead*, Waters makes Betty a fully rounded and key character. Moreover, by giving Betty a voice, *The Little Stranger* subverts the myth of 'happy workers' who give their labour 'spontaneously' (Kelsall 1993: 34, 139). Betty complains about having to use the creepy back stairs and her old-fashioned uniform, an 'awful old dress and hat' (Waters 2009a: 13). Indeed, Betty is so 'unhappy' that she fakes a stomach ache in the hope of being sent home (ibid.). Undermining the Ayres' romantic myth that service transforms working-class girls from 'specks of grit' into 'pearls', Betty's hard work gives her 'calluses' (Waters 2009a: 73, 79). Even though Faraday notes that Betty's hands have become 'thickened and stained' since she started work at the Hall, he romanticizes the disfiguring effects of hard labour: '"Go on," I said [. . .] "They're good country hands, they are"' (Waters 2009a: 79). Defying a tradition of country house literature that tends to sentimentalize or mask social and economic deprivation, *The Little Stranger* acknowledges the horrors of poverty as well as the harshness of labour. When Faraday attends a man with an inflamed appendix, he discovers a family of unemployed squatters living in 'the worst sort of place imaginable – an abandoned hut, with holes in its roof and gaps in its windows, and without light or water' (Waters 2009a: 469).

As in the tradition of country house literature that presents grand houses inhabited by great people, Caroline is brought up to believe that her family is 'better and braver' than most (Waters 2009a: 398). Faraday's reference to the Ayres' 'good breeding', and Roderick's description of Caroline and himself as 'prize heifer' and 'prize bull', suggest that their superiority is natural and innate (Waters 2009a: 188, 190). However, this idea is challenged by an emphasis on material conditions. By linking illness to social factors such as poverty, Waters suggests that physical superiority is the product of culture rather than nature. As Faraday notes about a sick labourer, 'living conditions were against him – his home was a cramped terraced cottage with a damp brick floor' (Waters 2009a: 108). Further, the parallel between the labourer and Roderick, both made ill by working 'too hard' and drinking 'too freely', indicates that the same physical conditions have a similar effect on people from different classes (ibid.). A sense of superiority is also undermined by Caroline's recognition that Betty is 'brave' (Waters 2009a: 207). In contrast, when exhorted to be 'brave' at her mother's funeral, Caroline's courage fails: 'I don't know if I can be' (Waters 2009a: 421).

Like Charles in *Brideshead*, Faraday finds the country house set 'charming' (Waters 2009a: 70). Yet, the Ayres' charm is called into question by their arrogance, selfishness and class prejudice. Like her namesake, Caroline Bingley in Jane Austen's *Pride and Prejudice* (1813), another unmarried woman who lives with her brother in a country house, Caroline is a shallow snob. The resentful tone of her observation that Betty 'eats the same food as us' indicates a contempt for social equality, and Caroline self-centredly objects to rationed oranges being given to children (Waters 2009a: 16, 92). A sense of entitlement is likewise conveyed when she expresses relief at still being able to 'ring for a servant in the old-fashioned way, instead of having to traipse down to the kitchen for a jug of hot water, or something, ourselves' (Waters 2009a: 46). Despite his developing intimacy with the Ayres, Faraday remains 'Other' to his new friends in terms of social class. Roderick doubts the trustworthiness of a doctor 'like him', and Caroline acerbically reminds Faraday of his lack of social standing when she remarks that gossip would not matter 'to someone like you' (Waters 2009a: 179, 398). Caroline also snobbishly disdains the *nouveaux riches* Baker-Hydes as 'people like that' (Waters 2009a: 111). Similarly, Mrs Ayres dismisses a maid as 'no one', and Roderick demonstrates the superciliousness that earned him the moniker 'Ayres-and-Graces' at school when he calls Maurice Babb, the local builder, a 'grubby little businessman', refers to future inhabitants of the new council estate as 'the mob', and cruelly mocks Betty's Warwickshire accent: '*No, zir*' (Waters 2009a: 111, 152, 187, 190, 195).

Although Faraday initially feels 'impatience' for the snobbish, clannish Ayres, he is soon 'seduced' by the 'charm' of the Hall, and later says 'nothing' but sits 'enjoying the tea and cake' as they demean their staff (Waters 2009a: 73, 79). In this way, the novel implicitly points to the dangers of a heritage industry that, as Smith explains, typically invites visitors to appreciate the aesthetic qualities of a country house while overlooking social inequality (Smith 2009: 37). Moreover, the novel demonstrates that the country house fosters certain values in its occupants. As Faraday spends more time at Hundreds and becomes 'one of the family', he grows increasingly wedded to class hierarchy (Waters 2009a: 131). He is 'faintly unsettled' by Betty's move from a bedroom on the third floor, in the servants' quarters, to the second floor alongside Caroline and Mrs Ayres, and 'enraged' by the sight of Caroline setting a fire 'like a servant' after their engagement (Waters 2009a: 233, 312).

Waters' most significant challenge to the idealization of the country house and its class comes through the 'malevolent thing' that haunts Hundreds Hall (Waters 2009a: 164). In contrast to *Brideshead*, the Ayres' ancestral seat is no 'arcadia' (Waugh 2000: 15). Where Brideshead is touched by 'divine grace' (Waugh 2000: ix), Hundreds is in the grip of something 'diabolical' (Waters 2009a: 423). It is not a place of stability and serenity, but increasingly a site of chaos and terror. Instead of offering its owners a sanctuary, it is the location of their persecution and demise. Moreover, the parallel between the sense of menace that pervades the house and that felt by the Ayres beyond their home in the face of changes instigated by a Labour government committed to greater democracy suggests the spectre that haunts Hundreds Hall functions as a metaphor for class unrest. Stressing Waters' interest in the 'materiality' rather than the 'textuality' of history in her recent work, Katharina Boehm explores the way in which history, materiality and haunting are 'enmeshed' in the novel (Boehm 2011: 252). As in *Affinity* (1999), in which a servant masquerades as a medium's spirit guide in order to divest the rich of their wealth, the political subtext of *The Little Stranger* is clear in the ghost's implicit evocation of the opening words of *The Communist Manifesto* (1848): 'A spectre is haunting Europe – the spectre of Communism' (Marx and Engels 2004: 218).

The novel's title further connects the theme of haunting to issues of class. Seeley's reference to the 'childish' creature that disturbs the Hall as 'the little stranger', a once common euphemism for a newborn child, appears to support Mrs Ayres' view that the house is haunted by her daughter Susan (Waters 2009a: 298, 380). However, whereas Susan died aged seven, the ghost seems younger; listening to the speaking tube, Mrs Ayres hears 'something like the wail of a siren, or the cry of a hungry baby' (Waters 2009a: 344). The idea that Susan is the little stranger is further compromised by the latter's gender: Faraday compares the tapping sound it makes to 'a schoolboy idly drumming with a stick', and Betty refers to it as 'he' and 'him' (Waters 2009a: 130, 301, 335). Moreover, by echoing John Stuart Mill's observation that the proletariat tend to be 'governed or treated like children', the novel's title suggests that the little stranger that haunts Hundreds is not Susan but the insurgent spirit of the oppressed working-class (Mill 1965: 763). Waters' novel points to the infantilization of the lower orders through the proximity of servants' bedrooms to the nursery and the patronizing manner in which Caroline speaks to Betty: 'Good girl' (Waters 2009a: 207). The gender and class of the figure that haunts Hundreds Hall thus suggests that the little stranger is Faraday, who is not only one of the 'little people' – in contrast to the Ayres: 'big people in the district' (Waters 2009a: 1) – but also an outsider (or stranger) at Hundreds Hall.

Faraday's status as the little stranger is further suggested by Caroline's theory that uncanny events in the house can be attributed to a poltergeist, which – drawing on the work of Frederic Myers – she describes as 'some sort of energy, or collection of energies. Or something inside us [. . .]. Unconscious parts, so strong or so troubled they can take on a life of their own' (Waters 2009a: 364). The psychic pain and distress that are physically manifested in the poltergeist could emanate from any member of the Ayres family, who are all haunted by sadness and anger. However, while Roderick's war trauma, Mrs Ayres' grief, and

Caroline's bitterness at her secondary status (as a girl and second child) enable the reader to feel sympathy for characters that do not inspire affection, they also function as red herrings in a mystery. Like Agatha Christie's 'unsnobbish' whodunits and psychological thrillers, which tend to be set in upper-middle-class rural homes rather than aristocratic country houses and stimulate 'neither class envy nor deference', *The Little Stranger* suggests numerous possible explanations for the mystery at the heart of the novel before its resolution (Light 1991: 76, 78). As in Christie's *The Murder of Roger Ackroyd* (1926), in which a country doctor relates his story in a distinctively flat voice, and the killer turns out to be the narrator, the denouement of Waters' novel suggests that the poltergeist that disturbs the house and causes Caroline's death is the product of Faraday's psyche, his 'shadow-self' (Waters 2009a: 380). At the close of the novel, Faraday returns to Hundreds Hall in the hope of discovering the identity of the little stranger only to see his own face reflected in a mirror. Although Faraday (like the Ayres) represses painful feelings, he is bitter about the sacrifices his parents made to ensure his rise from 'labouring stock', which bring debt, ruined health and premature death (Waters 2009a: 246). Disappointment in the progress of his career feeds Faraday's bitterness, and a sense of grievance is exacerbated by having been 'thrown over' by a girl from a 'good Birmingham family' on the grounds that he was not deemed 'a suitable match' (Waters 2009a: 39). As indicated by the 'peasant blood' he initially feels 'rising' in response to the Ayres' snobbery, Faraday's social background suggests that the poltergeist embodies his fury at class inequality (Waters 2009a: 27).

Additional evidence that Faraday is the little stranger is his ambivalent attitude to the Ayres, which stems from anger and envy, emotions that Melanie Klein associates with infancy. According to Klein, infancy is dominated by feelings of love and hate towards the mother's breast. Idealization of the breast generates envy and frustrated desire for the idealized object leads to the 'sadistic expression of destructive impulses', as well as a sense of 'grievance', 'despondency' and 'guilt' (Klein 1997: 176, 183, 190). Because anger and hostility are difficult to acknowledge, they are 'split-off' from the self (Klein 1997: 208). Denial, Klein explains, is another form of defence (Klein 1997: 216). The novel's opening chapter, in which Faraday recounts his theft of the acorn, a breast-shaped object, from the house where his mother once worked as a nursery maid, suggests that Hundreds Hall inspires in him feelings of love and hate, and envy and anger, similar to that which, according to Klein, the infant feels toward his mother. As a child, Faraday is beguiled by the beauty of the house, and when he steals the plaster acorn he simultaneously seeks to take possession of the object he idealizes and attacks what he is formally denied, as indicated by the 'rope' or 'ribbon' across open doors, barring entrance to the house (Waters 2009a: 1). Foreshadowing the violence to come, hostility is conveyed by Faraday's use of a knife to force the acorn from the wall. An unconscious wish to spoil or destroy what he cannot possess is suggested by the revelation that the acorn does not come away 'cleanly', as well as by Faraday's later playful admission to Caroline that he once tried to 'vandalise' the house, an endeavour repeated in the fire that follows his humiliating ejection from the Hall by Roderick (Waters 2009a: 3, 64). The acorn incident also reveals Faraday's capacity for denial. Unconscious of the hostility that motivates what he later casually refers to as an 'attack' on the plaster, Faraday insists 'I didn't do it in a spirit of vandalism. I wasn't a spiteful or destructive boy' (Waters 2009a: 18, 3). When his mother discovers and confiscates the acorn, a sense of deprivation and grievance – 'it seemed very unfair' – ignites one of his 'secret' rages, demonstrating repression and self-concealment, likewise intimated by Faraday's omission of his first name (Waters 2009a: 4). Following his return to Hundreds as an adult, Faraday's repressed feelings resurface, symbolized by his lifting of the lid of the biscuit tin that stores old 'papers and family keepsakes, put together by my parents', and in which he finds 'odd little fragments from my own past' that leave him in a 'fit of discontentment' (Waters 2009a: 41). The return of the repressed is equally intimated by Faraday's later remark that the 'thing' that haunts the house is 'in some way *familiar*: as if its bashful advance towards us was more properly a *return*' (Waters 2009a: 393).

Like all the uncanny incidents that follow, the first strange event at Hundreds Hall – docile Gyp's savage attack on Gillian Baker-Hyde – is motivated by Faraday's envy and anger. Faraday, who is 'ashamed' of his working-class parents and thinks the Ayres occupy 'a rather rarer realm', tells Betty that she is 'lucky' to live at Hundreds, and informs Roderick, 'Plenty of men would envy you' (Waters 2009a: 13, 75, 153, 250). An unconsciously envious desire to remove Roderick is suggested by Faraday's failure to mention his absence from the party, revealed only by Mrs Baker-Hyde's remark that she would like to meet her host's missing son. The anger that accompanies Faraday's envy is exemplified by the poltergeist's attack on Roderick in his bedroom during the party. Roderick is menaced by something 'extraordinarily purposeful and vicious' that wishes him 'harm' (Waters 2009a: 163, 164). The later fire constitutes another unconscious attempt to eradicate Roderick, whom Faraday eventually has committed to an asylum. Thus, while the absence of a first name aligns Faraday with Stevens, the butler in Kazuo Ishiguro's *The Remains of the Day* (1989), his surname, which he shares with Stevens' American employer and the new owner of Darlington Hall, indicates his desire to become master of the house.

Concerned that he is not 'grand enough' to be accepted as a doctor by either the gentry or the working-class, Faraday's upward aspirations are clear. Thus reminders of his social inferiority are a source of humiliation and anger (Waters 2009a: 36). When Caroline invites him to the party, Faraday notes 'the briefest of hesitations' in Mrs Ayres (Waters 2009a: 77). He acknowledges that the guests are not 'the sort of people

I usually mixed with', and feels excluded from the conversation: 'there was little that I could contribute' (Waters 2009a: 85, 94). Already resentful of Baker-Hyde, who has assigned the care of his family's health to a rival, Dr Seeley, Faraday is embarrassed by Baker-Hyde's assumption that he attends the party as an employee rather than a guest: 'You're the family doctor, I gather. They like to keep you on hand, do they, for the sake of the son?' (Waters 2009a: 95). In addition, the realization that the party has been organized to introduce Caroline to Mrs Baker-Hyde's brother, Morley, leaves Faraday with a 'curiously dark and cheated feeling' that indicates both his unacknowledged designs on Caroline and his frustration at seeing them dashed (Waters 2009a: 88). The novel's opening chapter makes clear that the house is the true object of Faraday's affection. Stealing the plaster acorn, he compares himself to a man 'wanting a lock of hair from the head of a girl he had suddenly and blindingly become enamoured of' (Waters 2009a: 3), a passage that directly echoes but subtly revises Charles' description of the consummation of his relationship with Julia in *Brideshead*: 'I was making my first entry as a freeholder of a property I would enjoy and develop at leisure' (Waugh 2000: 243). The equation of women with houses suggests that in both novels the former provides access to the latter and, as Waters' narrative develops, it becomes increasingly clear that Faraday seeks to become master of Hundreds Hall by removing Roderick and marrying Caroline.

The suggestion that Faraday is the source of the poltergeist that prompts Gyp's attack on Gillian is endorsed by Roderick's later description of the 'thing' that haunts the house as 'a sly, spiteful child', which recalls Faraday's admission of his 'pointless, almost spiteful urge to make life difficult' for Baker-Hyde (Waters 2009a: 96, 165). Likewise, Roderick's comment about the thing that attacks him – 'I knew it hated me, really hated me' – evokes Faraday's admission that the Ayres stimulate a 'dark dislike', and is echoed by Caroline's later remark to Faraday that 'you must hate us slightly [. . .] on your parents' behalf' (Waters 2009a: 27, 164, 250). Faraday's astonishment – 'Hate you?' – only illustrates his repression of difficult feelings (Waters 2009a: 250). Betty's description of the poltergeist as 'a wicked servant' might support Faraday's suspicions about her trustworthiness but it also points to Faraday himself, who is not only mistaken for a member of staff but treated like one by Mrs Rossiter when she asks him to fetch her a drink (Waters 2009a: 361). Gyp's function as a conduit for Faraday's feelings is endorsed by the dog's name, which is slang for 'a cheat or swindle', and echoes Faraday's own sense that his presence at Hundreds Hall makes him a 'fraud' (Waters 2009a: 47). Faraday's later feelings about the incident also suggest his unconscious sense of responsibility. He looks back on Gyp's attack on Gillian, as on the fire and Caroline's death with a sense of 'guilt' (Waters 2009a: 96).

Gyp's attack on Gillian avenges Faraday's humiliation as well as venting his anger. Just as he metaphorically loses face at the party, so her face is almost torn off by the dog. Also, having been dismissed by Morley as insignificant, the incident renders Faraday not just essential – 'Thank God you were there last night!' – but heroic: word spreads that he 'practically saved the child's life' (Waters 2009a: 106, 121). Retribution is a feature of other mysterious events, too. By giving 'birth' to the little stranger, Faraday avenges the multiple miscarriages that killed his mother (Waters 2009a: 400). Caroline recognizes that the poltergeist seeks to 'punish and spite' her family, a point illustrated by the fire, which breaks out after Roderick's drunken revelation that Faraday has only been invited to dinner because his mother is 'too embarrassed to let any of our real friends see us as we are now' (Waters 2009a: 190, 352). Just as his cheeks burn with shame and humiliation, so his anger has an incendiary effect. The little stranger also punishes the Ayres for being 'frightful' by making them frightened, subverting the established social order by reducing those who assume the role of parents to the state of terrified children (Waters 2009a: 28). After being attacked by the mirror on the night of the party, Roderick clutches at his mother's hand 'like a child' and retreats to bed where he curls up 'like a baby' (Waters 2009a: 163, 164). Likewise, during the incident in the nursery, Mrs Ayres starts 'shrieking like a child' and, afterwards, Faraday speaks to her as he would 'a child or an invalid' (Waters 2009a: 346, 395). Class hierarchy is also subverted when Caroline and her mother are forced to perform domestic chores themselves, 'as if they had no servants at all', after the wire to the call-bell is cut to stop it ringing inexplicably (Waters 2009a: 331).

Revenge is again suggested by Caroline's death, punishment for breaking her engagement to Faraday, which deprives him of the house. However, allusions to *A Stranger Walked In* (1947), a film released the year in which the novel is set, based on an Agatha Christie short story about a woman who comes to realize that her husband married for money and plans to murder her, suggests that Faraday was unconsciously planning to kill Caroline all along. The notion that he means to dispense with Caroline is endorsed by Betty's comment that the ghost 'wanted the house all for its own' (Waters 2009a: 485). Like the judge who discredits Betty's account of the night that Caroline dies by referring to it as a 'most extraordinary tale', Faraday repeatedly dismisses what Betty says as 'pure silliness' (Waters 2009a: 130, 485). However, as in the novels of Agatha Christie, in which what servants see and say is often crucial, *The Little Stranger* makes Betty's apparently minor voice major in terms of its significance. Betty is the first person to identify a supernatural force at work in the house – a 'bad thing' that 'makes wicked things happen' – and the novel offers ample evidence to support her view, thus calling into question the authority exerted by a middle-aged, middle-class man over a working-class young woman (Waters 2009a: 129). In this regard, the novel offers a counterpoint to *The Franchise Affair*, in which Betty is ultimately exposed as a malicious, manipulative liar.

Although *The Little Stranger* follows *The Night Watch* (2006) in a further movement away from the lesbian focus that characterizes Waters' first three novels, it maintains an interest in gender and sexuality, and the text's feminist and queer sensibility highlights the limitations of Williams' Marxist critique of the country house. Like the typical country house, Hundreds Hall is a heteropatriarchal sphere in which the norms of gender and sexual desire are regulated as tightly as class boundaries. In this respect, the house resembles the gentleman's club 'the Old Hundredth' in *Brideshead*, where Sebastian and Charles seek to allay the suspicion that they are 'fairies' (Waugh 2000: 105, 110). Interactions between Faraday and Roderick echo the homoeroticism that underpins the relationship between Charles and Sebastian. Like Charles, Faraday finds his new acquaintance 'handsome' and 'charming', and just as Sebastian calls Charles to Brideshead to nurse his broken ankle, so Faraday is invited to Hundreds to treat Roddy's injured leg (Waters 2009a: 6, 62). Faraday, a 40-year-old bachelor who has had a small number of 'passionless embraces' with women, warms and works the muscles of Roddy's leg with his fingers before administering 'electrical therapy' in his patient's bedroom (Waters 2009a: 34, 39). The sexual subtext of this scene is underscored when Seeley later compares the 'sexual impulse' to 'an electrical current' (Waters 2009a: 381). Roderick's discomfort at Faraday's touch and accusation that he was 'making a grab' at him with his 'filthy doctor's fingers' illustrate the hostility provoked by same-sex desire in the period (Waters 2009a: 197). Like L. P. Hartley's *The Go-Between* (1953), in which a cross-class affair functions as a screen (Hartley's own repressed homosexuality might suggest) for other forms of forbidden love, *The Little Stranger* indicates the unspeakability of homosexuality when Faraday and Roderick both refer to desire between men simply as 'that' (Waters 2009a: 156). The importance attached to normative expressions of sexuality in the context of the country house is underlined by Roderick's family name: 'Ayres', a reminder that for the landed classes the production of heirs is crucial to the transmission of property and possessions. Since the country house demands the expression of desire in socially approved ways, Faraday redirects his desire to Caroline, just as Charles turns to Julia in *Brideshead*. The suggestion that a sister functions as a substitute for her brother, conveyed by the likeness of the siblings in both novels, is amplified in *The Little Stranger* by Faraday's fascination with Caroline's 'boyish' sandals, 'unshaven', 'muscular' legs, and 'masculine features' (Waters 2009a: 9, 24, 65). In contrast to his relationship with Roderick, Faraday struggles to feel a sexual connection – 'some charge or current' – with Caroline, and attraction is constantly complicated by aversion (Waters 2009a: 284). Their relations are 'strained and unnatural', and the pair find themselves 'blushing and awkward' (Waters 2009a: 286, 287). Thus, unlike Waugh, Waters refuses to replace homoeroticism with heteronormativity or expunge sexual uncertainty.

Traditionally, the country house demands the regulation of the norms of gender as well as sexuality. In contrast to Julia in *Brideshead*, who is 'exquisite' (Waugh 2000: 103), Caroline is shabby and 'eccentric', and while Faraday is initially fascinated by her masculinity, he grows increasingly irritated by her refusal to embrace an acceptable model of femininity as their courtship develops (Waters 2009a: 118). When Faraday and Caroline talk to men working on the houses being built near the Hall, he senses that they are the subject of speculation and suddenly wishes that she 'wasn't wearing that ridiculous hat' (Waters 2009a: 249). Likewise, at the district hospital dance, Faraday feels 'the sting of something that was almost anger' at the sight of Caroline, who looks a 'fright', and is 'relieved' when she tidies herself, making 'a neat, conventional mask of her face and throat with lipstick and powder' (Waters 2009a: 266). It is clear that, once married, Faraday expects Caroline to embody the dominant feminine ideal: 'I planned to take her into Leamington and quietly kit her out with some decent dresses' (Waters 2009a: 324).

However, Caroline persistently resists Faraday's attempts at coercion and ultimately rejects the role of country 'lady' when she breaks off their engagement and prepares to leave the Hall. Like the first Mrs de Winter in Daphne du Maurier's *Rebecca* (1938), who has a string of affairs that cross the boundaries of gender and class, Caroline is punished by death for her rebellion against the dominant model of womanhood. *The Little Stranger* invokes *Rebecca* through a number of parallels and allusions. The absence of Faraday's first name connects him not only to the servant Stevens in *The Remains of the Day* but also to the second Mrs de Winter.[2] Further, like Faraday, du Maurier's protagonist has a romance with an upper-class owner of a haunted (metaphorically in the case of *Rebecca*) country house. In addition, Faraday and Caroline plan to honeymoon in Cornwall, the location of Manderley. Yet, in contrast to *Rebecca*, whose narrator (with whom the reader is encouraged to identify) is strikingly indifferent to the revelation that her husband murdered his first wife, *The Little Stranger* refuses to condone Caroline's death. Also, as indicated by the switch in the gender of the protagonist, Waters resists du Maurier's 'conservative vision of sexual difference' (Light 1991: 169). This is emphasized not only by the ambiguity and incoherence of Caroline's gender but also its performativity. Caroline admits that, since it is 'exhausting to be a woman', she seldom does it 'properly' (Waters 2009a: 270). When she does assume feminine poses, as when flirting with Faraday after the district hospital dance, he notes 'something false about her' as if she is trying out 'another personality', one modelled on 'the pictures' (Waters 2009a: 269).

Waters further challenges dominant ideologies of gender by giving the role of hysteric, traditionally reserved for women, to men. In this sense, *The Little Stranger* departs from a tradition of ghost stories set in a country house epitomized by Henry James' *The Turn of the Screw* (1898) and Shirley Jackson's *The Haunting of Hill House* (1959), two novels in which the 'debilitated sexuality' of 'neurotic' heroines wreaks havoc (Haggerty 2006: 131). Seeley ascribes the mysterious events at Hundreds to 'hysteria', a phenomenon he associates with 'girls' (Waters 2009a: 377, 378). He proposes Mrs Ayres, 'the menopausal mother', or Betty, the 'teenage housemaid', as the poltergeist's most likely source (Waters 2009a: 380). Heilmann posits that Noel Coward's *Blithe Spirit* (1941), first a play and later a film (1945) in which it transpires that ghosts are being conjured by the maid, encourages readers to see Betty, alongside Faraday, as a figure that summons up a spirit that represents class protest (Heilmann 2012: 50). However, the novel questions rather than endorses a tradition that aligns women with hysteria. Faraday presents himself as a champion of reason and rationality. He makes 'sensible deductions' and rejects Caroline's theory of the poltergeist as 'superstitious' nonsense (Waters 2009a: 353, 365), just as Charles dismisses Catholicism as 'mumbo-jumbo' in *Brideshead* (Waugh 2000: 307). Yet, Faraday's perspective is rendered profoundly unreliable, not only by repression but also conjecture, the uncertainties of memory and third-hand accounts of events. Also, although the inquest concludes that the cause of Caroline's death is suicide, motivated by 'mental derangement', Roderick is admitted to hospital in a 'near-hysterical state' (Waters 2009a: 227, 490). Likewise, by making Faraday, a middle-class man, the agent of disruption rather than a working-class woman, Waters complicates established assumptions about gender, class and hysteria.

To conclude, through her 'adaptation' of *Brideshead,* Waters subverts the tradition of country house literature. By presenting Hundreds Hall as a house haunted by a spirit fuelled by envy and anger, *The Little Stranger* explores the destructive effects of class hierarchy, while also challenging dominant ideologies of gender and sexuality. In this way, the novel extends rather than abandons the feminist and queer politics of Waters' earlier work. Further, although set in the past, Waters' treatment of the country house has a powerful contemporary resonance. In 1990, John Major asserted that he sought to make Britain a 'classless society' (Marwick 2000: 335) and in 1998 Tony Blair claimed 'we're all middle-class now' (Jones 2011: 139). Yet, throughout the noughties numerous reports, including one published by The Sutton Trust (2007), illustrated that social mobility has *declined* since the end of World War Two and Britain remains a country in which economic success and social status are determined by birth rather than worth. Through its critical engagement with a range of historical representations of the country house, *The Little Stranger* protests the class divisions that – as the veneration of the country house in contemporary culture attests – continue to haunt Britain.

Notes

1 Thanks to Victoria Stewart for pointing out that Tey's desire to preserve the country house and its class is reflected in the fact that she left the proceeds of her books to the National Trust.

2 While the absence of a first name reflects the outsider status of all three protagonists, like *The Little Stranger* Ishiguro's novel is critical of the class politics that underscore the country house tradition of literature.

CHAPTER EIGHT

The Death of the Lady: Haunted Garments and (Re-) Possession in *The Little Stranger*

MONICA GERMANÀ

Chapter Summary: In constructing her narrative as a self-conscious palimpsest of Gothic texts such as Daphne Du Maurier's *Rebecca* and, in turn, Charlotte Brontë's *Jane Eyre*, in *The Little Stranger* Sarah Waters combines questions of social realism with the supernatural themes of its predecessors. In *The Little Stranger*, therefore, the supernatural, which emerges in the form of unexplained, fantastic – in Todorov's sense of the word – poltergeist occurrences, conceals the (socialist) spectre of political change that invested England after the Second World War. The disquieting events that lead to the decline of British aristocracy, symbolized by the crumbling decay of Hundreds Hall, are underpinned by significant references to the cultural overlapping of fashion, gender and class. Set in 1948, the narrative sets the gentry's 'old-fashioned' style in contrast with the rise of a new fashion, signalling, simultaneously, the rise of the middle- and working classes and stylized femininity. This chapter offers an interdisciplinary reading of the postwar cultural concerns raised in *The Little Stranger* through a focused analysis of dress and fashion references: these highlight the irreversible changes to class and gender norms, which Hundreds and its female owners attempt to resist.

Keywords: *The Little Stranger*, Christian Dior, Gothic, class, queer sexuality, Josephine Tey.

> But words [. . .] They seduce us in darkness, and the mind clothes and fleshes them to fashions of its own. (Waters 2002: 216)

With these words Mr Lilly, the pornography collector of Sarah Waters' *Fingersmith* (2002), defends the powerful effects of language over those of photography for the representation of erotic materials. The choice of fashion as a metaphor to highlight the invisible hold of words is here significant: in Waters' novels clothing serves to convey the intricate hauntology of desire and self. In *Fingersmith*, the acts of dressing and undressing facilitate the development of a sexual relationship between Maud and Susan through a complex convergence of their personal stories and overlapping identities. In *Affinity* (1999), clothes perform multiple functions: the apparently magical exchange of garments is a medium of communication between Margaret and Selina; the voyeuristic search for the box holding Selina's clothes at Millbank Prison catalyses Margaret's growing attraction to Selina and, simultaneously, her desire to 'fashion' Selina to be her lover. Clothes function ambiguously in relation to the spiritualist context of the novel and their spectrality challenges the stable boundaries of self (Spooner 2007: 366).

Constructing her narrative as a self-conscious palimpsest of Gothic texts such as Daphne Du Maurier's *Rebecca* (1938) and, in turn, Charlotte Brontë's *Jane Eyre* (1947), in *The Little Stranger* (2009) Waters combines questions of social realism with the supernatural themes of its predecessors. In *The Little Stranger* the supernatural, which emerges in the form of unexplained poltergeist occurrences, conceals the (socialist) spectre of political change that invested England after the Second World War. The disquieting events that lead to the decline of British aristocracy, symbolized by the crumbling decay of Hundreds Hall, are underpinned by significant references to the cultural overlapping of fashion, gender and class. Primarily set in 1947–48, the narrative revolves around the tragic vicissitudes of the remaining members of the Ayres family – the elderly Mrs Ayres and her children, Roderick and Caroline. While Waters self-consciously follows the Gothic conventions of recognizable predecessors, she also deploys the supernatural poltergeist plot to offer a historical commentary on postwar Britain through the novel's fashion subtext. Narrated from the point of view of Faraday, the family doctor, the novel presents the Ayres family's 'old-fashioned' style in contrast with the rise of a new fashion, signalling, simultaneously, the rise of the middle- and working classes and a return to stylized femininity.

As noted of her earlier fiction, Waters' fascination with her literary models frequently emerges in the intertextual fabric of her novels. *The Little Stranger* is no exception and, as reviews of the novel have not failed to emphasize, many a reference in Waters' fifth novel points to the Gothic subtext of her narrative. The novel's intertextual structure draws on some recognizable references to the Gothic canon, with a particular emphasis on (late) nineteenth-century texts dealing with pathology and sickness, both of a biological and social nature: Caroline compares the device used by Faraday to treat Roderick's war leg-injury to Dr Frankenstein's machine (Waters 2009a: 60); the name of the Ayres' neighbours, Baker-Hyde, contains a dual reference to the address of Arthur Conan Doyle's Sherlock Holmes and the name of the infamous character from Robert Louis Stevenson's *Strange Case of Dr Jekyll and Mr Hyde* (1886). References to the medical profession are embedded in the décor of Hundreds Hall, which pays homage to Charlotte Perkins Gilman's *The Yellow Wallpaper* (1899) (Waters 2009a: 66, 225). As in Perkins Gilman's novella, *The Little Stranger* projects the notion of malaise on to the body of the 'sick' house, a strategy also exposed by Emily Brontë's *Wuthering Heights* (1846) and Charlotte Brontë's *Jane Eyre*, with whom the Ayres of Waters' novel share a near homonymic surname. Along with a pervasive engagement with the theme of madness, with *Jane Eyre* and Du Maurier's rewriting of Brontë's novel, *Rebecca*, Waters' country house Gothic romance shares the focus on class and gender politics and dual aesthetics of the novel, which combines social realism with the supernatural tropes of the Gothic. The fire, an important episode in all three novels, completely destroys Maxim de Winter's Manderley and significantly tarnishes the social position and masculine authority of the legitimate owners of Thornfield and Hundreds Hall. In *The Little Stranger*, the allusion to Edgar Allan Poe's 'The Fall of the House of Usher' (1839) through the name of Roderick Ayres further amplifies this notion of decaying masculinity: with Poe's characters and plot, *The Little Stranger* shares the theme of illness, a malaise simultaneously interpreted as individual psychosis and symptom of class anxiety. Beyond the nineteenth-century tradition, Faraday's name establishes another intertextual link, as noted by Blake Morrison in an article on the significance of the country house in the English novel, with Kazuo Ishiguro's *The Remains of the Day* (1989), where Farraday is the name of Steven's new American employer (Morrison 2011: 3).

As in all these texts, the architectural space of *The Little Stranger* forms a symbiotic relationship with the novel's characters, encouraging a reading of the decaying mansion as organic entity, not simply accommodating the supernatural episodes that take place within its walls, but nurturing the malevolent force that ultimately drives all of its inhabitants away: 'it's a sort of lovely monster! It needs to be fed all the time, with money and hard work', Caroline admits to Faraday, upon one of his earlier visits to Hundreds Hall (Waters 2009a: 69). The dark smudges that mysteriously appear to tarnish various surfaces (ceiling, door, leather ottoman) are suggestive of the house's malignant drive – much like Manderley, which, haunted by Rebecca's spirit, might have self-ignited at the end of the story – prompting Caroline to question its rational foundations: 'A chemical reaction that can make antique oak panels and plaster ceilings start smouldering all by themselves?' (Waters 2009a: 145). Roderick, similarly, describes the strange poltergeist occurrences as a 'filthy thing', supporting a reading of the house as infected body (Waters 2009a: 155). As Faraday is a doctor, it is perhaps natural for him to conceive of the house as a body, providing a diagnosis which relates the strange marks scattered on the house surfaces to the scars on Roderick's body. The doctor's reading of the stains as pathological manifestations of the family's damaged psyche reveals Faraday's anxiety about Roderick's emasculated condition:

> They were like the burns, I realised suddenly, on Rod's own face and hands. It was as if the house were developing scars of its own, in response to his unhappiness and frustration – or to Caroline's, or her mother's – perhaps, to the griefs and disappointments of the whole family. (Waters 2009a: 148)

Prior to the uncanny occurrences, the house exercises – on the readers as much as on the characters – the strange attraction of the 'good old days'. Towards the beginning of the novel, Caroline remembers an old aunt of hers who used to compare well-run houses to oysters: 'Girls come to one as specks of grit [. . .]; ten years later, they leave one as pearls' (Waters 2009a: 73). The significance of the gentry's attitude towards their servants will be discussed later, but the simile is not lost on Faraday, who picks up on it, when he muses about his own feelings about the mansion: 'if the house, like an oyster, was at work on Betty, fining and disguising her with layer after minuscule layer of its own particular charm, then I suppose it had already begun a similar process with me' (ibid.). Hundreds' appeal for the doctor, whose working-class origins have had a lingering impact on his conflicted class consciousness, is particularly important, because, through his point of view, Hundreds emerges as an otherworldly space:

> I never let myself into the park and closed the gates behind me, then made my way along the overgrown drive, without a small, adventurous thrill. Arriving at that crumbling red house, I'd have the sense, every time, that ordinary life had fractionally tilted, and that I had slipped into some other, odder, rather rarer realm. (Waters 2009a: 75)

We get the sense that Hundreds Hall is, as its name suggests, not just an elegantly decrepit Georgian mansion, but the uncanny embodiment of one of Michel Foucault's 'heterotopias', and, in particular, those defined as 'slices in time, [. . .] heterochronies' (Foucault 1986: 26). As Fred Botting reminds us, 'Gothic remains ambivalent and heterotopic, reflecting the doubleness of the relationship between past and present' (Botting 2000: 12). The mansion, then, serves the purpose of enacting the tension, central to the novel's treatment of class anxieties and social change in postwar Britain, between old and new.

The conflict arises, towards the beginning of the novel, with a disastrous party, which juxtaposes the old-style gentry represented by the Ayres and endorsed by Faraday's own class interests, and the modern middle-class, the Baker-Hydes. The clash between the Ayres' archaic aristocracy and the Baker-Hydes' bourgeois trendiness could not be more blatant. Even before the party, we understand that Peter Baker-Hyde is a 'London man', 'an architect working on Coventry [. . .] drawn to Standish as a country retreat by what he considered to be its "out-of-the-way charm"' (Waters 2009a: 71). In spite of his penchant for Elizabethan architecture, Baker-Hyde's modern sensibility is, Caroline feels, a threat to the historical heritage of England: 'He's a town planner, isn't he? He'll probably knock Standish down and build a roller-skating rink' (ibid.). In this respect, Baker-Hyde's social role is closer to Maurice Babb's, the 'big local builder', than it is to the Ayres'. As Babb's new houses are being built on the grounds that Roderick has been reluctantly forced to sell (Waters 2009a: 149), the social changes brought in by the war are viewed with suspicion by the Ayres, conscious of the impact these may have on their lawful rights. Since the war, the grounds of Hundreds have been 'intruded' on by 'ramblers wandering in', suggesting that Hundreds is subject to a tangled range of intrusions (Waters 2009a: 74). Roderick's anxiety about the changes occurring to what he still perceives as his legitimate property is rather clear: 'we must have a fence to keep out the mob. Not that that will stop them, mind. They'll soon be scaling the walls of the house at night, with cutlasses between their teeth' (Waters 2009a: 189–90). By setting the Ayres – and their decaying mansion – in adjacent contrast with the 'mob' of new incomers and their newly built homes, the novel outlines how social changes brought in during the war, the rise of a stronger middle- and working-class, are directly responsible for the collapse of that section of upper-class families unable to cope with such changes.

The Baker-Hydes represent one such set of middle-class intruders; the night of the party, from the start, sets the two social groups apart; as Faraday notes, 'Bill Desmond, Mr Rossiter and I were dressed in old-style evening clothes, and Mrs Ayres and the other ladies were all in floor-length gowns'. The Baker-Hydes, on the other hand, turn up in lounge suits, though Faraday does not fail to observe that 'it was the rest of us who ended up feeling badly dressed' (Waters 2009a: 87). The comment stems from Faraday's own class preoccupations; later, he will admit that, being a medicine student of working-class stock meant that 'all I learned was that my accent was wrong, my clothes were wrong, my table manners – all of it, wrong' (Waters 2009a: 250). While his education, paid for by his parents' financial sacrifices, would seemingly facilitate his climb up the social ladder, it leaves him, in fact, in an uncomfortable liminal position. As for the hosts, the Ayres' financial weakness, for which the maintenance of the ailing house is partly responsible, is reflected in their sartorial style, which, at best, retains the residual traces of pre-war charm. Upon seeing Mrs Ayres for the first time, Faraday remarks upon her old-fashioned attire:

> Something about her – perhaps the scarf, or the fit of her dress, or the movement of her slender hips inside it – something, anyway, seemed to lend her a Frenchified air, slightly at odds with her children's light brown English looks. [. . .] They [her shoes] were dark patent leather with a cream stripe,

> too well made to be anything other than prewar, and like other well-made women's shoes, to a man's eye absurdly over-engineered – like clever little nonsense gadgets – and faintly distracting. (Waters 2009a: 20)

In contrast to Mrs Ayres' dated sophistication, from the beginning of the story Caroline's appearance is noted for her shabby disregard of feminine elegance: her legs are bare and unshaven, her feet in flat sandals and her body generally clad in shapeless blouses and badly fitting skirts. On the night of the party, Caroline's awkward style becomes more apparent because of her conscious effort to perform a role that no longer belongs to her, that of the English lady:

> She was wearing a blue chiffon evening gown and silver shoes and gloves; her hair was pinned up at one side with a diamanté clasp. The gown was an old one and, to be honest, not quite becoming. [. . .] I thought, actually, how much nicer and more like herself she would have looked with a scrubbed face, and in one of her shapeless old skirts and an Aertex blouse. (Waters 2009a: 82)

The politics of style – and, in particular, the advent of new fashions – becomes, in this context, the site of convergence of the important questions about gender and class that postwar Britain's economy produced. It is unsurprising that Gillian, the Baker-Hydes' seven-year-old child, is scared of Betty's maid's outfit: just like Betty, she finds the costume strange and unfamiliar in relation to the modern attire she is used to see (Waters 2009a: 87). While Faraday notes that 'her cuffs, collar and apron were blindingly white, and her cap was fancier than usual, with a stiff vertical frill like the wafer on an ice-cream sundae', Baker-Hyde's snide remark on Betty's uniform is a commentary on the Ayres' old-fashioned habits: 'I like the fancy headgear [. . .]. I'd like to see the look on our maid's face, if we tried one of those on her' (Waters 2009a: 83, 95). That the Baker-Hydes represent the new trends – as opposed to the Ayres' anachronistic lifestyle – and that their appreciation of modernity embodies a radically different ethos is emphatically expressed by Caroline, who, after Gillian's incident, claims that:

> There's no reasoning with people like that. [. . .] Not only are they getting rid of practically all the panelling at Standish, they mean to rip open the entire south wing of the house! They're going to make a sort of cinema of it for their friends. (Waters 2009a: 111)

Concurrent with the events occurring at the party, the poltergeist events in Roderick's chamber disclose the shared discourse of social anxiety in relation to attire. Following the appearance of strange marks on the door to his quarters and the ceiling of his bedroom, later, his personal objects begin to act out of his control: his collar and cufflinks temporarily vanish only to reappear in the sink, covered in water. Roderick's reaction, which does not display concern about the apparently paranormal nature of such phenomena, reveals instead his self-conscious paranoia about the mismatch of class and ownership that his lack of adequate clothing denotes 'there I was – the host, supposedly; the master of Hundreds! – keeping everyone waiting, chasing around the room like a twit, because I only owned one decent stand-up collar!' (Waters 2009a: 158).

As the plot unfolds, there are further suggestions that the poltergeist haunting Hundreds Hall is linked to the family's material possessions and, in particular, their garments. Echoing the evocative ways in which the nameless narrator in *Rebecca* is haunted by the psychological ghost of the first wife, whose residual presence continues to possess Manderley through the clothes and personal objects that had belonged to her, in *The Little Stranger* garments embody the anachrony of spectrality; as Jacques Derrida puts it, '[t]he apparition de-synchronizes. It recalls us to anachrony' (Derrida 1994: 6–7). Subverting the logic of sequential time, the spectral apparition, representative of the paradoxically absent presence of an earlier time, disrupts linear chronology, forcing its witnesses to confront the residual traces of their past in their present. That clothing, like spectrality, is qualified by anachrony at Hundreds Hall, becomes particularly manifest when Mrs Ayres' psychological collapse starts with the discovery of handwritten 'S's – possibly drawn by Susan, her dead daughter. These appear in her dressing room, which becomes the inner sanctum of the house, the place which holds its darkest secrets and the buried memories of the family's past sins. As Mrs Ayres is intensely aware, what haunts her old clothes is the spectre of social injustice:

> I feel so guilty [. . .] with the war on, hanging on to all this. I gave away what I could, but some of these, oh, I just couldn't see them go, to be hacked about and so on, made into blankets for refugees and goodness knows what. Now I'm awfully glad I kept them. Do you think it very wicked of me? (Waters 2009a: 315)

That Mrs Ayres' closet represents her class' (fashion) excesses in pre-war Britain is further emphasized when Faraday's narrative records 'the smell [. . .] of camphor, maiden-auntish [. . .] and the bed [. . .] heaped with gowns and furs, and with the loose silk bags, like deflated bladders, in which the furs had been stored' (ibid.). Suggestive of the spectral quality that these clothes from the past embody, the emphasis placed on their 'camphor' scent and 'deflated' containers concurrently reminds us of their past glory and current physical decay. Their ephemeral condition – itself a function of fashion's trend-led *raison d'être* – discloses the awareness that the war has definitively eroded the social model Mrs Ayres has lived by, thus signalling the beginning of the end for the whole family. Pre-war social roles are caught in the process of renegotiation to accommodate the increasing permeability of class boundaries in post-war Britain. This becomes obvious in the scene when Mrs Ayres encourages Betty to try on her old pair of gold slippers, which the maid models in a parody of a catwalk:

> So the girl unlaced her stout black shoes and shyly slipped on the gold leather slippers; then, encouraged by Mrs Ayres, she walked from the dressing-room door to the fireplace, and back again like a mannequin. She burst out laughing as she did it, raising a hand to cover up her crooked teeth. Mrs Ayres laughed too, and when Betty stumbled because the slippers were too big, she stuffed the toes of them with stockings to make them fit. (Waters 2009a: 316)

The carnivalesque performance of the scene conceals the kernel of social subversion that leads to the tragic demise of the Ayres family. In drawing attention to the clash between Betty's 'crooked' teeth and her temporary appropriation of Mrs Ayres' aristocratic glamour, as explained further later, the episode prefigures the disruption of established social hierarchy, pointing to a more permeable social structure. The masquerade, therefore, defines a pivotal moment in the story: not long after the discovery of Susan's handwriting in her dressing room, Mrs Ayres hangs herself with the cord of her dressing gown (Waters 2009a: 412). Her death is foreshadowed by the recognition that her spectral memories of the past hold more value in her mind than her present existence. Raving about Susan, she admits to Faraday: 'She has always been real to me. More real, sometimes, than anything else' (Waters 2009a: 317). The recognition that the ghostly memory of her dead daughter is 'more real [. . .] than anything else' reinforces the idea that the old-style British aristocracy is approaching its demise. As their family name suggests, the Ayres are mere spirits from the past, a past that is being swiftly swept away by a new way of living.

If the Ayres represent the past which, by the end of the novel, is buried with the bodies of Mrs Ayres and Caroline, the novel clearly points to the outsiders as representative of the future to come. Although the slippers are too big for Betty's feet, the act of wearing Mrs Ayres' *gold* shoes discloses the subversion of linear genealogy by which the maid replaces Susan, the dead heiress, and becomes the potential usurper of the Ayres' inheritance. As Katharina Boehm observes, '[t]he violent objects in *The Little Stranger* are directly linked to domestic labour' (Boehm 2011: 254). As well as being the only person who participates in both the poltergeist scene and the party scene, Betty is also responsible for Faraday's first visit. Rather than referring to physical illness, on that occasion her complaints relate to her working conditions, epitomized by a reference to her servant's outfit: 'You ought to see the awful dress and cap they makes me wear!' (Waters 2009a: 13). Betty's resistance to the rules of Hundreds is received by the Ayres with a patronizing attitude:

'Poor Betty', Caroline comments, 'Not a natural parlourmaid' (Waters 2009a: 73). As Hilary Mantel observes in her insightful review of *The Little Stranger*, the novel's use of the uncanny is closely linked to the politics of class; like the threatening 'mob' mentioned by Roderick, Betty is associated with the superstitious, irrational, 'inhuman' force at work at Hundreds Hall:

> In a classic ghost narrative, it is often the children and the dogs who are first to feel the cold draught, the creep and slither of the uncanny. It is a mark of the author's perfect understanding of her period that Dr Faraday and her employers regard Betty as being hardly on the human level. (Mantel 2009)

When Betty initially claims that there is something 'queer' about Hundreds, her fears are dismissed by the housekeeper, Mrs Bazeley, whose acquaintance with the house is ten years old. Against Mrs Bazeley's reassurance, Betty's insistence highlights the possibility that 'It might be a – *new* thing' (Waters 2009a: 130, my emphasis).

At the time of the novel's historical setting, 'new' grew to be a keyword in fashion journalism: Christian Dior's 'New Look' collection was launched on 12 February 1947. From the end of the 1940s and for the rest of the following decade, the influence of Dior's vision would revolutionize the world of fashion in relation to both gender and class. Disregarding the austerity measures put in place during and immediately after the Second World War, his designs, which required large amounts of fabric to be produced, were a lavish slap on the face of the rigid orthodoxy of the British 'Utility scheme'; '[a]usterity was the keyword of the later forties; the New Look kicked austerity in the teeth' (Wilson and Taylor 1989: 148). Moreover, Dior was one of the first designers to sell his patterns to authorized retailers who could reproduce his designs with cheaper materials, thus making the fashionable garments more affordable: this marked the development of a new phase in the fashion industry, one which increasingly catered to the mass market. As fashion historians have noted, despite the proactive attempts made by certain British institutions to 'educate' British women to consume these new fashions sensibly, '[w]orking-class women did not keep away from the frivolous or the impractical, even at work' (Partington 1992: 158). In fact, between the late 1940s and the early 1950s fashion became the site of complex class discourses and the relationship between taste and class suffered progressive, but radical changes (Partington 1992: 146). This process is further demonstrated by the resurrection of an important fashion magazine, *Vanity Fair*, which, re-launched in 1949, aimed to offer stylistic advice that catered to the *new* needs of a *new* breed of fashion consumers, as the editorial reads:

> The periodical *Vanity Fair* flourished from 1868 until some time before 1914. It is chiefly remembered because of its cartoons of personalities by Spy and

> other artists. Over two thousand of these cartoons were published – and only eighteen were of ladies [. . .] it was a man's world. Times have changed and this issue pretends in no way to be a strict revival. Our world is now very much in the hands of what we may term the Younger Smarter Woman. We salute the past – and present our salutations to the future too! (*Vanity Fair* 1949: 13)

In aiming to address the 'Younger Smarter Woman', the re-launch of *Vanity Fair* pointed to some of the complex cultural changes swept in by the end of the war. In particular, it is not unreasonable to link the magazine's admission of its previous gender bias to the social changes that affected gender roles in 1940s Europe and America. As with the Great War, the Second World War had accelerated social changes that meant, for instance, wider female employment and participation in domains that had previously been exclusively male. Combined with fabric shortages and necessary rationing of cloth and energy to produce garments, 1940s ladies fashion produced a kind of feminine attire that was – in the absence of unnecessary frills – both practical (shorter skirts ensured easier mobility in the work space, public transport, etc.) and androgynous (Cawthorne 1996: 13). Significantly, while the launch of Dior's New Look was immediately regarded as a sartorial revolution that 'gave women back their natural shape' (Cawthorne 1996: 111), it also prompted the indignation of feminist campaigners who saw the return to long and cumbersome dresses as the unwanted reinstatement of more conservative gender politics (Palmer 2009: 27). Under the pretence of enhancing women's 'natural femininity', the technology behind Dior's newly stylized femininity drew attention, in fact, to the artificial quality of gender essentialism: '[i]ronically, the curves of this 'natural' shape were completely artificial. [. . .] Dior's garments did not just hang on the body. They were constructed' (Cawthorne 1996: 111).

While the class implications of a new style in women's fashion, which will be discussed later, seem more evident in the subtext of *The Little Stranger*, the intricate tensions introduced by the complex gender politics of the 1940s underpin the construction of the novel's central female character. Caroline's uneasiness with, and unwillingness to conform to, a model of femininity that either follows her mother's old-style charm or the more modern embodiments of stylized femininity introduced in the late 1940s, also conceals wider anxieties about the construction of heteronormative femininity which would dominate the 1950s. Significantly, on the night of the district hospital dance, the night that ends in an awkward kiss in Faraday's car, Caroline's effort to perform a conventional feminine role is tinted with ambiguity. Upon seeing her, Faraday notes that she was 'dressed very unshowily, in an olive-coloured sleeveless gown, with her hair hanging loose and uncurled, her throat and hands, as usual, bare, and her heavy face almost free of make-up' (Waters 2009a: 253). At the dance, Caroline's interest seems to focus mainly on Brenda

Graham, the daughter of another doctor in the district. It is after meeting Brenda, who is, according to Faraday, 'worldly-looking' and whose hips swing 'impatiently' to the rhythm of the music, that Caroline shows more vitality and the hint of her queer sexuality. Paradoxically, it is then that Faraday first feels the strange attraction for the woman who was previously too plain to flatter his masculine ego:

> The heightened colour suited her, I thought. For all that her dress was unshowy and her pose so plain, she looked very young – as if her youth had been whipped to the surface, by motion and laughter, along with her blood. (Waters 2009a: 262)

Yet Faraday pursues his affair with Caroline, and Hundreds, his passion driven seemingly more by the latter than by an authentic affection for Caroline. The wedding preparations, which Faraday undertakes with queer 'girly' enthusiasm, conceal in fact his desire to refashion Caroline into the perfect bride. On choosing the dress, Faraday's smug satisfaction unveils a self-conscious effort in the display of the right kind of taste: 'The dress was exactly what I'd wanted: pure, crisp, unfussy, and seeming to shine with newness' (Waters 2009a: 443). While the implied simplicity of the design does not suggest the excessive luxury of the designs inspired by Dior's 'New Look', in choosing Caroline's wedding dress for her, Faraday's desire to lay the foundations of a patriarchal marriage fits with the conservative gender politics associated with Dior's couture. His anxieties are also supported by his conscious effort to display his credentials as the 'bread-winner' in the socially hybrid marriage between the penniless aristocrat and middle-class doctor; in choosing the ring, the emphasis is placed more on the weight, than the symbolic value carried by this piece of jewellery: '[t]he ring was weightier than I remembered, which reassured me no end; it sat snugly in a ruffled silk mount, inside an expensive-looking little shagreen box' (ibid.). The romance between Caroline and Faraday is made impossible by the same double set of factors that drives Caroline to her grave. From a class point of view, based on Faraday's conservative desire to belong to a British aristocracy which, as the decaying condition of Hundreds Hall suggests, has no real future, their union would represent yet another anachrony, an attempt to preserve the status quo at any cost. But what Gothic frequently unveils – as seen in other Gothic novels concerned with class, such as *Jane Eyre* and *Rebecca* – is the destabilization of social order and, in frustrating Faraday's ambition, *The Little Stranger* performs a similar function. From a gender point of view, reminiscent of Jane's resistance to Rochester's attempt to fashion her into a lady in Brontë's novel, Caroline's reaction to the gift of the wedding dress – 'When she lifted off the lid and parted the folds of tissue paper and saw the simple gown beneath, she sat in silence' (Waters 2009a: 44) – foreshadows her final rejection of conventional marriage with the intention of moving away from Britain, aware that 'England's no good anymore for someone like me. It doesn't want me' (Waters 2009a: 448). While the sentiment in Caroline's statement may refer to her redundant social status, it also conceals a reference to the queer woman, whose sexuality, stemming from the gender politics of wartime Britain, is forced underground by the dominant heteronormativity of the 1950s.

As well as disclosing an ambiguous narrative about the construction of gender, the aesthetic changes unveiled by postwar sartorial discourse refer to the important shifts in the relationship between fashion and class. Between the end of the 1940s and the beginning of the first post-war decade, style becomes particularly relevant in relation to class and national identity. It is interesting to note that in January 1947, one month before Dior's iconic launch, articles such as Robin Fedden's 'The Future of the British Country House', lamented that:

> The English country house has fallen on evil days. Lunatics peer from the windows of Georgian asylums; bars and golf-club bores are installed in Adam drawing-rooms; pigtails and hockey sticks invade what once were formal lawns. On all sides a hungry urban development swallows rectories and Tudor manors. There are even country houses – where generations lived and died – that are labelled like merchandise and sent across the Atlantic in the holds of ships. (Fedden 1947: 71)

As Fedden concludes his article warning that 'Income tax, dry rot, and the jerry builder wait for no man', one cannot help but think of Hundreds Hall, and Maurice Babb whose newly built housing estate looms over the mansion at the end of the novel (Fedden 1947: 97). Remarkably, the conservative nostalgia of Fedden's article echoes in the words of Scarlett Thomas, who reviewed *The Little Stranger* for *The New York Times*:

> Does a house ask to be vandalized or, indeed, taken by force? And, more to the point, do its inhabitants somehow 'ask' to be destroyed because they have become redundant in a society that needs public housing and health centers more than rich families and country piles? If death is a harsh sentence for all but the flattest fictional characters, then one is left with the uncomfortable sense that the Ayres have been needlessly murdered by progress and social change, which doesn't feel quite right either. (Thomas 2009)

Tangled with wider questions of national pride in postwar Britain, the impact of Dior's designs on mass consumption and the politics of class in Britain was long-lasting and far from simple. To begin with, the arrival of these luxurious garments created a stronger sense of inequality, widening the gap between the affluent women who could afford the New Look and deprived women who would still wear wartime Utility clothes. Carolyn Steedman's historiographic memoir, *Landscape for a Good Woman* (1986) draws attention to such tensions remembering her mother's financial struggles in 1950s Britain:

> I was born in the year of the New Look, and understood by 1951 and the birth of my sister, that dresses needing twenty yards for a skirt were items as expensive as children – more expensive really, because after 1948 babies came relatively cheap, on tides of free milk and orange juice, but good cloth in any quantity was hard to find for a very long time. (Steedman 1986: 29)

To begin with, the Board of Trade and Chancellor of the Exchequer disapproved of the wasteful approach to fashion and dress-making displayed by Dior's designs (Cawthorne 1996: 120). The British reaction was to put in place an even stricter rationing system, which would make it virtually impossible for a woman to acquire one of his garments. In spite of this, the New Look eventually took off in Britain. In 1947, for instance, John Lewis Partnership organized a private New Look fashion show, and as early as October 1948, the impact of the New Look – and what it entailed with regard to its constructed femininity – became available on the Utility scheme (Cawthorne 1996: 119–22).

While they certainly did not eradicate class divisions in Britain, the changes in the ways of consuming fashion introduced after the war pointed to a new approach in an industry that increasingly sought to cater to the needs and aspirations of the modern middle-class. Increasingly, the market widened to integrate a more fashion-conscious working-class, who, as Partington explains, rapidly developed sophisticated ways of adopting the new 'frivolous' and 'impractical' style in their daily routines: 'it was sampled and re-mixed with the comfortable and the serviceable, rather than kept separate and used on 'decorative' occasions only, as advised by fashion experts' (Partington 1992: 158). The profound impact of the influential changes brought in by Dior's 'New Look' – and the proliferation of less expensive variations of his designs – became visible in the shifted politics of magazines such as *Vogue*. As early as 1950 the magazine published articles such as 'The 1950s body line' (*Vogue* 1950: 115) and 'More Taste than Money' (*Vogue* 1950: 46–53), which proposed the view that fashion, no longer the privilege of a few, might be a gateway to anyone's renewed identity, regardless of the size of one's body or pockets. The 'New Look' woman looked confidently ahead. The new trend, in Dior's words, 'became symbolic of youth and the future' (Ewing 1974: 155).

The fashion subtext of *The Little Stranger* helps untangle the intricate embroidery of this ghosted text. As mentioned earlier, spectrality – viewed in post-structuralist terms – becomes synonymous with anachrony, the disruption of linear time caused by the coexistence of past and present brought in by the apparitional ghost of the past. While Hundreds Hall is haunted by the ghostly traces of pre-war Britain that its doomed dwellers embody, the house is also disturbed by another, more destructive, spectre. What possesses the mansion and his inhabitants, in the end, is the ghost of the future, a future made of significant social changes to the class structure of Britain and foreshadowed by the rise of a new fashion. At the end of the novel, when the Ayres ladies are not yet cold in their graves, on his visit to the house, Faraday meets Betty: 'She was wearing a cheap summer frock with a fashionable swing to its skirt. Her colourless hair had been lightened and permed, her lips and cheeks were red with rouge' (Waters 2009a: 497). Now a factory girl, Betty models a refashioned identity which strikes us for the vitality that her new persona seems to embody. As Catherine Spooner reminds us in her seminal interdisciplinary work on Gothic fashion and fiction, 'the Gothic novel is historically linked to fashion through the emergence of modern consumerism in the eighteenth century' (Spooner 2004: 1). Read against the conventions of the Gothic canon, which Waters self-consciously adopts in the intertextual body of *The Little Stranger*, the novel's fashion subtext supports the discourse of spectrality throughout the novel. As in the literary predecessors that Waters' novel gestures towards – and, in particular, Brontë's *Jane Eyre* and Du Maurier's *Rebecca* – the performative function of clothing and the consumption of fashion expose and simultaneously destabilize the paradigms of gender and class identity. Like the ghostly apparition, the changeable surface that negotiates the body in a social context is able to enhance or conceal the body underneath, thus creating an unsolved tension between visibility and invisibility, the real and the imagined (dreamed of, ideal, fetishized) body.

Ultimately, the insight offered by the cultural context underpinning the historical setting of *The Little Stranger* may help advance the hypothesis that Betty is in fact the 'little stranger'. This is suggested also by another intertextual reference in the novel: Josephine Tey's *The Franchise Affair* (1948), which, as Waters admitted, first inspired the plot of *The Little Stranger* (Waters 2009b). Tey's novel, which revolves around a charge of abduction made against two reclusive middle-class women by a working-class girl called Betty Kane, was in turn inspired by a real case, the abduction of Elizabeth Canning in 1753. Like her historical predecessor, Waters reminds us, 'Betty Kane is an inflammatory figure because she's such a powerful meeting point for anxieties about gender, sexuality and class – all categories that the war had done a great deal to disturb' (ibid.). It is precisely these disruptive tensions that the 'other' Betty's intrusion in the static world of Hundreds Hall produces through the poltergeist activities she is associated with. By the end of the novel 'the most popular tale [. . .] is that the Hall is haunted by the spirit of a servant girl who was badly treated by a cruel master, and who jumped or was pushed to her death from one of the upstairs windows' (Waters 2009a: 495). While searching for the ghost, in the last line of his narrative, Faraday becomes aware 'that what I am looking at is only a cracked window-pane, and that the face gazing distortedly from it, baffled and longing is my own' (Waters 2009a: 499). While this may point to the identification of the ghost with Faraday, it could be suggested that the line invites a more complex reading. Earlier, Faraday's narrative hints at the possibility of an 'uncanny return', the presence of a revenant haunting Hundreds, on using the house's speaking tube: 'I had the bizarre impression that this thing, whatever it was, was in some way *familiar*: as if its bashful advance towards us was more properly a *return*' (Waters 2009a: 393). As pointed out by Claudia FitzHerbert, 'all the odd happenings are connected to the disappearance of a world which is no longer feasible: a speaking tube connecting the nursery to the servant's quarters emits strange sounds, demanding to be disconnected; call bells ring for no reason' (FitzHerbert 2009). Read together with Faraday's earlier reflection on using the tube – 'I had the sudden irrational idea that, in putting my ear to the cup, I would hear my mother's voice. I had the idea that I'd hear her calling my name, exactly as I'd used to hear her, calling me home' (Waters 2009a: 334) – these clues lead to a composite reading of the little stranger's identity. What generates the poltergeist is the synergy created by Faraday's desire channelled through his mother's revenant and the representative of a 'new' working-class, who, in her ability to re-fashion herself, embodies the resilient vitality of the most powerful kind of Gothic 'undead'. Just like the 'jerry-built' houses erected on the grounds of Hundreds Hall, Betty's 'new-look' body rises confidently over the ashes of the English aristocracy, apparently 're-vamped': 'she was still small', Faraday notes on their last encounter, 'but her slightness had gone, or else she'd found some artificial way to improve her figure' (Waters 2009a: 497).

'I'd love to write an anti-*Downton*!': An Interview with Sarah Waters

KAYE MITCHELL

Kaye Mitchell: I'd like to start by asking you about the earliest fiction, *Tipping the Velvet* in particular; what was it about the late Victorian period that was attractive to you, that made you think that you could write *into* that the history that you wanted to write?

Sarah Waters: The late Victorian material came out of work I did for the early chapters of my PhD thesis. The thesis moved on through the twentieth century to look at different points in the representation of the lesbian and gay past, but it started with all that Greek Love stuff in the late nineteenth century. I'd been looking at London's queer underworld, and could see that there was a lot of material there which felt very exciting and which I wasn't really seeing outside of an academic context. Actually, one place I did see it was in the novels of a writer called Chris Hunt, and they, in a way, were my biggest inspiration. Hunt is a female writer, apparently, but is more or less marketed as male by Gay Men's Press because she writes gay men's historical fiction, and she wrote two novels set in late Victorian London – *Street Lavender* and *N for Narcissus*. They're romps, and bit soft porny really, but they are really thoughtful and well done and I absolutely loved them. The combination of those with the academic work I'd done, along with finishing the thesis and not quite knowing what to do next, produced this moment in which I began to think about writing a novel. I suppose that what had drawn me to the late Victorian period was a potential in it for that kind of 'naughty nineties' thing: it felt like there was a queer potential there already, a ripeness, I suppose, for lesbian appropriation. It also seemed like a bit of a hinge point. I had done my academic work in the 1990s and was very much in that post-Foucault/Jeffrey Weeks tradition of thinking about heterosexuality and homosexuality as having emerged in the late nineteenth century. The late Victorian moment seemed to be one in which identifiably modern lesbian and gay things were going on, but at the same time it still belonged to an older tradition. That's what I mean by its being a 'hinge point': it felt close enough to feel familiar and meaningful, but distant enough to be interesting, to have that historical edge to it. All of that really made it very appealing.

KM: Was it then very much an *appropriation*, in the sense that you were taking stories of a gay male subculture and rewriting them with a lesbian focus?

SW: That was a big part of it, definitely. I started writing the middle of the novel first, precisely because I'd been reading about Oscar Wilde and all that 'renter' culture and, yes, I wanted to take that for lesbians – which is what I felt I did. But then, I was also interested in male impersonation – I'd been collecting images of male impersonators and had been really intrigued by what surrounded that performance, what erotic charge it might have had for people at the time, whether it had had any lesbian charge. If you look at those images now, images of performers like Vesta Tilley and Hetty King – well, they just look like drag kings. At the time, of course, they were part of mainstream entertainment. Nevertheless I still think there might have been something going on, some sort of queer element to them. Anyway, that [interest in male impersonation] produced the first section of the novel, and then in the later section I explored interests in socialism and women's networks and suffrage. So it was a bit of everything really!

KM: It seems there's something in the theatricality of the setting too, the music hall scenes, that precisely allows for that playful treatment of gender and sexuality?

SW: Yes, I started the novel in the mid-1990s and that was a time in which the lesbian community that I was part of, in London, seemed to be becoming a bit more playful and a bit more sexualized, in what felt like a very exciting way. There was a lot about drag kings around, there was a lot about performativity, queer theory – not that I was ever madly *au fait* with queer theory – but it was all around, and inevitably it fed into the story.

KM: When *The Night Watch* came out you talked about the different kind of research that you had to do for that novel, the greater availability of material, particularly first person accounts. Did you feel that your research processes changed, or that your attitude to history changed? There are suggestions in recent criticism on your work that that the earlier neo-Victorian material has a self-conscious, playful aspect to it, that it is very much about appropriation and re-invention, and that when you get to *The Night Watch* and *The Little Stranger* there's a rather different attitude to history evident, that is more about evoking the material presence of history and more concerned with forms of documentary evidence. I've been teaching *The Night Watch* again recently and I'm always struck by the level of intense sensual detail in it, not only the sights and sounds of London in wartime but the smells as well; there's a real attention to that historical detail in a way that – the critical suggestion is – is less ironized, I suppose. Is that something you're aware of or is that just about the change of period?

SW: Well, it is about a change of period, yes, but it's also about a change in my relationship with writing, my own writing. When I look back at *Tipping the Velvet*, though I can see that in many ways it's the least accomplished of the books, I can also see that it's doing something more sophisticated with history [than the subsequent novels], which is to be more playful with history, to 'parade' history and to parade its own status as a historical fiction. I was very interested in that issue – in how of course we can't reconstruct the past or capture the past, we can only reinvent it, so I wanted the novel to be very self-consciously a piece of lesbian historical fantasy; it is full of little gestures to other canonical lesbian novels, for example. But increasingly as a novelist I've found myself becoming much more interested in character and motivation and emotional dynamics, which means that I'm *less* interested in writing a kind of metafiction, I'm less interested in *playing* with history than with creating a kind of *emotional experience* for my reader. So it is partly that I have become more of an old fashioned novelist. But it's also to do with the shift of period. When I moved to the forties, the kind of characters I was writing about felt more life size, they felt more *my* size, they felt like they were living in a world that was very close to mine, rather than a sort of stage set, rather than a piece of period drama, which I'd always enjoyed playing with in the early books. Suddenly I was very conscious of people who had lived in London not that long ago, in conditions of war, and yes, I became very interested in the daily experience of wartime life: smells and textures and things like that.

KM: Because the research for *The Night Watch* had involved reading memoirs and first person accounts, did coming up against those other voices invite ethical considerations, even when you were creating fictional characters, about not misrepresenting those experiences?

SW: It did, yes. Or I suppose, to put it another way, I found myself trying to do them justice, trying to capture something of the reality of their lives. I read a lot of diaries and that was fantastically helpful because lots of '40s diaries give you amazingly vivid accounts, day-by-day accounts, of wartime life. *The Night Watch* is set at very precise moments in the war, so I was reading diaries covering the very days that my characters were operating in and it was a very different experience from writing about 'the Victorians', which is a much more diffuse kind of idea. We've absorbed a sort of mish-mashy Victorian landscape from things like period dramas, but the war was more discrete, it had a timetable, it had a very specific shape and movement. And I did feel that I wanted to do justice to that, but also that I had to operate within it. At the same time, I was aware that we have many stereotypes about the war and that they are overwhelmingly heterosexual ones. And I wanted to try to play with those, to overturn them or to use them – to use that landscape but put gay men and lesbians into it.

KM: Was that something you found evidence of when you were doing your research?

SW: I get the sense that it was a bit of a golden age, really – for all the obvious reasons: women were moved around, away from the surveillance of their families, they were in barracks, they had permission to be a bit butch if they wanted to be. I found references to lesbianism in Joan Wyndham's diary – not that she was gay, but she was definitely aware of some women in the services who were lesbians; Naomi Mitchison mentions it in her diaries; there's the wonderful Barbara Bell memoir, *Just Take Your Frock Off*, in which she talks about being in the police force during the war and making the most of every opportunity to meet women. So there was a lot going on, and again that was different from the Victorian period, where really we've just got glimpses and fragments to work with. Suddenly I was very conscious that here were real lives, real experiences; and that the women who had had them might still be alive. I had to get it right.

KM: In the last couple of decades there's been something of a boom in historical fiction. How much do you feel implicated in that? How much do you think about that as a development and what do you think the appeal of historical fiction is?

SW: It's amazing isn't it? I remember thinking when I first started writing, 'Oh, God, this is going to be out of fashion any minute, nobody's going to want to read historical fiction any more'. I'd been very influenced by people like Chris Hunt and Philippa Gregory, who I thought had done very intelligent things with popular fictional forms, and by those more literary writers like Peter Carey, A.S. Byatt and Peter Ackroyd, who had done very clever reappropriations of the past. I'd been interested in all that, but I felt like it must be the end of that wave. And one of the agents I first sent *Tipping the Velvet* to said, 'I have to be honest, I think historical fiction is going out . . .'. Since then it has just been year after year of neo-Victorian fiction in particular. I don't know what I think about it really. I love writing historical fiction but I don't want everybody to be doing it – not because of the competition, I just don't want all British literature to be historical as it seems a bit reductive; but I can never really quite explain the appeal of it.

KM: Do you still read historical fiction?

SW: Well no, I rarely do. I'll read the occasional novel, if it sounds a bit special – *Wolf Hall*, for example, which I loved. But on the whole the genre feels too close to home – I can 'see the strings', as it were – and I'd rather read just about anything else. That's sad, really, because it was my absolute passion for historical novels that got me writing in the first place.

KM: Do you watch *Downtown Abbey* and other popular period dramas? And do they give you pause in any way, considering how history as a 'resource' for popular culture, for literature, might be, not misused, but used for quite conservative or conciliatory ends?

SW: I love *Downton Abbey*, but I also have big problems with it. I heard Alison Light talking about *Downton* a few months ago on the radio and she was speaking in support of it, saying that most of our ancestors were servants and that we've got a very legitimate interest in servants and servants' lives – and I think that's fair enough. I think *Downton*'s popularity is symptomatic of an opening-up in history and an allowing-in of working class lives and working class voices, which is great. But the cosiness of it I find terribly depressing. I completely understand the appeal of cosiness right now, when the world feels so full of antagonism, when there are so many crises going on, on such a huge scale – political, financial, environmental. I understand the appeal of a show like *Downton*, which is so much about people *doing their duty*. That's not a bad thing, doing one's duty. We do have a duty to other human beings – to respect them, to treat them fairly. But I wish that *Downton* didn't present that duty in terms of class deference and benevolent capitalism. It misrepresents the past; the past is more interesting than that. I wish there was an anti-*Downton*. I'd love to write an anti-*Downton*: something that had the same laudable values but was approaching them in a completely different way and showing the complexity of historical relations.

KM: Perhaps this could bring us on to talking about *The Little Stranger*. In reading that novel I'm struck, obviously, by the influence of the 'country house' tradition of writing and your use of that to puncture some of the more conservative messages that you would expect to get from that kind of fiction and, in particular, to offer quite an acute portrait of class relations and anxieties about the falling away of an old order.

SW: I worried when I was writing *The Little Stranger* that it would end up being conservative – having a conservative message about how upwardly mobile people would destroy you and suck the life out of you. I thought, 'God, is it really any different from that vision of Hooper's Britain in *Brideshead Revisited*? Is Doctor Faraday just a malign Hooper?' This is another thing that's happened to my writing. *Tipping the Velvet* has a very clear class agenda – a sort of pantomime class agenda, really; it was great fun to write. And I always start each new book wanting it to have a very clear class message, too. But these days the class relations in my novels end up muddied – more complex. There aren't class heroes and class villains in the way there are in *Tipping*. *The Little Stranger* ultimately I felt was a novel about class conflict, about waste and failure really; it's about the failure of the Ayreses and of Faraday to evolve. The only person who evolves is Betty: she's the image of the working class future, she's on her way up, she's on her way out, she's unharmed by what's happened; but both the Ayreses and Faraday in their different ways are trapped in an older structure. I was very conscious of novels like *Brideshead Revisited* and *The Franchise Affair* – the latter was my starting point, in fact, I was absolutely fascinated by that novel and how horrid it is, how horrid and compelling it is and how skewed it is in a very conservative direction and how it completely demonizes the working class girl, Betty. What I really wanted to do was to retell the story, to tell Betty's story if I could; I thought a lot about how I could do it – whether it was a legitimate thing to do and even whether there would be issues with Josephine Tey's Estate. By that point I was beginning to move in a slightly different direction anyway: it became this haunted house story and Faraday took over from Betty as the underground agent of the house's decline. But *The Franchise Affair* was the absolute starting point for the whole book.

KM: Writing historical fiction obviously requires you to do the kind of research that is not required – to the same extent – for the writing of fiction set in the contemporary world. Do you think that research-based approach suits you?

SW: Yes, I think that's partly why I write historical fiction: it's almost as if the novel is the excuse for the research, not the other way around. In a way it is very much the PhD writing process over and over, the long period of research, the turning of research into something else, something that's mine. I love both those processes: the research and then, once you've got the information, figuring out how you might do something with it.

KM: In your use of different genres – sensation fiction, the country house novel, etc. – are you trying to bring particular genres or particular authors back into public view to some extent? I'm thinking particularly here of the influence of women's writing of the interwar and postwar periods, particularly the middlebrow woman's novel and how that figures as part of your research, but also as something that you might be paying homage to.

SW: Yes. That's never something I plan at the start – although actually it probably was with *Fingersmith* because before I started the book I'd been reading a lot of Victorian fiction and I knew about sensation novels and just adored them. When I moved to the 1940s I really didn't know that much about the period. I knew enough to take me there, if you know what I mean, I knew enough about women's experiences during the war and just after it to know that that was very interesting, and again I had the impulse to take on a familiar landscape and put lesbians into it and see what that did. But it was only once I turned my attention to it and began to read *fiction* from the period and to look at *films* from the period – I was already a big fan of *Brief Encounter* and other films of the period – that I began to get into the middlebrow women's novel in a big way and loved it. It was just at that time when Persephone Books were (re)publishing a lot of writers – Jocelyn Playfair, Dorothy Whipple, and there are some old Viragos as well, such as Betty Miller – and they're just wonderful, I absolutely love them, along with authors like Elizabeth Taylor and Elizabeth Bowen. It was a great time for fiction and there was a very consistent tone across those novels which is very similar to the tone of something like *Brief Encounter,* very much about middle-class women's daily life and lots of female feeling. I suppose all my books have an element of homage to them and that was definitely something I wanted to pay my respects to in *The Night Watch* and *The Little Stranger* – not necessarily that I wanted to draw attention to [those authors], but just that it felt right to me. That's the other thing about genre for me, and period: I go to a period not necessarily knowing what the generic feeling will be, what will emerge as the idiom or the generic feeling, but once I get a handle on it, it somehow feels right to use that in representing the period, it feels natural to do that.

KM: So certain genres fit with certain periods.

SW: Yes, exactly. Something about the mentality of the period I suppose. Even though *The Night Watch* was written in the third person, I still wanted the tone to feel like a forties tone. That felt appropriate to how my characters would operate in the world.

KM: I was reading your piece about Sylvia Townsend Warner recently, the introduction to the new edition of *Lolly Willowes.* Are there other authors who you would want to hold up as interests or influences?

SW: One of the reason I enjoy being with Virago is that I love their Modern Classics list, which has got some fabulous writers on it – Sylvia Townsend Warner being one example. There are many women writers who have been rather overlooked and, while nobody could call Sylvia Townsend Warner a forgotten writer, she's definitely an under-read writer and, for me, one of the great writers of the twentieth century. It just maddens me that she's so under-read while male writers like Evelyn Waugh (an interesting writer but not a great writer) and Graham Greene (a fantastic writer, but certainly not more impressive than her) have remained firmly in the canon. Ivy Compton Burnett is another one: she was seen in her own day as a really great literary novelist, but how many people are reading her now? Barbara Comyns' novel *The Vet's Daughter* is an absolute masterpiece: it's just very odd and unsettling and gothic, it's a great modern gothic novel. So there are heaps of great Virago writers and some Persephone ones too. And there are many male writers I can think of – someone recommended William Gerhardie to me recently, for example; I'd never heard of him. But his novel *Futility,* about the Russian revolution, is just fabulous. I think he has been republished now by Faber Finds, and it's great that writers like that are being reprinted in a small way or in a print on demand capacity, but there are a lot [of these under-read writers] – like Patrick Hamilton, or Olivia Manning – again, neither of whom is exactly a forgotten writer, but they're very under read, I think, underappreciated.

KM: Have you found being described as a 'lesbian novelist' a blessing or a curse – or both?

SW: I've certainly never felt it as a curse. And in lots of ways, yes, it has been a blessing, because lesbian readers tend to be very enthusiastic and very generous and welcoming. I've gone all over the place, done events in lots of different countries, and there's always been a lesbian element in the audience – women who are really, really happy to see me. Who wouldn't want that kind of response from their readers? I understand it, too. There's this extra political and emotional element to lesbian readings or lesbian books – it's inevitable. We just don't see ourselves represented in respectful ways often enough for it not to be a big deal when it does happen.

KM: Martha Vicinus suggests that the lesbian is 'everywhere and nowhere' and, as you and Laura Doan point out in your co-authored article ['Making Up Lost Time'], there are crucial differences between writing lesbian history and writing gay male history. If you look at the fiction of someone like Alan Hollinghurst you see very clearly that imbrication of male homosexuality with establishment networks of power – the gentleman's club or the colonial service or Oxbridge or whatever it might be – and all of those networks of power also support, tolerate, conceal and facilitate male homosexual relationships; but lesbian history is just not like that, or doesn't appear to be like that. Is that an advantage in the sense that you can do what you did with *Tipping the Velvet* and write lesbians *into* history, rewrite the history to include them? Or is writing lesbian historical fiction made more difficult by the fact that lesbian histories are such contested histories?

SW: The lack of evidence, or the fragmentary nature of it, and the undecidability of lesbian relationships, for a historian is very frustrating; but as a novelist it's fantastic, you're liberated because, precisely as you were saying, it gives you a licence to make things up. Lesbian historians might agonize over whether women in the past had sex with each other, but if I want my lesbians in the 1860s to have sex, then they just do. I'm in charge. I do try to be sensitive – of course I do; that's what motivates me to write historical fiction – I do try to be sensitive to the complexity of the past, the changing nature of sexuality and the way people feel about sex and about their bodies, but at the same time, on the whole, my lesbian characters do tend to be pretty much people like me, people for whom experiencing same-sex desire means something about their identity. I don't see that as ahistorical, exactly. Think of someone like Anne Lister: that's clearly how she felt about it – that desiring other women wasn't just a question of sexual *acts*; it made her *a certain kind of person*. The book I'm writing now has a lesbian having an affair with a married woman and that's been interesting, because obviously the married woman is much more tentative about what's going on and what it means – what, if anything, it *says* about her. I'm still figuring that out, really.

KM: How far on is the latest book?

SW: I've written two-thirds of it, but I'm already re-writing that before I go on to write the end. It's set in the early 1920s, in London, so it's another post-war one, but a different kind of post-war. If anything it is a bit like *The Night Watch* in that it's just about human dramas and about people figuring things out. It's very domestic, though, as well – I'm worried it's too domestic at times.

KM: On your website you say if the writing's not going very well you go out for a walk and that you like walking through London and getting inspiration from that. What, for you, is the significance of London, what kind of backdrop does that provide you with? Obviously you've lived here for years . . .

SW: I have and this [the National Theatre] is a nice place to be talking about London, because I often walk back and forth across the river when I'm going into town and out again, and I like the South Bank a lot. In some ways there's nothing to say about it except that I love London and that that love leaks into the books. The characters, especially the characters I feel closest to, tend to respond to London in the same way that I do: they enjoy walking across London because of its mixture of life and anonymity – the fact that there's room for you to be in a crowd but for you to be untouched by the crowd at the same time. And I love the fact that London's history is still very visible on its streets, that you can 'read' a street as a piece of social history. Then, too, there's the fact that there are sites in the city that *resonate* – for particular communities; for the nation; or for individuals, in very personal ways. It's all freighted with layers and layers of meaning. It's a joy to tap into that, when you're writing a book about London – to evoke those very different atmospheres belonging to different parts of the city. I've always felt the settings of *The Night Watch*, for example, to make little nods to those Ealing comedies, those great London films like *The Lavender Hill Mob*, *Passport to Pimlico* and *The Ladykillers*. For me, that's an example of the real city and the imaginary, mythicized city coming together. And to put lesbians into that mix was, for me, very exciting – like saying, London belongs to us lesbians, too!

KM: And the different cultures and subcultures of the city as well?

SW: Absolutely: those spaces, perhaps private, individual ones, perhaps to do with couples or communities; the spaces that the city has room for even if they've been hidden in a vest pocket: pockets of love and desire and contact and affinity. I love all that about London.

KM: Do you, as well as thinking about location, place or the city, think about the kinds of *spaces* your characters are moving through? I'm thinking particularly of Millbank prison in *Affinity*, Duncan's prison experience in *Night Watch*, the madhouse in *Fingersmith*, Hundreds Hall in *The Little Stranger* – the kinds of intimacies that are either afforded or precluded by those kinds of spaces.

SW: Yes, I seem to always end up enacting relationships in spatial terms. I'm very conscious of that at the moment with the book I'm writing now: it's set mainly in a suburban house in which two households have to share the space, so it's all a bit fraught. Everything seems to happen at a threshold: in a doorway, or on the stairs or the landing. It's made me realize that, of course, thresholds are loaded with significance: somebody crossing a threshold, whether you've invited them to, or whether they're invading your space; or glancing across a threshold, what you can see and what you can't see; it just keeps happening again and again in this novel. But I think that does come up in my novels as a whole, there tend to be significant houses or structures. Millbank Prison had those very odd angles in its wards. While I was writing *Affinity* I literally laid the angles out on my study floor and thought about what you'd be able to see at what point. I thought about what you'd see through the spyhole of a prison door, what the inmates would see if they looked out the window. People often stand at windows in my books, looking out – which means, of course, that then there's the potential for them to be observed, too. I can't quite rationalize it, but I guess it's to do with houses and spaces being an extension of subjectivity.

KM: And I suppose those things are also historically specific, in that the kinds of spaces that we inhabit and move through change. We're much more 'spaced out' now, as it were, and those things are relative to class and wealth as well.

SW: I think about that an awful lot. The house I live in now was built in the 1790s; it's not a huge house, I share it with my partner and my cat, but I know, from having looked at censuses, that in 1901 there were, I think, 13 people living there – at least two separate households. If you go back more than about 40 years you are instantly in a landscape in which people shared intimate spaces all the time, and you think about toilets and bathrooms and the completely different sorts of relationships that people would have had with those spaces. And of course this is local to our culture, there are plenty of cultures where people still share spaces like that. But what that meant in terms of basic things like sounds and smells, what you saw or what you weren't supposed to see, your own personal space and how you related to your own body if you were in continual contact with other bodies – again, that's part of the excitement for me in writing about the past, trying to get into that world and hopefully take a reader with me.

KM: Do you think the literary world has changed since you've been publishing?

SW: It has changed, I would say, in the last five to ten years. It has changed enormously recently because of e-books and the internet; it's also changed because of publishers wanting bestsellers, and a corresponding falling away of mid-list writers. I don't know if there ever really was a time when it was possible to be a career novelist, without ever having a huge hit – maybe there was – but certainly there is the idea among authors that there was once a time like that and now there isn't; now you're just as good as your last book; publishers don't take risks any more and don't nurture you; they give you your chance and if you don't live up to it you're out the window. Another change, of course, is the rise of reading groups and prizes – both great things in their way, especially reading groups (I'm in a reading group myself), but, at the same time, I think they've contributed to a certain narrowing of focus in publishers and bookshops. The dominance of chain bookshops and of Amazon, together with the loss of so many independent bookshops, has only added to that. And then there's the rise of literary festivals, which means that writers have to be personalities in the way they never used to have to be.

KM: Do you feel there's more pressure on you to do that?

SW: Well, funnily enough there's less pressure on me now than there was, say, five years ago, because I'm that bit more established. At one point I think I felt that I had to say yes to every invitation, and my publisher would encourage that; but now that I'm a bit more established, I *can't* literally say yes to everything because there are an awful lot of requests, so I can be a bit more selective about what I do and what I don't do.

KM: How involved with the adaptations of your novels have you been?

SW: I've not been creatively involved and I've not wanted to be. I have once or twice been approached to adapt or co-adapt but I've always been much happier to sell the rights and let them get on with it – although of course I only sell the rights to a book once I've met the production company and have a good sense that they're not going to muck around with it. I met Andrew [Davies] very early on with *Tipping* and I really liked him and was just bowled over, basically, that someone of his stature wanted to be involved. *Tipping* was the most exciting one, of course, because it was the first adaptation and it was a very fun project, everybody was very welcoming; *Fingersmith* was nice as well. So I've always enjoyed being included in the process – going to the read-throughs, meeting the actors, going on set, etc. But, of course, by the time a novel's being adapted it's usually, for me, a few books old; it feels a bit like an old project. It's great to see it getting a new lease of life, but creatively I don't think I've got anything to add to the process, really.

KM: Does it feel hard to let go of it and think, 'well actually this isn't my project, it's theirs and their vision may be different from mine'?

SW: No, no it doesn't. I have always been very sanguine about it actually. You do always have to hand the book over and yet, ultimately, the adaptation's never going to replace the book. The book is always there; the adaptation just becomes this other thing, which on the whole has a very positive impact, in that it brings new readers to the book. It's also, to be honest, a great source of income. It's fascinating to see how the scriptwriter does it: what has to stay, what has to go, the compromises that get made, all the things the adaptation can bring to the novel. I think TV adaptations can sometimes tidy up messy books, so, for example, I think *Tipping the Velvet* benefited from that – I think Andrew brought something to it that made it work very well on screen and made it lots of fun. Some things do get lost on the way but that's inevitable – it's a translation.

KM: Are there any plans for an adaptation of *The Little Stranger*?

SW: There are; it's in development as a feature film, so that's quite exciting. It's with a company called Potboiler productions, a British company who seem very keen and optimistic. A draft of the script has been written and they're about to take it to directors.

KM: When you write do you think in terms of framing and focalization – or in a 'filmic' way?

SW: Yes, definitely. Not that I'm writing *for* the screen – I'd be lying if I said that it didn't occur to me now, these days, that a book might get picked up and that it might get adapted for the screen, but it doesn't affect the way I write the book or the choice of material or anything like that. When I was writing *The Night Watch* I thought, 'nobody is going to want to adapt this because it's so gloomy and there are too many lesbians, there are too many of the wrong kind of lesbians, they aren't young and nubile and corset-wearing. They're too butch, and they're a bit miserable'. But it didn't mean that I wanted to write the book in a different way. But yes, I do find myself effectively thinking in terms of close-ups, long shots, etc. I'll definitely *see* a scene before I write it. That might be a generational thing: like lots of people my age, I grew up watching telly absolutely non-stop. Also, my writing is pretty old-fashioned in the sense that it's about story and character and it unfolds often like a film does, so that lends the books to adaptation, I think.

KM: Is that the kind of writing that you read, do you think?

SW: Yes, probably. I certainly find an emotional satisfaction in reading older writers – writers like Elizabeth Taylor, Anthony Powell, Winifred Holtby – that I don't always get from contemporary fiction. Then again, I can think of many contemporary writers that I admire immensely – Hilary Mantel, Colm Toíbín, Damon Galgut, Kazuo Ishiguro. Ishiguro, in particular, is quite an important writer for me because I often have terrible doubts about the whole historical fiction writing project, I often think 'why am I devoting myself to these small historical stories, especially now when we're living in a time when there are very pressing and distressing things going on in the world, why not write about them?' And then I think about Kazuo Ishiguro, whose novels are all about 'small', inarticulate lives; they're never set in the contemporary world, exactly; and yet they feel incredibly pertinent and important and as though they are tackling big issues. I like to remember him as somebody who provides a model of writing about pressing things without engaging, in obvious ways, with the contemporary moment.

This interview is the edited transcript of a conversation that took place on 16 March 2012, at the National Theatre, London.

Bibliography

Works Cited by Contributors

Abraham, J. (1996), *Are Girls Necessary? Lesbian Writing and Modern Histories*. New York: Routledge.

Ahmed, S. (2006), *Queer Phenomenology: Orientations, Objects, Others*. Durham, NC: Duke University Press.

Apollodorus (1997), *The Library of Greek Mythology*. Trans. Robin Hard. Oxford: Oxford University Press.

Arias, R. (2009), 'Female confinement in Sarah Waters' neo-Victorian fiction', in J. Alber and F. Lauterbach (eds), *Stones of Law, Bricks of Shame: Narrating Imprisonment in the Victorian Age*. Toronto, ON: University of Toronto Press, pp. 256–77.

Armitt, L. (2007), 'Interview with Sarah Waters' (CWWN Conference, University of Wales, Bangor, 22 April 2006). *Feminist Review*, 85, 116–27.

— (2009), *Twentieth-Century Gothic*. Cardiff: University of Wales Press.

Armitt, L. and Gamble, S. (2006), 'The haunted geometries of Sarah Waters' *Affinity*'. *Textual Practice*, 20(1), 141–59.

Auerbach, J. A. (1999), *The Great Exhibition of 1851: A Nation on Display*. New Haven, CT: Yale University Press.

Austen J. (2003), *Pride and Prejudice*. London: Penguin Classics.

Barrett Browning, E. (1857), *Aurora Leigh*. London: Chapman and Hall.

Barthes, R. (1990), *S/Z*. Trans. R. Miller. Oxford: Blackwell.

Bauer, H. (2009), *English Literary Sexology: Translations of Inversion, 1860–1930*. London: Palgrave.

Bell, B. (1999), *Just Take Your Frock Off: A Lesbian Life*. Brighton: Ourstory Books.

Bentley, N. (2008), *Contemporary British Fiction*. Edinburgh: Edinburgh University Press.

Boehm, K. (2011), 'Historiography and the material imagination in the novels of Sarah Waters'. *Studies in the Novel*, 43(2), 237–57.

Boehm-Schnitker, N. and Gruss, S. (2011), 'Introduction: Spectacles and things – visual and material culture and/in neo-Victorianism'. *Neo-Victorian Studies*, 4(2), 1–23.

Botting, F. (2000), 'In gothic darkly: Heterotopia, history, culture', in D. Punter (ed.), *A Companion to the Gothic*. Oxford: Blackwell, pp. 3–13.

Bowen, E. (1949), *The Heat of The Day*. London: Cape.

— (1999), 'Postscript to the demon lover' [1945], in H. Lee (ed.), *The Mulberry Tree: The Writings of Elizabeth Bowen*. London: Virago, pp. 94–9.

Braid, B. (2010), 'Victorian panopticon: Confined spaces and imprisonment in chosen neo-Victorian novels', in A. Ciuk and K. Molek-Kozakowska (eds),

Exploring Space: Spatial Notions in Cultural, Literary and Language Studies, Volume 1: Space in Cultural and Literary Studies. Newcastle: Cambridge Scholars, pp. 74–82.

Brannigan J. (2003), *Orwell to the Present: Literature in England, 1945–2000.* Basingstoke: Palgrave.

Briggs, J. (2006), *Virginia Woolf: An Inner Life.* London: Penguin.

Brindle, K. (2009/10), 'Diary as queer malady: Deflecting the gaze in Sarah Waters' *Affinity*'. *Neo-Victorian Studies*, 2(2), 65–85.

Brooks, P. (1984), *Reading for the Plot.* Cambridge, MA: Harvard University Press.

Brown, B. (2003), *A Sense of Things.* Chicago: University of Chicago Press.

Butler, J. (1993), *Bodies that Matter: On the Discursive Limits of 'Sex'.* London: Routledge.

— (1999), *Gender Trouble*, 2nd edn. London: Routledge.

— (2004), *Undoing Gender.* London: Routledge.

Calinescu, M. (1998), 'Orality in literacy: Some historical paradoxes of reading and rereading', in D. Galif (ed.), *Second Thoughts: A Focus on Rereading.* Detroit, MI: Wayne State University Press, pp. 51–74.

Cardwell, S. (2002), *Adaptation Revisited: Television and the Classic Novel.* Manchester: Manchester University Press.

Carroll, R. (2006), 'Rethinking generational history: Queer histories of sexuality in neo-Victorian feminist fiction'. *Studies in the Literary Imagination*, 39(2), 135–47.

— (2007), 'Becoming my own ghost: Spinsterhood, heterosexuality and Sarah Waters' *Affinity*'. *Genders* 45.

Carroll, S. J. (2010), 'Putting the "neo" back into neo-Victorian: The neo-Victorian novel as postmodernist revisionist fiction'. *Neo-Victorian Studies*, 3(2), 172–205.

Carter, A. (1979), *The Sadeian Woman.* London: Virago Press.

Castle, T. (1994), *The Apparitional Lesbian: Female Homosexuality and Modern Culture.* New York: Columbia University Press.

Cawthorne, C. (1996), *The New Look: The Dior Revolution.* London: Hamlyn.

Chevalier, T. (2009), 'Class-ridden Britain gives up the ghost'. *The Observer*, 31 May.

Christie, A. (2007), *The Murder of Roger Ackroyd.* London: Harper.

Ciocia, S. (2005), '"Journeying against the current": A carnivalesque theatrical apprenticeship in Sarah Waters's *Tipping the Velvet*'. *Literary London: Interdisciplinary Studies in the Representation of London*, 3(1).

— (2007), '"Queer and verdant": The textual politics of Sarah Waters' neo-Victorian novels'. *Literary London: Interdisciplinary Studies in the Representation of London*, 5(2).

Currie, M. (2007), *About Time: Narrative, Fiction and the Philosophy of Time.* Edinburgh: Edinburgh University Press.

Davies, H. (2012), *Gender and Ventriloquism in Victorian and Neo-Victorian Fiction.* Basingtoke: Palgrave.

De Certeau, M. (1984), *The Practice of Everyday Life.* Trans. Steven Rendall. Berkeley, CA: University of California.

de Groot, J. (2008), *Consuming History.* London: Routledge.

— (2009), *The Historical Novel*. London: Routledge.

Deer, P. (2009), *Culture in Camouflage: War, Empire, and Modern British Literature*. Oxford: Oxford University Press.

Derrida, J. (1994), *Spectres of Marx: The State of the Debt, the Work of Mourning, and the New International*. Trans. Peggy Kamuf. New York: Routledge.

Dinshaw, C. (1999), *Getting Medieval*. Durham: Duke University Press.

— (2009), 'Temporalities', in P. Strohm (ed.), *Oxford Twenty-First Century Approaches to Literature: Middle English*. Oxford: Oxford University Press, pp. 107–23.

Dinshaw, C., Edelman, L., Ferguson, R. A., Freccero, C., Freeman, E., Halberstam, J., Jagose, A., Nealon, C. and Tan Hoang, N. (2006), 'Theorizing queer temporalities: A roundtable discussion'. *GLQ*, 13(2–3), 177–95.

Doan, L. and Waters, S. (2000), 'Making up lost time: Contemporary lesbian writing and the invention of history', in D. Alderson and L. Anderson (eds), *Territories of Desire in Queer Culture*. Manchester: Manchester University Press, pp. 12–28.

Du Maurier, D. (2003), *Rebecca*. London: Virago.

Edelman, L. (2004), *No Future: Queer Theory and the Death Drive*. Durham: Duke University Press.

Emmens, H. (2009), 'Taming the velvet: Lesbian identity in cultural adaptations of *Tipping the Velvet*', in R. Carroll (ed.), *Adaptation in Contemporary Culture*. London: Continuum, pp. 134–46.

Ewing, E. (1974/ 2005), *History of 20th Century Fashion*. London: Batsford.

Feay, S. (2006), 'You can't do that in a Victorian novel!' *Independent on Sunday*, 1 January.

Fedden, R. (1947), 'The future of the British country house'. *Vogue*, January 1947, 103(1), pp. 70–1 and 97.

FitzHerbert, C. (2009), '*The Little Stranger* by Sarah Waters: Review'. *The Telegraph*, 29 May.

Fleishman, A. (1972), *The English Historical Novel: Walter Scott to Virginia Woolf*. Baltimore: John Hopkins University Press.

Fludernik, M. (1999), 'Carceral topography: Spatiality, liminality and corporality in the literary prison'. *Textual Practice*, 13(1), 43–77.

Foucault, M. (1986), 'Of other spaces'. Trans. J. Miskowiec. *Diacritics*, 16(1), 22–7.

— (1995), *Discipline and Punish: The Birth of the Prison*. Trans. Alan Sheridan. New York: Vintage.

Fox, C. (2011), '*The Night Watch*: set report'. *The Telegraph*, 3 July.

Freeman, E. (2010), *Time Binds: Queer Temporalities, Queer Histories*. Durham: Duke University Press.

Freud, S. (1955), 'The psychogenesis of a case of homosexuality in a woman', in *The Standard Edition of the Complete Works of Freud*, Vol. 18. Trans. James Strachey. London: Hogarth Press, pp. 145–74.

Gamble, S. (2009), '"You cannot impersonate what you are": Questions of authenticity in the neo-Victorian novel'. *Literature Interpretation Theory*, 20, 126–40.

Gardiner, J. (2003), *From the Closet to the Screen: Women of the Gateways 1945–85*. London: Pandora Press.

Garland, R. (1995), *The Heart in Exile* [1953]. Foreword by N. Bartlett. Brighton: Millivres-Prowler Group Ltd.

Gill, R. (1972), *Happy Rural Seat: The English Country House and the Literary Imagination*. New Haven: Yale University Press.

Gilman, C. Perkins (2009), *The Yellow Wallpaper*. London: Virago

Grafton, P. (1981), *You, You and You: The People Out of Step with World War Two*. London: Pluto Press.

Green, H. (1991), *Caught* [1943]. London: Harvill.

Haggerty, G. E. (2006), *Queer Gothic*. Urbana and Chicago: University of Illinois Press.

Halberstam, J. (2005), *In a Queer Time and Place*. New York: New York University Press.

Hall, R. (1934), *Miss Ogilvy Finds Herself*. London: Heinemann.

— (1999), *The Well of Loneliness*. London: Virago.

Halperin, D. M. (1995), *Saint Foucault*. Oxford: Oxford University Press.

— (2004), *How To Do The History Of Homosexuality*. Chicago: University of Chicago Press.

Hartley, L. P. (2004), *The Go-Between*. London: Penguin.

Harvey, D. (1990), *The Condition of Postmodernity*. Oxford: Blackwell.

Heilmann, A. (2009/10), 'Doing it with mirrors: Neo-Victorian metatextual magic in *Affinity*, *The Prestige* and *The Illusionist*'. *Neo-Victorian Studies*, 2(2), 18–42.

— (2012), 'Specters of the Victorian in the neo-forties novel: Sarah Waters's *The Little Stranger* (2009) and its intertexts'. *Contemporary Women's Writing*, 6(1), 38–55.

Heilmann, A. and Llewellyn, M. (2010), *Neo Victorianism: The Victorians in the Twenty-First Century 1999–2009*. Basingstoke: Palgrave.

Heise, U. K. (1997), *Chronoschisms*. Cambridge: Cambridge University Press.

Hensher, P. (2006). 'Smoother than velvet'. *The Observer*, 8 January.

Hewison, R. (1987), *The Heritage Industry: Britain in a Climate of Decline*. London: Methuen.

Hillis Miller, J. (1987), *The Ethics of Reading: Kant, de Man, Eliot, Trollope, James, and Benjamin*. New York: Columbia University Press.

Hutcheon, L. (1989), *The Politics of Postmodernism*. London: Routledge.

— (1998), *A Poetics of Postmodernism*. London: Routledge.

Ishiguro, K. (1989), *The Remains of the Day*. London: Faber

Jagose, A. (2002), *Inconsequence: Lesbian Representation and the Logic of Sexual Sequence*. Ithaca: Cornell University Press.

Jameson, F. (1991), *Postmodernism, or, The Cultural Logic of Late Capitalism*. London: Verso.

Jardine, L. (2005), 'Sarah Waters: sex and the Victorian city'. BBC2, 4 May.

Jeremiah, E. (2007), 'The "I" inside "her": queer narration in Sarah Waters' *Tipping the Velvet* and Wesley Stace's *Misfortune*'. *Women: A Cultural Review*, 18(2), 131–44.

Jones, O. (2011), *Chavs: The Demonization of the Working Class*. London: Verso

Jordan, J. (2006), 'Through the bomb-sites, backwards'. *The Guardian*, 4 February.

Keats, J. (1980), *Keats: Poems Published in 1820* (ed.) M. Robertson. Oxford: OUP.

Keen, S. (2006), 'The historical turn in British fiction', in J. F. English (ed.), *A Concise Companion to Contemporary British Fiction*. Oxford: Blackwell, pp. 167–88.

Kelsall, M. (1993), *The Great Good Place: The Country House in Literature*. New York: Columbia University Press.

Klein, M. (1997), *Envy and Gratitude and Other Works, 1946–1963*. London: Vintage.

Kohlke, M.-L. (2004), 'Into history through the back door: The "past historic" in *Nights at the Circus* and *Affinity*'. *Women: A Cultural Review*, 15(2), 153–66.

Koolen, M. (2010), 'Historical fiction and the revaluing of historical continuity in Sarah Waters' *Tipping the Velvet*'. *Contemporary Literature*, 51(2), 371–97.

Kurth, P. (1999), 'Tipping the Velvet'. *Salon*, 30 July.

LaCapra, D. (2001), *Writing History, Writing Trauma*. Baltimore: Johns Hopkins University Press.

Light, A. (1989), '"Young Bess": Historical novels and growing up'. *Feminist Review*, 33, 57–71.

— (1991), *Forever England: Femininity, Literature and Conservatism between the Wars*. London: Routledge.

Llewellyn, M. (2004), '"Queer? I should say it is criminal!": Sarah Waters' *Affinity* (1999)'. *Journal of Gender Studies*, 13(3), 203–14.

— (2009), 'Spectrality, s(p)ecularity, and textuality: Or, some reflections in the glass', in R. Arias and P. Pulham (eds), *Haunting and Spectrality in Neo-Victorian Fiction*. Basingstoke: Palgrave, pp. 23–44.

Lo Dico, J. (2009), '*The Little Stranger* by Sarah Waters'. *The Independent*, 31 May.

Love, H. (2007), *Feeling Backward: Loss and the Politics of Queer History*. Cambridge, MA: Harvard University Press.

Macpherson, H. (2004), 'Prison, passion, and the female gaze: Twentieth-century representations of nineteenth-century panopticons', in M. Fludernik and G. Olson (eds), *In the Grip of the Law: Trials, Prisons and the Space between*. Frankfurt: Peter Lang, pp. 205–21.

Mallet-Joris, F. (2006), *The Illusionist* [1951]. Berkeley, CA: Cleis Press.

Mantel, H. (2009), 'Haunted by shame'. *The Guardian*, 23 May.

Margaronis, M. (2008), 'The anxiety of authenticity: Writing historical fiction at the end of the twentieth century'. *History Workshop Journal*, 65, 138–60.

Mars-Jones, A. (2002), 'Inner steel', *The Observer*, 27 January.

Marwick, A. (2000), *A History of the Modern British Isles, 1914–1999*. Oxford: Blackwell.

Marx, K. and Engels F. (2004), *The Communist Manifesto*. London: Penguin.

Maurier, D. du (1938), *Rebecca*. London: Victor Gollancz.

Maxwell, R. (2010), *The Historical Novel in Europe, 1650–1950*. Cambridge: Cambridge University Press.

McManus, C. (2004), *Right Hand, Left Hand: The Origins of Asymmetry in Brains, Bodies, Atoms and Cultures*. Cambridge, MA: Harvard University Press.

Mengham, R. (1982), *The Idiom of the Time: The Writings of Henry Green*. Cambridge: Cambridge University Press.

Merck, M. (2000), *In Your Face: 9 Sexual Studies*. New York: New York University Press.

Middleton, P. and Woods, T. (2000), *Literatures of Memory*. Manchester: Manchester University Press.

Mill, J. S. (1965), *Principles of Political Economy*, Books III–V. Toronto: University of Toronto Press.

Miller, K. A. (2008), 'Sarah Waters's *Fingersmith*: Leaving women's fingerprints on Victorian pornography'. *Nineteenth Century Gender Studies*, 4(1), npg. Accessible at: www.ncgsjournal.com/issue41/miller.htm

Mitchell, Kate (2010), *History and Cultural Memory in Neo-Victorian Fiction*. Basingstoke: Palgrave.

Mitchell, Kaye (2013), '"That library of uncatalogued pleasure": Queerness, desire and the archive in contemporary gay fiction', in Sas Mays (ed.), *Literatures, Libraries and Archives*. London: Routledge (not yet published).

Morrison, B. (2011), 'They capture the castle'. *The Guardian*, 11 June.

Muller, N. (2009/10), 'Not my mother's daughter: Matrilinealism, third-wave feminism and neo-Victorian fiction'. *Neo-Victorian Studies*, 2(2), 109–36.

Myerson, J. (2002), 'Corsets and cliffhangers'. *The Guardian*, 2 February.

O'Callaghan, C. (2012), 'The equivocal symbolism of pearls in the novels of Sarah Waters'. *Contemporary Women's Writing*, 6(1), 20–37.

Ovid (1955), *Metamorphoses*. Trans. M. M. Innes. Middlesex: Penguin.

Owen, A. (1989) *The Darkened Room: Women, Power and Spiritualism in Late Victorian England*. London: Virago.

Palmer, A. (2009), *Dior*. London: V&A Publishing.

Palmer, B. (2009), 'Are the Victorians still with us? Victorian sensation fiction and its legacies in the twenty-first century'. *Victorian Studies*, 52(1), 86–94.

Palmer, P. (2007), 'Queer transformations: Renegotiating the abject in contemporary Anglo-American lesbian fiction', in K. Kutzbach and M. Müller (eds), *The Abject of Desire: The Aestheticization of the Unaesthetic in Contemporary Literature and Culture*. Amsterdam: Rodopi, pp. 49–67.

— (2008), '"She began to show me the words she had written, one by one": Lesbian reading and writing practices in the fiction of Sarah Waters'. *Women: A Cultural Review*, 19(1), 69–86.

Partington, A. (1992), 'Popular fashion and working-class affluence', in J. Ash and E. Wilson (eds), *Chic Thrills: A Fashion Reader*. London: Pandora, pp. 145–61.

Pauli, M. (2002). 'Fingersmith is book-buyer's Booker choice', guardian.co.uk, 22 October. www.guardian.co.uk/books/2002/oct/22/bookerprize2002.bookerprize.

Perry, J. (2003). 'Quick fingers'. *The Observer*. 23 February.

Rees, J. T. (1955), *They Stand Apart: A Critical Survey of Homosexuality*. London: Heinemann.

Renault, M. (2003), *The Charioteer* [1959]. New York: Vintage.

— (2005), *The Friendly Young Ladies* [1944]. London: Virago.

Roberts, M. (2006), 'Oh what a lovely, lonely war'. *The Independent*. 27 January.

Schofield, M. (1952), *Society and the Homosexual*. London: Gollancz.

Scott, W. S. (1948), *Bygone Pleasures of London*. London: Marsland Publications.

Sedgwick, E. Kosofsky (1990), *Epistemology of the Closet*. London: Penguin.
— (1993), *Tendencies*. Durham: Duke University Press.
Shute, N. (1955), *Requiem For A Wren*. London: Heinemann.
Smith, L. (2009), 'Deference and humility: The social values of the country house', in L. Gibson and J. R. Pendlebury (eds), *Valuing Historic Environments*. Aldershot: Ashgate, pp. 33–50.
Southgate, B. (2009), *History meets Fiction*. Harlow: Pearson.
Spooner, C. (2004), *Fashioning Gothic Bodies*. Manchester: Manchester University Press.
— (2007), '"Spiritual garments": Fashioning the Victorian séance in Sarah Waters' *Affinity*', in C. Kuhn and C. Carlson (eds), *Styling Texts: Dress and Fashion in Literature*. Youngstown, NY: Cambria, pp. 351–67.
Steedman, C. (1986/2005), *Landscape for A Good Woman*. London: Virago.
Steele, M. (1998), 'Books: Fiction in brief'. *Independent on Sunday*, 22 March.
Suyin, H. (1962), *Winter Love*. London: Jonathan Cape.
Tait, T. (2006). 'Sarah Waters's richness in austerity'. *Times Literary Supplement*, 1 February.
Tew, P. (2008), *The Contemporary British Novel*. London: Continuum.
Tey, J. (1948), *The Franchise Affair*. London: Peter Davies.
The Sutton Trust (2007), *Creating a High Aspiration Culture for Young People in the U.K.* www.suttontrust.com/research/creating-a-high-aspiration-culture-for-young-people-in-the-uk/ [accessed 29 June 2011].
Thomas, S. (2009), 'House Calls', *New York Times*, 29 May.
Thomson, I. (1999), 'Mistress of the hard task'. *The Guardian*, 15 May.
Thrift, N. (2008), 'Space – the fundamental stuff of geography', in Nicholas Clifford, Sarah Holloway, Stephen P. Rice and Gill Valentine (eds), *Key Concepts in Geography*. 2nd edn. London: Sage, pp. 85–96.
Turner, J. (2006). 'Charging about in brogues', *London Review of Books*, 28(4), 12–13.
Wallace, D. (2005), *The Women's Historical Novel*. Basingstoke: Palgrave.
Waters, S. (1995), 'Wolfskins and togas: Lesbian and gay historical fictions, 1870 to the present'. Unpublished PhD thesis, University of London.
— (1996), 'Wolfskins and Togas: Maude Meagher's *The Green Scamander* and the Lesbian Historical Novel'. *Women: A Cultural Review*, 7(2), 176–88.
— (1998), *Tipping the Velvet*. London: Virago.
— (1999), *Affinity*. London: Virago.
— (2002), *Fingersmith*. London: Virago.
— (2006a), *The Night Watch*. London: Virago.
— (2006b), 'Romance among the ruins'. *The Guardian*, Saturday, 28 January.
— (2006c), Email to the author. 30 October 2006.
— (2009a), *The Little Stranger*. London: Virago.
— (2009b), 'The lost girl', *The Guardian*, Review, 30 May, p. 2.
— (2010), Email to the author, 10 February 2010.
— (2011), 'Live webchat: Sarah Waters', *The Guardian*, 13 July. www.guardian.co.uk/books/booksblog/2011/jul/13/live-webchat-sarah-waters [accessed 29 July 2011].

Waugh, E. (2000), *Brideshead Revisited* [1959]. London: Penguin

White, H. (2007), 'Historical fiction, fictional history, and historical reality'. *Rethinking History*, 9(2/3), 147–57.

Willard, N. (2000), 'Blithe spirits'. *New York Times Book Review*, 23 July.

Williams, R. (1973), *The Country and the City*. Oxford: Oxford University Press.

Wilson, C. A. (2006), 'From the drawing room to the stage: Performing sexuality in Sarah Waters' *Tipping the Velvet'*. *Women's Studies*, 35(3), 285–305.

Wilson. E. and Taylor, L. (1989), *Through the Looking Glass*. London: BBC.

Vanity Fair. (1949), Autumn–Winter, p. 13.

'The 1950s body line', *Vogue*, 106(3), March 1950, p. 115.

'More Taste than Money' *Vogue*, 106(2), February 1950, pp. 46–53.

Woolf, V. (1919/92) *Night and Day*. London: Penguin.

— (1925), *Mrs Dalloway*. London: L. & V. Woolf.

— (1933), *Flush: A Biography*. London: L. & V. Woolf.

— (2005), *Street Haunting: A London Adventure*. London: Penguin.

Wyndham, J. (1985), *Love Lessons*. London: Heinemann.

— (1986), *Love is Blue*. London: Heinemann.

Yates, L. (2009/10), '"But it's only a novel, Dorian": Neo-Victorian fiction and the process of re-vision'. *Neo-Victorian Studies*, 2(2), 65–85.

Further Reading

I Works by Sarah Waters

Academic/critical writing

(1995), 'Wolfskins and togas: Lesbian and gay historical fictions, 1870 to the present'. Unpublished PhD Thesis. University of London.

(1996), 'Wolfskins and togas: Maude Meagher's *The Green Scamander* and the lesbian historical novel'. *Women: A Cultural Review*, 7(2), 176–88.

Doan, L. and Waters, S. (2000), 'Making up lost time: Contemporary lesbian writing and the invention of history', in D. Alderson and L. Anderson (eds), *Territories of Desire in Queer Culture: Refiguring the Contemporary Boundaries*. Manchester: Manchester University Press, pp. 12–28.

Journalism

(2002), 'Sarah Waters's top 10 Victorian novels'. *The Guardian*, 20 March.

(2006), 'Romance among the ruins'. *The Guardian*, 28 January.

(2006), 'Sensational stories: Sarah Waters on the echoes of sensation novels in *Fingersmith*'. *The Guardian*, 17 June.

(2007), 'Writers' rooms: Sarah Waters'. *The Guardian*, 26 January.

(2009), 'The lost girl'. *The Guardian*, 30 May.

(2009), 'My hero: Angela Carter'. *The Guardian*, 3 October.

(2010), 'Sarah Waters's rules for writers'. *The Guardian*, 23 February.

(2011), 'My favourite independent bookshop: Gay's the Word, London'. *The Guardian*, 1 October.

Novels

(1998), *Tipping the Velvet*. London: Virago.

(1999), *Affinity*. London: Virago.

(2002), *Fingersmith*. London: Virago.

(2006), *The Night Watch*. London: Virago.

(2009), *The Little Stranger*. London: Virago.

II Critical Material

Book chapters

Arias, R. (2009), 'Female confinement in Sarah Waters' neo-Victorian fiction', in J. Alber and F. Lauterbach (eds), *Stones of Law, Bricks of Shame: Narrating Imprisonment in the Victorian Age*. Toronto: University of Toronto Press, pp. 256–77.

Armitt, L. (2007), 'Dark departures: Contemporary women's writing after the gothic', in B. A. Brabon and S. Genz (eds), *Postfeminist Gothic*. Basingstoke: Palgrace, pp. 16–29.

Braid, B. (2010), 'Victorian panopticon: Confined spaces and imprisonment in chosen neo-Victorian novels', in A. Ciuk and K. Molek-Kozakowska (eds), *Exploring Space: Spatial Notions in Cultural, Literary and Language Studies*. Newcastle upon Tyne: Cambridge Scholars, pp. 74–82.

Davies, H. (2012), 'Sexual re-scripting: Ventriloquial repetitions and transformations in Sarah Waters' *Tipping the Velvet* and *Affinity*', in H. Davies, *Gender and Ventriloquism in Victorian and Neo-Victorian Fiction*. Basingtoke: Palgrave, pp. 114–38.

Emmens, H. (2009), 'Taming the velvet: Lesbian identity in cultural adaptations of *Tipping the Velvet*', in R. Carroll (ed.), *Adaptation in Contemporary Culture: Textual Infidelities*. London: Continuum, pp. 134–46.

Heilmann, A. (2009), 'The haunting of Henry James: Jealous ghosts, affinities and *The Others*', in R. Arias and P. Pulham (eds), *Haunting and Spectrality in Neo-Victorian Fiction*. Basingstoke: Palgrave, pp. 111–32.

Letissier, G. (2011), 'More than kith and less than kin: Queering the family in Sarah Waters's neo-Victorian fictions', in M.-L. Kohlke and C. Gutleben (eds), *Neo-Victorian Families*. Amsterdam: Rodopi, pp. 365–94.

Llewellyn, M. (2007), 'Breaking the mould? Sarah Waters and the politics of genre', in A. Heilmann and M. Llewellyn (eds), *Metafiction and Metahistory in Contemporary Women's Writing*. Basingstoke: Palgrave, pp. 195–210.

— (2009), 'Spectrality, s(p)ecularity, and textuality: or, some reflections in the glass', in R. Arias and P. Pulham (eds), *Haunting and Spectrality in Neo-Victorian Fiction*. Basingstoke: Palgrave, pp. 23–44.

— (2010), '"Perfectly innocent, natural, *playful*": Incest in neo-Victorian women's writing', in M.-L. Kohlke and C. Gutleben (eds), *Neo-Victorian Tropes of Trauma*. Amsterdam: Rodopi, pp. 133–60.

Madsen, L. H. (2010), 'Female same-sex relationships and the erotics of domination in Sarah Waters' *Tipping the Velvet*', in A. Anton-Pacheco Bravo, I. Duran Gimenez-Rico, C. Mendez Garcia, J. Neff Van Aertselaer and A. L. Rodriguez Redondo (eds), *Differences, (In)Equality and Justice*. Madrid: Fundamentos, pp. 79–92.

Mitchell, K. (2013), '"That library of uncatalogued pleasure": Queerness, desire and the archive in contemporary gay fiction', in Sas Mays (ed.), *Literatures, Libraries and Archives*. London: Routledge (not yet published).

Muller, N. (2012), 'Sexual f(r)ictions: Pornography in neo-Victorian women's fiction', in K. Cooper and E. Short (eds), *The Female Figure in Contemporary Historical Fiction*. Basingstoke: Palgrave, pp. 115–33.

Palmer, P. (2007), 'Queer transformations: Renegotiating the abject in contemporary Anglo-American lesbian fiction', in K. Kutzbach and M. Mueller (eds), *The Abject of Desire: The Aestheticization of the Unaesthetic in Contemporary Literature and Culture*. Amsterdam: Rodopi, pp. 49–67.

Pantuchowicz, A. (2010), 'In the furrows of translation', in A. Fawcett, K. L. Guadarrama Garcia, R. Hyde Parker and J. Boase-Beier (eds), *Translation: Theory and Practice in Dialogue*. London: Continuum, pp. 128–44.

Preston, P. (2008), 'Victorianism in recent Victorian fiction', in M. Knezevic and A. Nikcevic-Batricevic (eds), *History, Politics, Identity: Reading Literature in a Changing World*. Newcastle upon Tyne: Cambridge Scholars, pp. 91–109.

Spooner, C. (2007), '"Spiritual garments": Fashioning the Victorian séance in Sarah Waters' *Affinity*', in C. Kuhn and C. Carlson (eds), *Styling Texts: Dress and Fashion in Literature*. Youngstown, NY: Cambria, pp. 351–67.

Wieckowska, K. (2009), 'Dis/Locations: Images of London in Sarah Waters' fiction', in A. Rasmus and M. Cieslak (eds), *Images of the City*. Newcastle upon Tyle: Cambridge Scholars, pp. 204–15.

Wormald, M. (2006), 'Prior knowledge: Sarah Waters and the Victorians', in P. Tew and R. Mengham (eds), *British Fiction Today*. London: Continuum, pp. 186–97.

Journal articles

Armitt, L. and Sarah Gamble (2006), 'The haunted geometries of Sarah Waters' *Affinity*'. *Textual Practice*, 20(1), 141–59.

Bishton, J. (2008), 'Kissing women: The fiction of Sarah Waters'. *American, British and Canadian Studies*, 10, 91–105.

Boehm, K. (2011), 'Historiography and the material imagination in the novels of Sarah Waters'. *Studies in the Novel*, 43(2), 237–57.

Brindle, K. (2009/10), 'Diary as queer malady: deflecting the gaze in Sarah Waters' *Affinity*'. *Neo-Victorian Studies*, 2(2), 65–85.

Carroll, R. (2006), 'Rethinking generational history: Queer histories of sexuality in neo-Victorian feminist fiction'. *Studies in the Literary Imagination*, 39(2), 135–47.

— (2007), 'Becoming my own ghost: Spinsterhood, heterosexuality and Sarah Waters' *Affinity*'. *Genders* 45.

Carroll, S. J. (2010), 'Putting the "neo" back into neo-Victorian: The neo-Victorian novel as postmodernist revisionist fiction'. *Neo-Victorian Studies*, 3(2), 172–205.

Chialant, M. T. (2011), 'Dickensian resonances in the contemporary English novel'. *Dickens Quarterly*, 28(1), 41–51.

Ciocia, S. (2005), '"Journeying against the current": A carnivalesque theatrical apprenticeship in Sarah Waters's *Tipping the Velvet*'. *Literary London: Interdisciplinary Studies in the Representation of London*, 3(1).

— (2007), '"Queer and verdant": The textual politics of Sarah Waters' neo-Victorian novels'. *Literary London: Interdisciplinary Studies in the Representation of London*, 5(2).

Constantini, M. (2006), 'Faux-Victorian melodrama in the new millennium: The case of Sarah Waters'. *Critical Survey*, 18(1), 17–39.

Gamble, S. (2009), '"You cannot impersonate what you are": Questions of authenticity in the neo-Victorian novel'. *Literature Interpretation Theory*, 20, 126–40.

Heilmann, A. (2009/10), 'Doing it with mirrors: Neo-Victorian metatextual magic in *Affinity*, *The Prestige* and *The Illusionist*'. *Neo-Victorian Studies*, 2(2), 18–42.

— (2012), 'Specters of the Victorian in the neo-forties novel: Sarah Waters's *The Little Stranger* (2009) and its intertexts'. *Contemporary Women's Writing*, 6(1), 38–55.

Jeremiah, E. (2007), 'The "I" inside "her": Queer narration in Sarah Waters' *Tipping the Velvet* and Wesley Stace's *Misfortune*'. *Women: A Cultural Review*, 18(2), 131–44.

Kaplan, C. (2008), '*Fingersmith*'s coda: Feminist and Victorian studies'. *Journal of Victorian Culture*, 13(1), 42–55.

Kohlke, M.-L. (2004), 'Into history through the back door: The "past historic" in *Nights at the Circus* and *Affinity*'. *Women: A Cultural Review*, 15(2), 153–66.

Koolen, M. (2010), 'Historical fiction and the revaluing of historical continuity in Sarah Waters' *Tipping the Velvet*'. *Contemporary Literature*, 51(2), 371–97.

Letissier, G. (2006), 'Le texte Victorien à l'âge postmoderne: jouvence ou sénescence? *Fingersmith* de Sarah Waters et le mélodrame victorien'. *Cahiers Victoriens et Edouardiens*, 63, 277–93.

Llewellyn, M. (2004), '"Queer? I should say it is criminal!": Sarah Waters' *Affinity* (1999)'. *Journal of Gender Studies*, 13(3), 203–14.

Millbank, J. (2004), 'It's about this: Lesbians, prison, desire'. *Social and Legal Studies*, 13(2), 155–90.

Miller, K. A. (2008), 'Sarah Waters's *Fingersmith*: Leaving women's fingerprints on Victorian pornography'. *Nineteenth Century Gender Studies*, 4(1), npg. Accessible at: www.ncgsjournal.com/issue41/miller.htm

Muller, N. (2009/10), 'Not my mother's daughter: Matrilinealism, third-wave feminism and neo-Victorian fiction'. *Neo-Victorian Studies*, 2(2), 109–36.

Mundler, H. (2008), 'Seeming and being: The play of alterity in *Affinity* by Sarah Waters'. *Resonances*, 9, 103–15.

O'Callaghan, C. (2012), 'The equivocal symbolism of pearls in the novels of Sarah Waters'. *Contemporary Women's Writing*, 6(1), 20–37.

Palmer, B. (2009), 'Are the Victorians still with us? Victorian sensation fiction and its legacies in the twenty-first century'. *Victorian Studies*, 52(1), 86–94.

Palmer, P. (2004), 'Lesbian gothic: Genre, transformation, transgression'. *Gothic Studies*, 6(1), 118–30.

— (2008), '"She began to show me the words she had written, one by one": Lesbian reading and writing practices in the fiction of Sarah Waters'. *Women: A Cultural Review*, 19(1), 69–86.

Parker, S. (2008), '"The darkness is the closet in which your lover roosts her heart": Lesbians, desire and the gothic genre'. *Journal of International Women's Studies*, 9(2), 4–19.

Stevenson, S. (2007), 'Waters's *Affinity*'. *The Explicator,* 65(2), 124–7.
Voigts-Virchow, E. (2009), 'In-Yer-Victorian-Face: A subcultural hermeneutics of neo-Victorianism'. *Lit: Literature Interpretation Theory,* 20(1–2), 108–25.
Wilson, C. A. (2006), 'From the drawing room to the stage: Performing sexuality in Sarah Waters' *Tipping the Velvet*'. *Women's Studies,* 35(3), 285–305.
Yates, L. (2009/10), '"But it's only a novel, Dorian": Neo-Victorian fiction and the process of re-vision'. *Neo-Victorian Studies,* 2(2), 65–85.

Newspaper reviews

Charles, R. (2009), 'Book review: Ron Charles on *The Little Stranger* by Sarah Waters'. *The Washington Post,* 20 May.
Chevalier, T. (2009), 'Class-ridden Britain gives up the ghost'. *The Observer,* 31 May.
Feay, S. (2006), 'You can't do that in a Victorian novel!' *Independent on Sunday,* 1 January.
— (2009), '*The Little Stranger*: Sarah Waters'. *Literary Review,* 1 June.
FitzHerbert, C. (2009), '*The Little Stranger* by Sarah Waters: Review'. *The Telegraph,* 29 May.
Hensher, P. (2006), 'Smoother than velvet'. *The Observer,* 8 January.
— (2009), 'Straitened circumstances'. *The Spectator,* 23 May.
Jordan, J. (2006), 'Through the bomb-sites, backwards'. *The Guardian,* 4 February.
Kemp, P. (2009), 'Spirits of the age'. *The Sunday Times,* 31 May.
Kennedy, D. (2002), 'Finger-licking good'. *Mail on Sunday,* 17 March.
Leavitt, D. (2006), 'This is London'. *The New York Times,* 26 March.
Lo Dico, J. (2009), '*The Little Stranger* by Sarah Waters'. *The Independent,* 31 May.
Mantel, H. (2009), 'Haunted by shame'. *The Guardian,* 23 May.
Mars-Jones, A. (2002), 'Inner steel'. *The Observer,* 27 January.
McGrath, M. (2006), 'No love off limits'. *The Evening Standard,* 16 January.
Mosse, K. (2009), 'Plunge in to the best summer books, chosen by our top writers'. *The Times,* 27 June.
Myerson, J. (2002), 'Corsets and cliffhangers'. *The Guardian,* 2 February.
O'Brien, S. (2009), 'Sarah Waters's little stranger'. *TLS,* 29 May.
Pearson, A. (2009), 'Literary fiction'. *The Daily Mail,* 29 May.
Perry, J. (2003), 'Quick fingers'. *The Observer,* 23 February.
Preston, J. (2009), 'Fiction: Sarah Waters's old-style ghost story makes the hairs on the back of John Preston's neck stand up'. *The Telegraph,* 17 May.
Roberts, M. (2006), 'Oh what a lovely, lonely war'. *The Independent,* 27 January.
Sexton, D. (2009), 'Gothic house of horrors'. *The Evening Standard,* 14 May.
Steele, M. (1998), 'Books: Fiction in brief'. *Independent on Sunday,* 22 March.
Thomas, S. (2009), 'House calls', *New York Times,* 29 May 2009.
Thomson, I. (1999), 'Mistress of the hard task'. *The Guardian,* 15 May.
Thorne, M. (2002), 'Mrs Sucksby's house of crime'. *Independent on Sunday,* 2 February.

Toms, K. (2007), 'Love in the blackout'. *The Observer*, 28 January.
Turner, J. (2006), 'Charging about in brogues'. *London Review of Books*, 28(4), 12–13.
Wagner, E. (2009), 'Terror at every turn'. *The Times*, 30 May.
Wilson, A. N. (1999), 'Fiction'. *The Daily Mail*, 23 April.

General: On historical fiction and neo-Victorianism

Arias, R. and Pulham, P. (2009) (eds), *Haunting and Spectrality in Neo-Victorian Fiction*. Basingstoke: Palgrave.
Boccardi, M. (2009), *The Contemporary British Historical Novel*. Basingstoke: Palgrave.
Davies, H. (2012), *Gender and Ventriloquism in Victorian and Neo-Victorian Fiction*. Basingstoke: Palgrave.
de Groot, J. (2009), *The Historical Novel*. London and New York: Routledge.
Gutleben, C. (2001), *Nostalgic Postmodernism: The Victorian Tradition and the Contemporary British Novel*. Amsterdam: Rodopi.
Fleishman, A. (1972), *The English Historical Novel: Walter Scott to Virginia Woolf*. Baltimore: John Hopkins University Press.
Hadley, L. (2010), *Neo-Victorian Fiction and Historical Narrative*. Basingstoke: Palgrave.
Heilmann, A. and Llewellyn, M. (eds) (2007), *Metafiction and Metahistory in Contemporary Women's Writing*. Basingstoke: Palgrave.
— (2010), *Neo Victorianism: The Victorians in the Twenty-First Century 1999–2009*. Basingstoke: Palgrave.
Ho, E. (2012), *Neo-Victorianism and the Memory of Empire*. London: Continuum.
Hutcheon, L. (1998) *A Poetics of Postmodernism*. London and New York: Routledge.
Jones, N. W. (2007), *Gay and Lesbian Historical Fiction*. Basingstoke: Palgrave.
Kaplan, C. (2007), *Victoriana: Histories, Fiction, Criticism*. Edinburgh: Edinburgh University Press.
Keen, S. (2006), 'The historical turn in British fiction', in J. F. English (ed.), *A Concise Companion to Contemporary British Fiction*. Oxford: Blackwell, pp. 167–88.
King, J. (2005), *The Victorian Woman Question in Contemporary Women's Writing*. Basingstoke: Palgrave.
Kohlke, M.-L. (2012), *Neo-Victorian Gothic: Horror, Violence and Degeneration in the Re-Imagined Nineteenth Century*. Amsterdam: Rodopi.
Kohlke, M.-L. and Gutleben, C. (eds) (2010), *Neo-Victorian Tropes of Trauma*. Amsterdam: Rodopi.
— (eds) (2011), *Neo-Victorian Families*. Amsterdam: Rodopi.
Kontou, T. (2009), *Spiritualism and Women's Writing: From the Fin de Siècle to the Neo-Victorian*. Basingstoke: Palgrave.
Kucich, J. and Sadoff, D. (2000), *Victorian Afterlife*. Minneapolis: University of Minnesota Press.

Llewellyn, M. (2008), 'What is neo-Victorian studies?' *Neo-Victorian Studies*, 1(1), 164–85.

Lukács, G. (1962), *The Historical Novel*. Trans. H. and S. Mitchell. London: Merlin.

Margaronis, M. (2008), 'The anxiety of authenticity: Writing historical fiction at the end of the twentieth century'. *History Workshop Journal*, 65, 138–60.

Maxwell, R. (2010), *The Historical Novel in Europe, 1650–1950*. Cambridge: Cambridge University Press.

McWilliam, R. (2009), 'Victorian sensations, neo-Victorian romances: Response'. *Victorian Studies*, 52(1), 106–13.

Middleton, P. and Wood, T. (2000), *Literatures of Memory*. Manchester: Manchester University Press.

Mitchell, K. (2010), *History and Cultural Memory in Neo-Victorian Fiction*. Basingstoke: Palgrave.

Robinson, A. (2011), *Narrating the Past: Historiography, Memory and the Contemporary Novel*. Basingstoke: Palgrave.

Scanlan, M. (1992), *Traces of Another Time: History and Politics in Postwar British Fiction*.

Southgate, B. (2009), *History Meets Fiction*. Harlow: Pearson.

Wallace, D. (2005), *The Woman's Historical Novel*. Basingstoke: Palgrave.

White, H. (2007), 'Historical fiction, fictional history, and historical reality'. *Rethinking History*, 9 (2/3), 147–57.

Widdowson, P. (2006), 'Writing back: Contemporary re-visionary fiction'. *Textual Practice*, 20(3), 491–507.

III Interviews

Akbar, A. (2009), 'Sarah Waters: "Is there a poltergeist within me?"' *The Independent*, 29 May.

Anon (2003), 'Interview with Sarah Waters', *Virago Press*. [Accessible at: www.sarahwaters.com/ints.htm].

— (2009), 'Sarah Waters on *The Little Stranger*'. *BBC Newsnight*, 5 October. [Accessible at: http://news.bbc.co.uk/1/hi/programmes/newsnight/review/8291045.stm].

Allardice, L. (2006), 'Uncharted Waters'. *The Guardian*, 1 June.

Armitt, L. (2007), 'Interview with Sarah Waters'. *Feminist Review*, 85, 116–27.

Dennis, A. (2008), '"Ladies in peril": Sarah Waters on neo-Victorian narrative celebrations and why she stopped writing about the Victorian era'. *Neo-Victorian Studies*, 1(1), 41–52.

Ettinger, S., Beutner, K. and Estes, J. (2010), '3 authors interview Sarah Waters'. *Lamda Literary*, 21 July. [Accessible at: www.lambdaliterary.org/interviews/07/12/3-authors-interview-sarah-waters/].

Finding, D. (2007), 'Interview with novelist, Sarah Waters'. *Feminist and Women's Studies Association Newsletter*, 50, 4–5.

Greenstreet, R. (2005), 'Q&A'. *The Guardian*, 21 May.

Jardine, L. (2005), 'Sarah Waters: Sex and the Victorian city', BBC2, 4 May.
Mansfield, S. (2009), 'Interview: Sarah Waters – from queer to strange'. *The Scotsman*, 21 August.
McCrum, R. (2009), 'What lies beneath'. *The Observer*, 10 May.
Mechling, L. (2009), 'A poltergeist in the family'. *Wall Street Journal*, 25 April.
Moss, S. (2002), 'Hot Waters'. *The Guardian*, 26 September.
O'Connell, J. (2006), 'Sarah Waters: Interview'. *Time Out*, 7 February.
Ramaswamy, C. (2009), 'With gay abandon: Sarah Waters interview'. *The Scotsman*, 29 May.
Seajay, C. (2006), 'Sarah Waters' Victorian love affair'. *Lamda Literary*, 1 April. [Accessible at: www.lambdaliterary.org/interviews/04/01/interview-with-sarah-waters/].
Tiernan, S. (2006), 'The politics of lesbian fiction: Sonja Tiernan interviews novelist Sarah Waters'. *Irish Feminist Review*, 2, 148–59.

IV Filmography

(2002), *Tipping the Velvet*. Sally Head Productions for the BBC, adapted screenplay by Andrew Davies.
(2005), *Fingersmith*. Sally Head Productions for the BBC.
(2008), *Affinity*. Box Productions for ITV, adapted screenplay by Andrew Davies.
(2011), *The Night Watch*. BBC productions.

V Websites

www.sarahwaters.com/.

Index